THE RORSCHACH

A Developmental Perspective

To Lui

THE RORSCHACH

A Developmental Perspective

Martin Leichtman

 THE ANALYTIC PRESS

1996   Hillsdale, NJ   London

Published by
The Analytic Press, Inc.
    Editorial Offices:
    101 West Street
    Hillsdale, New Jersey 07642

Library of Congress Cataloging-in-Publication Data
Leichtman, Martin.
    The Rorschach : a developmental perspective / Martin Leichtman.
        p. cm.
    Includes bibliographical references and index.
    ISBN 0-88163-138-8
    1. Rorschach Test.   2. Projective techniques for children.   3. Psychological tests
for children.   I. Title.
    [DNLM: 1. Rorschach Test—in childhood.   2. Development Disorders—
psychology.   3. Child Development Disorders—diagnosis.   4. Child Psychology.
WM 145.5.R7 L526r 1995]
    BF698.8.R5L38   1995
155.2'842—DC20DNLM/DLC
for Library of Congress   95-35826
                                                                                   CIP

Printed in the United States of America
10 9 8 7 6 5 4 3 2 1

Contents

PART III
PSYCHOSOCIAL ASPECTS OF THE RORSCHACH TASK

PART IV
COGNITIVE ASPECTS OF THE RORSCHACH TASK

PART V
CLINICAL APPLICATIONS

Preface

Vanity and the vagaries of memory being what they are, I began this book believing that I had something original to say about the Rorschach test. As research progressed, however, I discovered that I owed much of that originality to an ignorance of the literature or to my having forgotten the sources of ideas. As I was completing the book, for example, I learned that the comparison of Card I and pictures of butterflies and jack-o-lanterns in Chapter 14, of which I was rather proud, was an exercise John Exner had done in his Rorschach workshops two decades earlier. I have tried to acknowledge debts of which I am aware with citations, but suspect others remain that will become clear only after this book is in print. Perhaps the best that can be done is to indicate where they have probably been incurred.

The application of Wernerian developmental theory to the Rorschach I owe to my graduate education at Clark University twenty-five years ago. There almost all psychology students—clinicians, developmentalists, social psychologists, and even an occasional wayward physiological type—internalized that perspective in one form or another. It is a testimony to the power of those ideas that after lying dormant for decades they could shape a book that was intended to be on a different theme.

I am uncertain about the specific source of the notion that the model of symbol formation advanced by Werner and Kaplan could be used with the Rorschach. Werner's own work on the Rorschach antedated that theory and treated the test as a perceptual task, as did the research of other Clark graduates such as Hemmendinger (1953, 1960) and Friedman (1953). To the best of my knowledge the Rorschach was first treated as a form of visual representation by Leonard Cirillo in a course on projective testing some time in the 1970s. However, it is quite possible that I first heard the suggestion that the test could be approached in this way from Bernard Kaplan or Roger Bibace a decade earlier. If they didn't actually advance the idea, they might well have. In any case, Clark faculty members prided themselves on teaching ways of thinking rather than specific ideas. The nature of my debt in that regard is clear.

I am no less indebted to the Psychology Postdoctoral Training Program at the Menninger Clinic, with which I have had the privilege of being associated as a fellow and teacher for over a quarter century. The program began as, and has remained, a bastion of the Rapaport tradition. Although I take issue with some of Rapaport's views, I have been deeply influenced by the emphasis of his students on understanding the Rorschach as a sophisticated form of a clinical interview, attending to interpersonal aspects of the test process, and analyzing test behavior.

I owe even more to Dorothy Fuller, Tom Cummings, and Cotter Hirschberg of the Menninger Children's Division, who have remained my teachers over the years and nurtured a conviction that careful attention to early development can make unique contributions to understanding general clinical problems. For all the sophistication of work done with adults, whether we deal with diagnostic schemes such as DSM-IV, theoretical perspectives such as psychoanalysis, or tests like the Rorschach, more may be gained by starting at the beginning of developmental sequences and looking forward than by seeking to extend back schemes created for adults.

A third general obligation I have incurred is to the Society for Personality Assessment. Much of the research on early Rorschachs, of which I have made liberal use, was done by members of the Society in its original incarnation as the Rorschach Institute and published in its journal, the *Rorschach Research Exchange*. Over the last half-dozen years, I have given workshops on the Rorschach at Society meetings and benefited from lively discussions with participants.

Finally, I am especially indebted to a number of individuals: to John Kerr, whom I initially came to know as a supportive and patient editor and have come to value even more as a scholar and friend; to Paul Lerner, who has shared his time generously and made numerous insightful comments about aspects of this manuscript; to John Exner and Irving Weiner for clarifying issues related to their work; to Charles

Fantz and James Kleiger, who have helped with the thankless job of puzzling out the scoring of protocols best left unscored; to Marge McElhenny for the care and attention she has given this manuscript and so many others; to Charlotte Adamson for the sketches that grace Figure 2; to Don Kaufman for the diagrams; to my children, Max and Alexandra, who have provided me with a rigorous postgraduate education on child development as well as necessary corrective experiences whenever I was under the illusion I might be an expert on the subject; and, above all, to my wife, Lui, for her suggestions and critiques and, even more, for her forbearance around this project and, I fear, much else in our lives.

Introduction

THE CENTRAL PROBLEM IN RORSCHACH THEORY

Over the last seventy years, the Rorschach test has been the subject of a massive body of literature. A variety of systems for administering, scoring, and interpreting the test have been put forward (Exner, 1969); a multitude of studies have examined the significance of particular test signs and patterns of test performance; and innumerable books and papers have described clinical applications of the instrument (Stein, 1956; Lang, 1966; Exner, 1986). Yet what is most striking about this literature is not what it includes, but what it lacks. In these tens of thousands of pages, there is remarkably little discussion of the most significant question that can be asked about the test: What is the nature of the Rorschach task itself?

Rorschach himself touched on the question only briefly. In the introduction to *Psychodiagnostics* (1921), he stressed that his book was "predominantly empirical," an attempt to describe a technique and the results of its application. He did devote a few pages to outlining his view that the test measured a particular form of perception, but acknowledged at the outset: "The theoretical foundation for the experiment is, for the most part, still quite incomplete" (p. 13). Dying in 1922 shortly after the publication of his study, Rorschach was not to complete that foundation.

With a few notable exceptions (e.g., Frank, 1939; Rapaport, Gill, and Schafer, 1946), those advancing Rorschach's technique in the three decades after his death followed his example. Accepting his formulation that the test was based on perception, they sidestepped serious consideration of the response process and focused on issues of administration and scoring, interpretations of scores and responses, and ways of using such a framework to understand personality and psychopathology. Consequently, in the early 1950s, Holt (1954) began a paper on the rationale of the test with Rorschach's statement about its "incomplete" theoretical foundation and observed:

> When one considers the fact that these words were written more than 30 years ago, and that some thousands of persons have worked with Rorschach's test since then, producing a bibliography that now runs to over twelve hundred items, it is sobering to note how well the last sentence quoted could describe the situation today [p. 501].

Similarly, in describing this 30 years of research, Hertz (1951, p. 308) admitted that proponents of the test could be justly criticized for "failure to develop a basic underlying theory for our method and paying little attention to the theoretical and conceptual side of our problem."

A dozen years after Holt's paper, Ernest Schachtel (1966) opened his book on "the experiential foundations of Rorschach's test" with the same quotation from its originator and the same observation about the state of Rorschach theory. He noted:

> Of the extensive literature on the test, by far the greatest part has been devoted to adding to these [Rorschach's] empirical observations and to refinements of technique; relatively few attempts have been made to inquire into the rationale of the test and contribute to its theoretical foundations [p. 1].

At best, he suggested, "the gap between empirical observations and theoretical understanding" was "somewhat narrower," but still "quite large."

In the next decade, Exner (1974) began the most influential recent work on the Rorschach in a characteristic fashion—with a book devoted entirely to administration and scoring. Only in his second volume (Exner, 1978) did he offer a chapter on "the response process." Here, again quoting Rorschach's introductory remark, he asserted:

> Whatever might have been had Rorschach lived longer, the question of how a Rorschach answer is formed and delivered remains one of the

fundamental mysteries of the test. It is an area of research that has been sorely neglected in the Rorschach literature; and this neglect may well have contributed considerably to the broad divergence that occurred among those attempting to extend Rorschach's work and "complete" the test [p. 37].

Coming after a half century of Rorschach research, such an observation can only be viewed as extraordinary.

Though the situation may not be quite so bleak today (Exner, 1986), there is still a paucity of studies of the response process. Certainly, the basic problem posed by Rorschach is no less with us. Now, as then, the fundamental question remains: What is the nature of the Rorschach task?

PRESCHOOL RORSCHACHS AND RORSCHACH THEORY

At first glance, the study of the Rorschach performance of young children appears an unlikely avenue for approaching any significant issues in Rorschach theory. With no other group have there been as many questions about how the test should be administered, scored, and interpreted or, indeed, whether it should be given at all (Klopfer, Fox, and Troup, 1956; Spiegelman, and Fox, 1956; Klopfer, Ames, Metraux, Rodell, and Walker, 1974). Because of these methodological problems, a study of the application of the test to preschoolers might aptly be subtitled: "The use of the Rorschach with children for whom it may be inappropriate."

Yet it is in these difficulties themselves that the potential contributions of children's Rorschachs to Rorschach theory lie. If the world behaves according to expectations, we are prone to take it for granted. Only when our cars, our plumbing, our bodies, or our spouses act in problematic ways do most of us begin to take a fresh look at them and, in the process of trying to understand what is wrong, learn something about the principles governing their behavior. Similarly, in using the Rorschach with subjects who take it in familiar ways, we have little reason to ask questions about the instrument and instead we concentrate on what it reveals about those to whom it is given. In contrast, in borderline applications of the Rorschach, we encounter curious test behavior and responses, begin to doubt whether assumptions underlying usual modes of administration and scoring can be made, and face controversies about whether and how the test should be used. These phenomena demand explanations and these controversies require consideration of what constitutes "appropriate" technique and why. Hence, we are led to reflect on the nature of the test and how it works.

The promise the study of preschool Rorschachs holds for Rorschach theory, however, goes beyond simply calling attention to anomalous phenomena and raising questions about methodology. Even to ask why so many controversies surround the testing of young children is to recognize the answer. Disagreements about whether and how to give the test arise and atypical records occur because preschoolers are only in the process of mastering the test. But this answer, in turn, raises another question. How do children come to be able to "do" the Rorschach? And, with this question, the problem of preschool Rorschachs can be seen in a new light.

When we ask how children master the test, the primary issue is no longer what the Rorschach can teach us about young children, but rather what they can teach us about the Rorschach. Formulating the problem in this way, we need no longer be embarrassed by seemingly irreconcilable disagreements over test administration and scoring. Instead, these debates, which are, after all, disagreements about strategies for coping with the difficulties children experience with the test, become additional data for understanding the developmental sequence through which they come to be able to take the test in its standard forms.

More important, if we construct a developmental sequence of how children master the test, new questions arise. How do they progress from one stage to another? Why do they produce the curious responses they do? Why do these responses (e.g., the perseverations and confabulations) occur in a particular order? And, underlying these questions, the fundamental one: What is the task they are mastering?

In addition to leading us back to the central problem in Rorschach theory, the study of preschool Rorschachs enables us to approach that problem in new ways. The questions that must be asked about children's handling of the test are a fertile field for generating new theories; the fact that we are dealing with developmental processes in young children encourages us to draw on a major body of psychological theory for concepts upon which to build those theories; and accounting for the ways in which the Rorschach is mastered provides a testing ground for evaluating alternative conceptions of the test. In short, adoption of a developmental perspective may be the key to solving "one of the fundamental mysteries" of the Rorschach.

THE RORSCHACH: A DEVELOPMENTAL PERSPECTIVE

The essay that follows examines the Rorschach from this perspective. Its point of departure is a review of the literature on preschool Rorschachs, highlighting methodological debates, differing conceptions of stages in the mastery of the test, and ways these controversies can be used to construct a new view of that developmental process. The second section outlines this conception of stages in mastering the test. The third considers explanations of psychosocial aspects of this developmental progression. The fourth inquires into the cognitive process involved, questioning the adequacy of theories that conceive of the Rorschach as a test based chiefly on perception and proposing a conception of the task as one of symbolic representation drawn from the work of Werner and Kaplan (1963). The concluding section suggests some applications of this theory to clinical issues, notably the assessment of preschoolers, the evaluation of profoundly disturbed early elementary school children, and the analysis of thought disorder at later stages of development.

At the outset, however, it should be stressed that this is a book on Rorschach theory, not practice. It does not advance a new Rorschach system, present a brief on behalf of any existing system, or advocate particular clinical uses of the test. Rather, its concern is with theoretical issues that underlie existing systems and with a conceptual framework for understanding clinical applications of the test.

I

Young Children and the Rorschach

Studies of the Rorschach in Early Childhood

THE RORSCHACH LITERATURE ON CHILDREN

In a library consisting of all that has been written on Rorschach's test, the section on young children would occupy only an alcove. Even at the height of the test's popularity in the 1950s and 1960s, its acceptance as an instrument for the assessment of preschool children was limited (Anderson and Higham, 1956). Certainly most studies of young children's Rorschachs have arisen out of scientific curiosity rather than conviction that the technique can make major contributions in diagnosis and treatment. Hence, it is hardly surprising to find that publications on preschool children constitute only a small fraction of those on the use of the test with children, which, in turn, constitute only a small fraction of the Rorschach literature as a whole (Levitt and Truuma, 1972).

Yet the number of publications in this area of Rorschach research is not a good measure of its significance. To the contrary, because of the developmental perspective it affords, the manner in which young children respond to the test was of considerable theoretical interest to Rorschach (1921) and Klopfer (1945, 1956) and the children's section of the Rorschach library includes at least items by most of the major systematizers of the test (e.g., Beck, 1930; Hertz, 1941; Hertz and Ebert,

1944; Beck and Molish, 1945; Piotrowski and Lewis, 1950; Bohm, 1958; E. Schachtel, 1966; Exner and Weiner, 1982). For these reasons alone, this alcove is worth exploring.

A HISTORICAL REVIEW

From the first, children have played a significant role in the history of the Rorschach. Long before there was such a test, making shapes from inkblots, *Klecksographie*, was a popular children's game. In fact, Rorschach, who was nicknamed "Klex" as a child, may well have first become interested in the idea for his test through such play (Ellenberger, 1954).

Children's responses to inkblots began to intrigue psychologists two decades before Rorschach's work (Tulchin, 1940). Soon after Binet and Henri (1895–1896) suggested that inkblot techniques could be used to investigate personality in 1895 (Klopfer and Kelley, 1942; Zubin, Eron, and Schumer, 1965), Kirkpatrick (1900) undertook a large-scale study of developmental trends in responses of elementary school children to these stimuli. Pyle (1915) and Parsons (1917) also published early empirical studies on the topic. Although Rorschach may not have been familiar with their work, his interest in the technique was stimulated by a friend's report of grade school children's reactions to inkblots when he showed them to his class. Moreover, it was Rorschach's dissatisfaction with a colleague's analysis of data from a study of children's responses to similar material that provided impetus to the work that culminated in *Psychodiagnostics*.

Although the 1921 monograph introducing what was to become the preeminent inkblot test was concerned chiefly with adults, Rorschach did include mention of developmental changes in children's responses. Over the next decade and a half, a number of the small group of European clinicians and researchers who kept interest in the test alive (e.g., Behn-Eschenburg, Dworetzki, Loepfe, Loosli-Usteri, Schneider, and Zullinger) applied the technique in a more systematic way to children and, on occasion, very young children (Bohm, 1958). As a relatively unknown emigrant during the Second World War, Margaret Mahler, a student of Rorschach's colleague Behn-Eschenburg, was able to establish a place for herself in the American psychiatric community quickly because of her familiarity with this body of work (Mahler, 1988).

The use of the Rorschach with preschool children increased with the growing popularity of the test. As the technique took root in the United States in the 1930s, the enthusiasm it generated led to curiosity about how early the test could be administered and what responses could be obtained from children (e.g., Sunne, 1936). This interest is best seen in a paper by Klopfer and Margulies, "Rorschach Reactions in Early Childhood" (1941), which reported a collaborative study involving a half-dozen major nurseries and child study centers in the East. In the early 1940s, a modest stream of articles on preschool Rorschachs appeared (e.g., Kay and Vorhaus, 1943; A. Schachtel, 1944; Swift, 1944a, 1944b, 1944c, 1945; Vorhaus, 1944; Klopfer, 1945) and, within ten years, two books presenting extensive normative data were published (Ford, 1946; Ames et al., 1952).

A steady flow of books and articles on the Rorschach performance of young children continued through the 1950s and 1960s. Klopfer and his colleagues offered detailed analyses of theoretical and methodological problems in the area (Klopfer, 1956). Ames (1959, 1960a, 1960b, 1965, 1966) extended the work of the Gesell Institute group on clinical and developmental applications of the test. Kiviluoto (1962), Johannessen (1965), and Norland (1966) offered normative data on children of different ages. Allen (1951, 1954, 1955) published a series of longitudinal studies of Rorschachs given repeatedly to individual youngsters between the ages of two and five. Halpern (1953, 1956) explored clinical applications of the test with young children. Continuing a line of experimental research begun by Meili-Dworetzki (1956), students of Werner studied children's Rorschachs in terms of principles of perceptual development (Hemmendinger, 1953, 1960; Goldfried, Stricker, and Weiner, 1971). Also viewing the Rorschach from the standpoint of perceptual development, Francis-Williams (1968) devoted sections of her book on children's Rorschachs to preschoolers.

In the last two decades, interest in preschool Rorschachs has waned. For example, this population has not benefited from the enormous spur to Rorschach research provided by Exner's work. In extending that system to children, Exner and Weiner (1982) simply begin with school-age children and make no reference to younger ones. Levitt and Truuma (1972) also do not consider preschoolers in their book on children's Rorschachs. Hence, it is not surprising that a survey of recent Rorschach research on children (Zlotogorski, 1986) hardly mentions work with this age group.

Nonetheless, the subject has not been entirely neglected. The Ames group published a second edition of *Child Rorschach Responses* (1974) with data from new normative samples. Aronow and Reznikoff (1983) and Rausch de Traubenberg (1986) contributed to methodological discussions of how the test may be used with children. The Rorschach continued to play a role in clinical studies of young children (e.g.,

Olesker, 1980). And, in a precursor to this book, Leichtman (1988) proposed a conception of developmental stages in the mastery of the test.

CRITICAL ISSUES

Even a cursory examination of this body of literature will allow the reader to recognize that two sets of issues take precedence over all others in any consideration of the Rorschach performance of preschool children.

The first issues are methodological. As will be seen, no applications of Rorschach technique are fraught with as much disagreement about ways in which the test should be administered, scored, and interpreted as those with young children. Without an appreciation of the nature of the controversies around these issues, it is difficult to evaluate and compare data produced by investigators of differing persuasions or weigh the arguments of those who question whether the test can be used appropriately with these children.

A second set of issues concerns how to understand normal development trends in children's Rorschach protocols. The protocols preschoolers produce are unique and quite extraordinary. Although the perseverations, confabulations, and other unusual phenomena typically found in these Rorschachs bear some resemblance to responses encountered in older clinical populations (Halpern, 1953), children's responses are nonetheless fundamentally different from those indications of serious psychopathology. They occur in a regular developmental progression in individuals who are often better adapted to their worlds than are those of us who test them. Understanding the nature of these responses and conceptualizing their developmental sequence are significant problems in their own right. They are also prerequisites for any clinical applications of the test with young children. Indeed, one of the few points upon which contending Rorschach authorities agree is that evaluation of children should be done within a developmental framework (Klopfer, 1945; Klopfer, Spiegelman, and Fox, 1956; Ames et al., 1974).

For the present purposes, a consideration of these issues is important in one critical respect. By analyzing them, we can use the Rorschach literature, controversies and all, to construct a comprehensive model of the stages through which children master the test.

Methodological Issues

ATTITUDES AND TECHNIQUE

Though we might prefer it otherwise, discussions of Rorschach methodology with preschool children have a comic dimension. To explore the topic is to enter a border region where the line separating science and farce is not always clear.

Threats of embarrassment arise from a variety of sources. In part, they are present because of the subjects. As parents and educators know only too well, it is hardly possible to engage in serious pursuits with young children for long and retain one's dignity. In part, such threats are inherent in any attempt to extend a technical procedure to the limits of its applicability. Inevitably as one approaches those limits, the undertaking begins to appear ludicrous. In part, they are related to the nature of Rorschach technique. Over the years, we have created esoteric systems of scoring and interpretation and prided ourselves on their complexity. To apply those systems to younger and younger children is to confront a growing contrast between the rigor and sophistication of the method and the increasingly meager and questionable nature of the data to which it is applied.

Such considerations may well affect decisions about using the Rorschach with young children. Concerns about looking ridiculous contribute to the reluctance of some to consider the test for children before the elementary school years. Others, one suspects, are prepared to venture beyond this point because of a playfulness that insulates them against these fears, a seriousness of purpose so intense as to blind them to the quixotic nature of their pursuits, or an interest in children greater than that in the test itself. Once acknowledged, however, such points are best set aside lest they interfere with a consideration of matters worthy, no doubt, of more sober analysis.

WHEN SHOULD THE RORSCHACH FIRST BE GIVEN?

Although Rorschach responses, or something resembling them, can be obtained from youngsters under the age of two (Klopfer, 1945), few would consider toddlers capable of "taking the test." Thus, a first question about the use of the test with children is that raised by Klopfer, Fox, and Troup (1956, p. 13): "What is the minimum chronological age at which the Rorschach can be successfully administered?"

Those expressing opinions on the matter fall into two camps. Most of the otherwise heterogeneous group of experts who work with preschoolers feel that the Rorschach begins to be a serious test at about the age of three. For example, although giving the test to younger children, Ames et al. (1952) contend that it is only at the age of three that children's protocols become rich enough to provide a differentiated picture of their functioning. Klopfer, Fox, and Troup (1956, p. 13) agree, noting: "Our own clinical experience seems to indicate that a meaningful Rorschach record can be obtained from any child who has reached a mental age of three." Similarly, Ford (1946) believes that this is the age at which it is reasonable to begin to use the test with children.

In contrast, a second body of opinion holds that the Rorschach is not an appropriate technique until children are of school age. For example, Aronow and Reznikoff (1983, p. 9) assert that with the "possible exception" of very mature four-year-olds, "the Rorschach test should not be administered to subjects under the age of 5." Klopfer (Klopfer, Fox, and Troup, 1956) and Ames (Ames et al., 1974) note that a significant group of experts share this view. Though rarely stated in print, these opinions are expressed in two other ways. First, the Rorschach is used infrequently with young children. In a survey of 104 child guidance clinics, Anderson and Higham (1956) found that only 9% considered the test useful with children under the age of five whereas almost three quarters did so with eight-year-olds. Second, the topic of preschool Rorschachs is simply ignored in much of the literature. For example, as has been noted, two otherwise comprehensive recent books on children's Rorschachs make no reference to the subject and consider the test only with children of five and older (Levitt and Truuma, 1972; Exner and Weiner, 1982).

Though this second position may be articulated rarely, its rationale is clear. In fact, Ames et al. (1952) outline objections to the use of the test with preschoolers at the beginning of their book because an appeciation of their work requires that those arguments be countered. Three points they address are worth considering in detail because they highlight technical issues that divide those authorities who are prepared to give the Rorschach to young children and allow the views of those who oppose the use of the test with this age group altogether to be seen as a logical extension of a wider body of opinion.

ADMINISTRATION AND INQUIRY

The first objection to the use of the Rorschach with young children addressed by Ames and her colleagues is that "the test is difficult to administer" (Ames et al., 1953, p. 29). Phrased in this way, the problem seems deceptively simple, as is the solution they offer. However, that solution does not so much settle questions of technique as provoke a debate touching on the essential questions about whether the test can or should be used with preschoolers.

That young children present a host of problems interfering with administration of the Rorschach is beyond dispute. Preschoolers are often uninterested in the test. They have difficulty grasping its nature. They are prone to redefine the task in their own idiosyncratic ways. If they do initially have some idea of what is expected of them, they have difficulty sustaining that set. They are distractible. They are impulsive. They are capricious. Even when they give responses, they dislike the inquiry process and resist it. And frequently they simply ignore adults' wishes and do whatever happens to catch their fancy at a given moment. In short, it is hard to elicit serious Rorschach responses from them and even harder to engage them in a serious dialogue about the location and determinants of those responses.

Those who favor the use of the Rorschach with preschoolers typically counter objections based on difficulties in administration by asserting that the test can nonetheless be given if suitable adaptations are made in test procedures. Accordingly, they propose a variety of modifications of technique with young children.

Hertz (1936), for example, recommends the use of an initial "trial inkblot" to orient children to the test. Ford (1946, p. 13) endorses Hertz's suggestion and, responding to "the grim necessity" of coping with children's readiness to treat cards as toys, suggests that inkblots be placed in an apparatus to restrict their rotation.

To establish rapport, Halpern (1953) recommends allowing some children to sit on the examiner's lap. She often conducts inquiry after each response because

> a young child rarely has the patience to go through the entire procedure a second time. Furthermore, even if his patience holds out, it is unlikely his memory will. Rather than explain what he said before, he is far more likely to give an entirely new Rorschach [p. 25].

Acknowledging difficulties with the inquiry process even with these modifications, she accepts a looser, more intuitive, albeit less objective, approach to scoring. In fact, she suggests encouraging associations during inquiry that could transform the Rorschach with some children into a test resembling the Children's Apperception Test (Halpern, 1960).

Ames et al. (1952) do not favor use of trial blots or restrictions on manipulation of Rorschach cards with young children, but advocate other modifications of test administration. First, through their attitudes and questions, they not only seek to establish rapport with children, but also actively encourage them to produce as extensive and rich a record as possible. Second, in order to offset restlessness and loss of interest in the test, they recommend conducting inquiry after each card. Third, to minimize frustration and distraction, they limit the inquiry process with many children, relying instead on examiners' sensitivity to nonverbal cues and intuition in scoring responses.

Although such modifications of technique do, in fact, make it easier to test young children, they stimulate debates about the applicability of the test, rather than end them. For example, there is no consensus among these authorities about which modifications of technique to adopt. More important, many question whether any significant changes in test procedures are necessary or desirable.

Klopfer, Fox, and Troup (1956) raise these objections in response to Ames's work. They note: "In our clinical experience, we have never encountered the need to depart from standard administrative procedure, except to gear language to the level of the child's comprehension" (p. 14). They oppose extensive encouragement and prodding of children to obtain "rich" records at the price of sacrificing standardization of administration procedures and validity. They find it unnecessary to inquire after each response or each card and favor waiting until all ten are presented. Above all, acknowledging difficulties in inquiring into determinants of responses, they nonetheless strenuously disagree with "intuitive" approaches to scoring that rely heavily on examiners' judgments based on nonverbal cues. "Guesswork," they assert, "has no place in the inquiry regardless of whether our subjects are adults or children" (p. 20). Instead, they prefer to simply score many responses with a question mark.

The gap between Ames and Klopfer is not quite as great as these arguments suggest. Klopfer can advocate methodological purity, in part, because his standard inquiry procedures are less restrictive than those of many Rorschach systems. He uses an "analogy period" and "testing-of-limits," which, he concedes, often provides the basis for scoring responses of children under the age of four (Klopfer et al., 1954; Klopfer, Fox, and Troup, 1956). Equally important, responding to Klopfer's critique in the revised edition of their book, Ames et al. (1974) stress the "objective" bases of judgments relying on nonverbal cues and use Klopfer's own work to illustrate the role of similar judgments in scoring in general (p. 13).

Nonetheless, Ames's and Klopfer's views do embody antithetical tendencies that provide a continuum along which methodological positions can be located. On one side are those who believe that, in order to remain faithful to the spirit of the Rorschach, it is necessary to alter the method of its presentation to accommodate to the characteristics of preschool children. On the other are those who believe that such alterations so change "the Rorschach" that they are unacceptable. Instead, they argue, the test should be administered in its standard form and problems in administration and uncertainty about scoring should be accepted as unavoidable consequences of working with young children.

At the liberal end of this continuum are clinicians such as Halpern (1953, 1960) who take substantial liberties with the form of the test in order to elicit any material that will be useful in understanding troubled children. Many other clinicians, while perhaps less extreme, are ready to modify standard procedures substantially in the interests of obtaining data. For example, Rausch de Traubenberg (1986) contends:

> It is difficult to set the conditions for test administration once and for all. Any experienced clinician must modify the administration in accordance with the goals she sets for herself. We believe that under no circumstances should the productivity of the child be sacrificed to procedure. . . [p. 143].

Ames's approach may be seen as a more conservative expression of this position in which there is a greater degree of standardization, but still a readiness to modify technique.

Moving toward the other end of the continuum, we encounter Klopfer's position with its emphasis upon standard procedures, but standard procedures flexible enough to permit young children's records to be obtained and scored. Many of those who do not favor the use of the Rorschach with children under school age fall at the far end. They adhere to more demanding methods than young children can manage and distrust data obtained under other conditions.

VALIDITY

A second set of arguments against preschool Rorschachs concerns validity. Ames et al. (1952, p. 29) note that objections are raised to the test because "results are not particularly valid, that is, determinants which indicate disturbance appear in children who on other grounds are considered quite undisturbed."

Again, there is agreement among major Rorschach authorities on the "facts" of the case. Ames, Klopfer, and others concur that preschool children not only give responses that are relatively poor in form, but also produce numerous perseverative, confabulatory, and odd responses that are likely to seem peculiar to anyone over the age of five. Commenting on children aged two to four-and-a-half, for example, Halpern (1953, p. 69) notes "In fact, children of this age have been characterized as 'healthy schizophrenics,' and their Rorschach protocols bear out this description." While this characterization, to which children and schizophrenics have good reason to object, is no longer used, preschool Rorschach protocols are replete with responses that would be considered pathological in older populations.

Ames and her colleagues argue that criticisms regarding validity are not a problem if children's protocols are interpreted with reference to children's norms. If so, for example, there is no more reason for considering their immature Rorschach responses pathological than for believing that three-year-olds are retarded because they have a mental age of only 36 months. Thus, Ames can point out that the very norms her study of children's Rorschach presents are sufficient to avoid mistaken attribution of pathology in young children when their responses differ from those of adults.

Yet questions about validity can still be raised. No problems arise when the seemingly pathological features of children's protocols lie on a continuum with adult protocols. For example, if very young children give responses with poor form, and form quality steadily improves as a function of age, it is reasonable to believe that interpretations based on the Rorschach concept of form level can be made at all ages. But the most distinctive features of young children's Rorschachs, especially their perseverative and confabulatory responses, do not fall on such a continuum. They are responses that differ in kind from normal Rorschach responses and they lead to doubts that the same modes of thinking underlie their formulation. Klopfer, Spiegelman, and Fox (1956), for example, believe that these responses reflect early forms of "concept formation" and that they are of such significance as to take precedence over other considerations in the interpretation of the preschoolers' Rorschachs. However, if the manner in which young children take the test is based on forms of thought different from those encountered later, then scores for location and form level, for example, may not mean the same thing they do for adults. The assumptions governing interpretations within many Rorschach systems may not hold for young children.

As with other questions regarding Rorschach methodology with preschoolers, these issues are far from settled. Hence, based on their respective positions on them, some authorities are prepared to use the test with this population and others are not.

THE "MEAGERNESS" OF DATA

The third objection to the use of the Rorschach with preschoolers examined by the Ames group concerns the data obtained. "Even when the test is administered successfully," they note, "the child's responses tend to be meager and his visual percepts do not as in the case of the adult reflect fully his individuality" (Ames et al., 1952, p. 29). Preschool Rorschachs, this argument runs, simply yield too little information to allow for the differentiated analyses we expect from "the Rorschach."

Judgments about the richness or meagerness of test results, of course, depend on who is making them and on what basis. Thus, for example, Ames and her colleagues acknowledge that preschoolers' Rorschachs are less revealing than those of adults, but still produce two editions of *Child Rorschach Responses* demonstrating that extensive data can be generated by testing them. They present table after table tracing changes over age in each scoring category, advance detailed analyses of these trends, and seek to establish correlations between Rorschach performance and the major features of development at each age outlined by Gesell and Ilg (1943, 1946).

Yet counterarguments can be advanced to these points as well. For example, Ames's data may be biased in the direction of fuller and more differentiated Rorschachs because of an overrepresentation of bright children from upper socioeconomic classes in her sample. More important, the data she presents are still too limited to permit the differentiated analyses done with older subjects. At two, her children produce an average of 10 responses and, when perseveration is taken into consideration, there are only one or two distinct responses. By five, children in her sample average only 14 or 15 responses, including some perseverations. Her analyses of these data do show statistical trends across age for basic determinants, yet the differences are usually so small that most of her tables are of little value as norms against which individuals' performance can be judged. For example, the average number of M responses in records changes from .1 at two years to .6 at five; m responses increase from .1 to .2; shading responses from .2 to .4; achromatic color responses from .1 to .2; FC responses from .1 to .2; and C responses decrease from .4 to .2. Although somewhat greater changes occur with a few determinants (e.g., CF responses, animal movement responses, and form level), the factors that best discriminate age groups over these years are number of responses, numbers of different content categories used, time required to administer the test (four minutes for two years; eight with five-year-olds), number of cards refused, and number of words used in giving responses. Needless to say, these are hardly the data upon which sophisticated Rorschach practitioners would like to base their interpretations.

In addition, although Ames and her associates offer comprehensive interpretations of personality characteristics of groups of children of different ages on the basis of these Rorschach signs, their inferences are vigorously criticized (Klopfer, Spiegelman, and Fox, 1956). They themselves are cautious about clinical applications of the test with preschoolers, as opposed to generalizations about age groups, because of a recognition of limitations of the data it provides.

CONCLUSIONS

Two conclusions can be drawn with some assurance from this review of methodological issues. First, the differences of opinion among Rorschach authorities about whether and how to administer the test to young children are as pronounced as any in the Rorschach literature. Second, over the course of a half century these disagreements have not been resolved and they are unlikely to be resolved soon. Indeed, they are not resolvable because there is no single correct position. Rather, these disputes are about options, each with a set of trade-offs that individual Rorschach practitioners evaluate differently.

For example, if modifications of standard technique such as those suggested by Ames are adopted, children produce more responses and examiners can generate a more comprehensive set of test scores. Those following this path are typically prepared to use the Rorschach with young children and make more elaborate interpretations of personality development on the basis of the test. However, they are also likely to be confronted by questions from their colleagues about the appropriateness of their procedures, the soundness of their data, and the value of their inferences.

If standard procedures are adhered to strictly, fewer questions arise about the purity of methods. Yet it is more difficult to test young children; test protocols are more barren; scoring responses is harder; examiners are more cautious in their conclusions; and many will see the enterprise as fruitless and prefer to give the test only to older subjects.

That a consensus has not emerged around these positions, then, is hardly surprising. Since the Rorschach is given for a variety of purposes by individuals with a variety of commitments, the presence of a wide range of opinions about the desirability of particular approaches to the use of the test with young children seems only natural.

Patterns of Early Rorschach Performance

MODELS OF DEVELOPMENTAL CHANGE

Although Rorschach authorities differ about how best to characterize changing patterns of Rorschach responses across the preschool years (Klopfer, Spiegelman, and Fox, 1956), their conflicts over these substantive issues have been far less intense than those over methodological ones. For example, in spite of their arguments around test administration, Ames and Klopfer agree about the types of protocols characteristic of particular periods of early childhood. The perseverative tendencies Klopfer and Margulies (1941) stress in their descriptions of the "Rorschach reactions" of two- and three-year-olds are prominent in Ames's description of the responses of these youngsters (Ames et al., 1952). In turn, her observations of confabulatory phenomena in the Rorschachs of three- and four-year-olds are used by Klopfer in advancing his later conception of stages in children's Rorschach responses (Klopfer, Spiegelman, and Fox, 1956).

Moreover, in contrast to assertions about methodology, conceptions of developmental stages are advanced in modest, even tentative ways. For example, Klopfer, Spiegelman, and Fox (1956) preface the presentation of their view of patterns of early Rorschach by acknowledging:

Future Rorschach research with children will have to contribute a great deal to the clarification and conceptualization of such phases of development. At the present stage of knowledge, or lack of it, it is difficult to give a systematic presentation of interpretation problems connected with age patterns [p. 25].

As a rule, schemes such as Klopfer's are offered as attempts to highlight salient features of a developmental process rather than definitive treatments of the subject that preclude others.

Consequently, the four major approaches that have been taken in describing developmental changes in the Rorschachs of young children need not be seen as conflicting. Rather, they may be viewed as models organized around different principles, each with its own strengths and limitations.

THE PERSEVERATIVE MODEL

The first conceptions of stages of "early Rorschach reactions" centered on the handling of a strong initial predisposition toward perseveration. In an influential exposition of this model, Klopfer and Margulies (1941) outline three successive "patterns of reactions." The most primitive stage, typically encountered in two-year-olds, is characterized by complete perseveration or "magic repetition." Ignoring differences in the inkblots, children simply repeat their first response on all 10 cards. The second stage, common in two-and-a-half- and three-year-olds, involves modified perseverations. Children still offer the same response to most cards, but now refuse some cards or give a few other responses. The final stage, which emerges between the ages of three-and-a-half and five, is that in which the hold of the perseverative tendency is broken and most cards "receive sufficient individual attention to merit a variety of responses" (p. 5).

Ford (1946) elaborates this model. She accepts Klopfer's stages and gives them names—the "pre-logic," "confused-logic," and "true logic" stages—reflecting what she takes to be the thought processes upon which they are based. In addition, she contends that between the latter two stages is one more, characterized by "perseverated logic." In this period, children still give the same response to most cards, but instead of doing so in an uncritical, automatic way, they now hunt for characteristics of the blot that fit the concept.

Two aspects of these views of early Rorschach patterns are noteworthy. On the one hand, by focusing on perseverative tendencies, they highlight what is undoubtedly the most salient feature of Rorschachs of children between the ages of two and three. All who write about preschool Rorschachs recognize their prevalence, even if disagreeing to some extent about the timing of shifts from stage to stage. On the other hand, a developmental model based on perseveration alone is too narrow to do justice to the range of phenomena encountered in preschool Rorschachs, especially those of three-and-a-half- to five-year-olds. Recognizing this limitation, Klopfer himself later proposed a more comprehensive scheme (Klopfer, Spiegelman, and Fox, 1956).

AMES'S APPROACH

In contrast to Klopfer's rather undifferentiated developmental model, Ames et al. (1952) offer a conception of changes in patterns of preschool Rorschachs that is extraordinarily variegated. Comparing records of groups of 50 children spaced at half-year intervals between the ages of two and six, they trace changes in test behaviors and in almost every Rorschach scoring category. Correlating these test signs with traits ascribed to children at each age level by Gesell and Ilg (1943), they suggest that striking transformations in personality can be seen in Rorschach performance at each six-month interval.

For example, in describing the "characteristics of 2½ years as shown by the Rorschach," the Ames group lists six developmental findings of Gesell and associated test signs. Egocentricity and unmodulated emotions, they contend, are seen in a preponderance of CF and C responses over FC responses (although the number of each of these responses is quite low); a limited interest in other people is seen in a very low H%; stubbornness and rigidity in a high A% and marked perseveration; a restricted psychic life in limited Rorschach content; inaccurate perceptions in a low F + %; and "psychic drives more at an instinctual than at a conscious level" in FM predominating slightly over M, although again the numbers are quite small (Ames et al., 1952, p. 122). A half year later, at age three, very different characteristics are ascribed to children and new Rorschach indicators are noted for each. Improved social relations are associated with an increase in human responses; an ability to distinguish between the personal and the physical in increased texture responses; efforts to please and conform in the increasing prominence of FC responses; thoughtfulness in semantic expressions such as "I think it is a . . ."; capacities for empathy in increased M responses; greater emotionality in more color responses; and so forth (p. 132).

Although providing a comprehensive description of a wide range of changes in the ways in which preschool children handle the Rorschach, Ames's research is subject to three sets of criticisms. First, it presents a multitude of continuous and discontinuous developmental trends, mixing together inferences based upon phenomena in which there are pronounced statistical differences and those in which differences are minute. As a consequence, it is often difficult to see which aspects of Rorschach performance are most significant at each stage. Second, rather than deriving characteristics attributed to a developmental stage from children's Rorschach performance, Ames and her colleagues begin with the Gesell and Ilg scheme and search for Rorschach signs that correlate with it. It is doubtful that skilled Rorschach practitioners working with test protocols alone would find the same signs significant or characterize the developmental period as Gesell did. Finally, objections can be raised to the model of personality itself. For example, in their critique of Ames's position, Klopfer, Spiegelman, and Fox (1956) are skeptical of the kind of shifts purportedly found in three-year-olds. They observe: "One wonders what kind of creature it is that in the space of six months changes its rigidity into flexibility, its inadaptability into adaptability. Perhaps this chameleon wasn't really 'rigid and inadaptable' at all . . ." (p. 22). Questions of this kind can be raised about comparable transformations at later ages.

PERCEPTUAL DEVELOPMENT MODELS

A third approach to understanding changes in children's Rorschachs is based on applications of principles of perceptual development. One such model is that of Meili-Dworetzki (1956). Drawing upon Gestalt theory and the genetic psychology of Claparède, she views the Rorschach as a perceptual task on which change proceeds in the direction of increasing differentiation, complexity, and integration. In conceptualizing major trends in children's responses, she proposes three stages. In the first, "syncretic perception" is dominant, resulting in a "general and confused perception of the whole"; in the second, responses reflect a "distinct and analytic perception of the parts"; and, in the final stage, more complex percepts are possible because the child now has the capacity for a "synthetic recomposition of the whole with awareness of the parts" (p. 112).

Hemmendinger (1953) offers a similar scheme. Assuming that children's Rorschach responses reflect a course of perceptual development embodying Werner's (1961) orthogenetic principle, he argues that they proceeded from an initial global, syncretic stage to ones involving increasing levels of differentiation and integration. Three-year-olds, Hemmendinger (1953, p. 168) suggests, are "whole-perceivers" whose mode of experiencing inkblots is "immature, inflexible, [and] un-differentiated"; four- and five-year-olds still exhibit relatively immature modes of perception, but begin to take notice of details; six- to eight-year-olds deal with details in a more refined way, but do not integrate them into wholes; and older children are increasingly capable of this integrative process.

The major contribution of these studies lies in their insistence on considering children's Rorschachs from the standpoint of a significant established body of theory and research in developmental psychology. Children's performance on the Rorschach, they stress, should be understood in terms of general developmental principles. Among their other strengths are Meili-Dworetzki's detailed analyses of the genesis of particular Rorschach determinants and Hemmendinger's use of a scoring system combining location and form level scores in ways that reveal basic developmental trends.

There are, however, potential problems in using these schemes alone to characterize changes in children's Rorschachs. Meili-Dworetzki's stages, for example, are relatively undifferentiated themselves in the sense that all preschool Rorschachs are included in her first stage. Children do not typically reach her second stage until they are six or seven. More important, both models focus chiefly on perceptual development and underestimate the significance of other aspects of the response process.

THE "CONCEPT FORMATION" MODEL

Reviewing the state of research on early Rorschach performance a decade and a half after Klopfer and Margulies (1941) presented the initial perseveration model, Klopfer, Spiegelman, and Fox (1956, p. 25) contend that only in the area of concept formation have age patterns "emerged sufficiently to be ready for conceptualization." Accordingly, they offer a conception of phases in children's handling of the test based on changes in modes of cognition.

The first stage, encountered in children between the ages of two and four, is that of "magic-wand perseveration." Struggling to cope with a perplexing task that seems beyond them, children simply repeat an initial concept on all subsequent cards or reject them.

The second stage, that typical of four-year-olds, is characterized by "confabulatory concept-formation." Different responses are given to most cards, but whole responses are usually based on a crude generalization from one detail of the blot "without any concern whether the form characteristics of the concept as a whole, or any major specifications, fit the blot in any conceivable way" (p. 27).

The third stage, one of "confabulatory combinations," is normal in four- and five-year-olds. Now two or more areas of the blot form the basis for reponses, although they may not be organized in a coherent form.

By the age of seven, these earlier patterns give way to efforts to meet "the minimum for requirements" for Rorschach performance found in older children and adults. At this point, records can be interpreted in standard ways and the presence of perseveration, confabulation, and confabulatory combination taken as indications of immaturity or pathology (p. 28).

This conception of early patterns of Rorschach performance has a number of attractive features. By emphasizing modes of thinking, it highlights processes that, there is good reason to believe, lie at the core of developmental changes in test responses. It subsumes Klopfer's earlier perseverative model and offers a richer characterization of the test performance of three- to five-year-olds. In addition, while focusing on test responses, it, nonetheless, occasionally suggests that the same concepts can be applied to the test process as well.

At the same time, by emphasizing concept formation alone, the scheme is too constricted to encompass many phenomena that deserve attention at each stage. There are only hints of the relationship between changes in test behavior and test protocols, relationships that warrant systematic elaboration. Furthermore, it is not clear that confabulatory combinations constitute a distinct stage rather than a sophisticated variation of the confabulatory processes encountered in the second stage.

As has been noted, however, Klopfer and his colleagues do not advance their views as the definitive treatment of early stages of Rorschach performance. Rather, their theory, like others, is put forward as a preliminary effort to encompass salient features of a developmental process that requires a broader and more comprehensive treatment in the future.

4

The Preschool Rorschach Literature: Consensus, Controversy, and Synthesis

It is impossible to survey the literature on preschool Rorschachs without becoming acutely aware of the persistent unresolved conflicts around basic methodological issues and the diversity of opinion around many substantive ones. In retrospect, such controversies appear inevitable. When an instrument already subject to dispute is used with a group on the fringe of the population to which it is usually applied, disagreements about how and with whom the test should be used are to be expected.

Yet this literature contains seeds of a synthesis encompassing opposing positions and revealing an order and regularity in the phenomena with which they grapple. The path toward this synthesis begins with a recognition of areas of the literature in which there is consensus, areas in which there are varieties of opinion, and areas in which there appear to be irreconcilable differences.

Rorschach authorities agree about how young children behave in the test situation and about the kinds of protocols they produce. Those who give the test to preschoolers describe that process, especially the problems encountered in it, in remarkably similar ways. Although differences in their techniques have some effect on results, the test protocols they obtain are very much alike. For example, for all their conflicts about scoring and interpretation, Ames and Klopfer accept each other's test records as characteristic of young children of particular ages. At the very least, their arguments are about the same children.

Differences of opinion about how to characterize developmental changes in Rorschach performance exist, but are not, for the most part, divisive. Beginning with early work such as that of Klopfer and Margulies (1941), descriptions of stages in young children's Rorschach performance have typically been presented as preliminary efforts to sketch salient features of the developmental process. How such stages are delineated—whether they are best understood in terms of perceptual development, concept formation, or broader transformations encompassing both types of processes—are treated as open questions. In any case, these problems are subordinate to methodological ones, since there can be little certainty about characterizations of data as long as the nature of the data and means by which they are gathered are in doubt.

The bitterest conflicts, as has been seen, are methodological ones centering on whether and how the Rorschach should be used with young children. These are controversies about the very definition of the test—about the purposes for which it can be used, the ways in which it should be administered, the manner in which it is to be interpreted, and the value of the results obtained. Those who have the least doubts about the applicability of the test with small children have been clinicians ready to use individualized, impressionistic modes of analysis (Halpern, 1953, 1960; Rausch de Traubenberg, 1986) and researchers for whom the Rorschach is an experimental task that can be scored and analyzed in terms of developmental schemes oriented as much around the primitive responses of preschoolers as the more advanced responses of adults (Hemmendinger, 1953; Meili-Dworetzki, 1956). Those who most question the use of the test with preschoolers are practitioners committed to sophisticated Rorschach systems used chiefly with adolescents and adults. They doubt that their norms and modes of analysis can be extended to a population that cannot take the test in a standard form, engage in a demanding inquiry process, or respond to the Rorschach task in ways that make it reasonable to assume that scores have the same meaning they do for adults. Between these extremes are a variety of positions that involve some degree of modification of administration and scoring procedures to accommodate to the special problems presented by children. Arguments among these groups are, above all, arguments about criteria for what constitutes "the Rorschach" and about the strictness or leniency with which those criteria are applied.

Whether a synthesis of differing positions can be achieved hinges on the manner in which these areas of consensus and controversy are approached. If the problem of preschool Rorschach performance is treated from the standpoint of what the Rorschach can reveal about young children, conflicts are inevitable. We must begin by making a commitment to a methodological stance, a commitment about which there is a maximum of controversy, in order to explain phenomena, such as children's behavior, about which there is considerably more agreement. However, if the terms of the problem are reversed, if the performance of preschool children is used to examine the Rorschach test, a very different situation arises. No longer is there a need to decide among competing methodologies. Instead differences in technique can simply be accepted and used as a basis for inquiring into what there is about the way in which children take the test that makes it so difficult for experts to agree about how it should be given.

Moreover, the answer to the question is obvious. Differences in method arise because young children do not take the test the same way older children and adults do. They are only gradually coming to understand and respond to the requirements of the Rorschach task. Controversies about method, then, can be seen primarily as controversies about strategies for dealing with these limitations. Although the strategies differ, the phenomena they address are the same.

Approached in this way, the problem of delineating "stages" in early Rorschach performance can be seen in a broader and more productive manner. The fundamental task is no longer that of describing patterns of early Rorschach responses; rather, it is that of articulating stages through which children come to master the test itself. Delineating patterns of responses remains important but is a subordinate aspect of this task.

When the problem is formulated in this way, each aspect of the Rorschach literature can be seen to have its own contribution to make toward a solution. On one hand, observations of test behavior and test protocols, about which there is consensus, can be emphasized properly. On the other hand, methodological controversies cease to be an obstacle to the study of preschool Rorschachs or a source of discomfort. They need no longer be viewed as factional disputes but now can be accepted as serious efforts to respond to ways in which children approach the Rorschach. Insofar as they are seen as alternative strategies for coping with children's problems in taking the test, it becomes possible to read back from them to the common characteristics of children's test behavior with which they are intended to cope.

In short, the key to understanding young children's Rorschachs lies in setting aside concerns about when the Rorschach is "the Rorschach" with them and viewing all of the phenomena encountered in the preschool literature—the behavior of examiners as well as that of children—as data for understanding stages through which youngsters come to be able to take the test in its standard form.

II

Stages in the
Mastery of the
Rorschach

5

Characteristics of the Model

If the Rorschach is given to normal children of younger and younger ages, a point will be reached at which they are so bewildered by the task and so unable to respond to its demands that the test appears meaningless. Conversely, if the test is given to children at later and later ages, another point will be reached at which they are so clearly able to understand the task, give a variety of responses to different cards, and participate in the inquiry process that Rorschach practitioners, regardless of their particular system, will be comfortable scoring and interpreting protocols in what they take to be standard ways. Because the Rorschach is a complex mental exercise, the distance between these two points is not traversed quickly or in a single step. To the contrary, mastery of the test occurs over a considerable period of time—the preschool years and beyond—and is reflected in a series of increasingly sophisticated, qualitatively different patterns of test performance. Thus, the problem of describing the manner in which children come to be able to take the Rorschach may be seen as one of delineating these patterns or stages.

Although the problem may be stated in a simple, straightforward way, its solution is more complicated. As Ames and her colleagues demonstrate in their detailed descriptions of shifts in the Rorschach performance of preschoolers at six-month intervals, the "average" child behaves in ever-changing ways in the test situation and produces test records that vary along many dimensions. Moreover, as she, Klopfer, and every other authority agree, this "average" preschool child is a fiction. Normal preschoolers differ considerably in how they approach the test and in the records they produce. For example, one three-year-old may adopt a predominantly perseverative approach to the test, while another adopts a confabulatory one without Klopfer considering either abnormal (Klopfer, Spiegelman, and Fox, 1956).

In order to impose on this complex array of data a scheme that highlights the most important changes in the ways children handle the test, we will advance a model organized around five working assumptions. For the most part, these assumptions are similar to those upon which earlier schemes have been based. Nonetheless, they should be acknowledged at the outset since they give this conception of stages in the mastery of the Rorschach its particular character.

First, a concept of stages will be used. Discussions of "stages" have so long been a part of the preschool Rorschach literature that it is easy to forget that the concept embodies a form of analysis that shapes data in distinct ways. Stages are constructs used to cast in sharp relief characteristics that make developmental processes at one point qualitatively different from those at another. They are "ideal types" intended to articulate principles governing modes of functioning, not descriptions of how any given youngster or group of youngsters of a particular age functions. Even though ages at which patterns of test performance typically emerge may be cited in examples, stages are defined by these patterns, not by age. As will be seen, a three-year-old can serve as a prime example of Stage I Rorschach phenomena usually found in children a year younger. Furthermore, individuals of any given age need not display pure characteristics of a stage; they may well present a "mixed" picture. The concept of stages, then, is a heuristic device intended to clarify theoretical issues—namely, steps in a developmental progression; questions of whether and in what ways the concept applies to any youngster or group of youngsters are empirical matters that the delineation of stages opens for exploration.

Second, it is assumed that the manner in which the Rorschach is given provides the best indicator of these stages. Insofar as conceptions of stages in preschool Rorschach performance go beyond simply imposing an intellectual scheme on phenomena arbitrarily, they should capture something "real" encountered in testing young children. As a first step in this direction, we will use shifts in how the test is given as signs that new stages have been reached. Hence, although Rorschach authorities may differ in their approaches to testing preschoolers, to the extent to which a new stage is present we expect that all will register this change in their own ways.

Third, new stages in Rorschach performance should be reflected in a wide variety of phenomena. If stages are intended to capture broad qualitative differences in how children take the test, they should be manifested in many different ways. In particular, each new stage should be characterized by significant shifts in the behavior of children *and* examiners in the test situation and in the production of fundamentally different kinds of test protocols.

Fourth, this model of stages in children's Rorschach performance should incorporate earlier ones. No theory of how an instrument used for almost three-quarters of a century is mastered should deal chiefly with "new" phenomena. If we are genuinely concerned with how young children handle the test, we should expect that others no less concerned with the issue have long ago recognized most of what is important in the process. As has been seen, the major differences of opinion that have arisen around delineating patterns or stages in preschool Rorschachs have centered on what is most salient in that process and how best to characterize it. Insofar as claims are advanced on behalf of a new model, they should be based on its capacity to subsume older ones in order to offer a more comprehensive picture of the process.

Finally, concepts of "transitional periods" or "substages" are needed. If the concept of stages is used to highlight broad qualitative differences in phenomena across development, problems arise around how to represent differences that, while significant, are less marked. In trying to characterize how children handle the Rorschach, for example, we encounter modified patterns of perseveration and confabulatory combinations that are both similar to and different from preceding patterns. They seem to be based on alterations rather than fundamental transformations of principles governing earlier approaches to the test. In such cases, concepts of substages are useful in representing both those similarities and differences.

Organized around these assumptions, the model of children's mastery of the Rorschach advanced here consists of three basic stages and two intermediate transitional periods. Each stage is demarcated by shifts in how the test is given and taken; each focuses on differences in behavior in the test situation *and* in the kinds of test protocols produced; and each seeks to integrate aspects of earlier models of stages in children's Rorschach performance.

Stage I: Perseverative Approaches to the Rorschach

THE RORSCHACH IN ITS EARLIEST FORM

Although Rorschach responses, or something resembling them, have been obtained for individual cards from subjects as young as 15 to 18 months (Klopfer, Fox, and Troup, 1956), it is not until the age of two that records have been gathered from substantial numbers of children. Among those who have worked with this age group, there is remarkable agreement about what the test process is like and about the kinds of protocols produced. Ford (1946), Allen (1951, 1955), and Ames et al. (1952) concur that the earliest approach to the test is the pattern of pervasive perseveration described by Klopfer and Margulies (1941).

The test process in this initial stage is conveyed vividly in one of the first cases in the American literature. At the age of three, Anna Schachtel (1944) reports, a young man named Colin was approached by his nursery school teacher who asked if he would like to see some pictures. He agreed but refused to be lured to a quiet office and insisted instead on remaining in the playroom. In the interest of doing the test, the examiner acceded to his wishes in spite of the distractions in that setting.

Shown the first "picture," he described it as "a mountain." Proceeding immediately to the second card, he said "That's a red mountain" and demanded to see the next one. Ignoring the examiner's encouragement to look at cards as long as he liked, he quickly described the third blot as a pink mountain and called for the next. This pattern was repeated on two more cards, both black mountains. However, by Card V, Colin noticed two girls nearby who were making a train out of chairs and singing a song. Pushing the sixth card away, he went off to join them. At this point the test had lasted four minutes.

Over the next hour and a half, the teacher coaxed Colin to return to the test, but he refused, having more interesting things to do. Finally, in an interlude while waiting his turn to paint, he consented to resume the test. On Cards VI, VII, and VIII, Colin again saw mountains. He also discovered that the eighth card would stand on edge if placed in a crack in the table. Both he and the teacher found this activity hilarious and he repeated it until Card IX slipped through the crack and fell on the floor. He continued playing in this manner on the last two cards, managing two more responses, both mountains, before completing the test and running off to paint.

THE TEST PROCESS

Obviously Colin's case cannot be used to illustrate the fine points of test administration. His teacher could have been firmer about structure. She might have persuaded Colin to go to a room without distractions or to focus on the task a bit more. She also might have tried to inquire into location and determinants. Yet, although such interventions would have elicited different behavior in Colin had he allowed himself to be tested under such circumstances, his responses would probably have differed little from those Schachtel reports.

In fact the work with Colin, problems and all, is representative of what it is like to test children who are just beginning to respond to the Rorschach. It highlights four distinctive aspects of the test process that are familiar to all who have given the Rorschach to two-year-olds.

First, for young children the nature of relationships overshadows the activities done within them. Hence, most Rorschachs obtained at this early stage have been given by familiar figures such as parents (Allen, 1951, 1954, 1955) or, as in Colin's case, teachers. Even when the test is administered by others, Klopfer and Margulies (1941, p. 3) note, it is often "advisable to use the mother or the nursery school teacher as an intermediary or interpreter."

Second, even under these conditions, whether or not a youngster responds to the test depends upon "the spirit of the moment." Klopfer and Margulies (1941, p. 3) observe: "One may get a Rorschach not only one day and not the next, but even one hour and not the next." As with Colin, the examiner must strike while the iron is hot or, perhaps, simply catch the child when he has nothing more interesting to do with his time.

Third, examiners typically have great difficulty keeping two-year-olds focused on the task and preventing Rorschach cards from being transformed into toys. For example, Ford (1946) notes:

> Early in the preliminary experimentation it was evident that the young child was unduly concerned with manipulation of the Rorschach card. He felt it, patted it, smelled it, and sometimes kissed it. Occasionally he pushed it off the table or threw it on the floor. More often he became engrossed in the manipulative possibilities. Not only did he inspect the card from all angles, but he was equally concerned with examining the back of the card. In fact, his interest in manipulation became primary and only secondarily, if at all, was he concerned with meanings [p. 33].

Ford is, in fact, so sensitive to the play potential of the Rorschach card that she recommends prohibiting children from turning it.

Finally, apart from occasional attempts to get a vague idea of location, most examiners have not found inquiry with very young children worth the effort. Describing the test process with two-year-olds, Ames et al. (1952) write:

> Any effort on the part of the Examiner to clarify the response by getting the child to indicate exactly where he sees something or to point out which part of the blot is the doggie or kitty, usually only confuses matters. The 2-year-old appears to be very suggestible, and at the same time quite unclear as to what he has seen or where he has seen it. If asked where he has seen something, he will point to some part of the card, apparently at random, to satisfy the Examiner; and if the Examiner departs from proper procedure to the extent of making a specific suggestion, the child is almost certain to accept it [p. 110].

Of course, inquiry is hardly necessary in cases where examiners know what responses will be *before* cards are even given to youngsters.

TEST PROTOCOLS

Although Colin was approaching the upper age at which such protocols are produced, his responses exemplify the pure perseverative pattern characteristic of the most primitive Rorschach records that can be obtained from children. These records have two noteworthy features.

That which is most striking and most often commented upon is the perseveration. As Klopfer and Margulies (1941, p. 4) observe: "With utter disregard for the differences between the ten cards, the child simply repeats the same word as his reaction to each card." They suggest that, perplexed by the Rorschach task, very young children treat their first response as a "magic key" to make the problem disappear. In later work, Klopfer, Spiegelman, and Fox (1956) and Fox (1956) use the term "magic wand."

A second feature of these records, which receives less attention, is how little idea examiners have of the basis for the first response. For example, Schachtel believes that Colin saw a mountain because of the upward slope of certain areas of Card I. She may well be correct, but with no clear indication from Colin of what he was in fact responding to, her belief is little more than speculation. Many examiners acknowledge frankly that they are uncertain about where the response comes from. Klopfer and Margulies (1941, p. 4) note: "The word chosen may or or may not be determined by some vaguely perceived features of the first card." They describe this initial response as "a 'magic key' that has been more or less accidentally encountered in the first situation." Concurring with their view, Ford (1946, p. 36) asserts that the word the child repeats on subsequent cards "may or may not be determined by some rather vague impression received from the first card or it may have no relation even to the first card." Hence, more often than not, the seeming arbitrariness of these first responses and their lack of congruence with blot characteristics leave examiners with little more than hunches about what led to the response and, in some cases, with a strong suspicion that the response may have little to do with the blot at all.

MODIFIED PERSEVERATIONS

By age two and a half, many children start to move away from the pattern of complete perseveration that epitomizes Stage I. The first in one of Allen's (1955) series of protocols obtained from individual children across early childhood exemplifies these changes.

When Allen initially gave the Rorschach to his two-and-a-half-year-old daughter, Ruth, she decided that the first card looked like a book that had chalk on it. The next six cards also looked like chalk of various colors. However, when Card VII was accidentally exposed early, she commented spontaneously, "Over here, that fire." Upon being given the following card, she said it was pink chalk and then, in a confabulatory response characteristic of the next stage, added, "This is a mouse going up to the top of the man's house, he's a funny man." She noted that Card IX was pink before trying to reject it and that Card X was pink fire.

Such records still clearly belong to Stage I. The way in which the test is taken is the same. For example, Allen does not bother inquiring into responses, although he will begin to do so with his daughter a few months later. Equally important, the predominant pattern remains a perseverative one. Even when Ruth starts to give new responses on the last three cards, she perseverates on her second response.

The beginning of a transition to a new stage is apparent, however, in the changes in the pattern of perseverations. Klopfer and Margulies (1941) describe two such modifications. Rather than repeating the same response on all cards, children may refuse some as Ruth tried to do on Card IX or, while perseverating on most cards, they may give new responses to a few of them. Ford (1946) identifies an additional pattern in which children still offer the same response to each card, but do so in a new way. They now search the blot for characteristics that justify the use of the concept. For example, after seeing butterflies on Cards I and II, a child may try to find aspects of Card III that make it, too, a butterfly.

Research on the ages at which these patterns are found is limited. Klopfer and Margulies (1941) had only 10 children aged two and a half in their sample. Four perseverated throughout the test, while the other six gave records based on modified forms of perseveration. Of the 27 three-year-olds, only 11% engaged in pervasive perseveration, 33% used modified forms, and a majority of children gave a variety of responses to at least seven of 10 cards. Ford (1946) encountered no cases of pervasive perseveration among the three-year-olds in her group, although a third still engaged in Klopfer's modified forms. Ames et al. (1952) found that 77% of their two-year-olds gave responses characterized by "magic repetition" and 72% of their two-and-a-half-year-olds gave perseverative responses, although most now in modified forms. By four years of age, Klopfer and Ford found that only about one-fifth of their groups still engaged in modified forms of perseverations, and the Ames group no longer treated them as a significant factor in their analysis.

Although limited samples and methodological problems suggest that statistics about the ages at which particular approaches to the test are typical should be treated cautiously, the Rorschach literature leaves no doubt about the nature of the earliest stage in children's response to the test. The most primitive pattern encountered in giving the test is one of pervasive perseverations, which, even before children reach age three, begins to give way to modified forms of perseveration that remain common in children well after their third birthday.

Stage II: Confabulatory Approaches to the Rorschach

THE APPEARANCE OF A NEW STAGE

A year after the initial Rorschach in which he offered five "mountain" responses, took a 90-minute break to play, and then gave another five "mountains," Colin was tested again (A. Schachtel, 1944). He now completed the test in a single sitting, albeit a brief one. On Card I he saw "a man with pinchers," and on Card II, "a bird with pinchers." Card III was "Peacocks. They are pulling something out of it and they are smack." On the next three cards, he gave single, unelaborated reponses ("fountain," "bird," and "another fountain," respectively), before the curious response to Card VII, "Goal that pinches." Becoming more volatile on the last three cards, Colin engaged in "playful fights" with them. As he hit each colored spot on Card VIII, he asserted, "That's a bang, bang, bang. Tigers walking all over it. A fountain." On Card IX he continued: "I hate that. That's a pound, pound, pound, that pounds people's heads. A hammer." And, on Card X, he exclaimed, "I hate that broken-down tree. See where it's chopped off?"

A detailed analysis of Colin's protocol is hardly necessary to grasp how much it differs from his earlier one. Although hints of perseverative tendencies are still present (e.g., the repeated themes of pinchers or pounding), perseveration is no longer the dominant mode of handling the test. Different responses are offered for most cards. At the same time, many of those responses, especially the ones that stand out most vividly, seem to be the product of a confabulatory process. The blot serves as a springboard for idiosyncratic associations (e.g., a goal that pinches) and fantasies, some of which are enacted during the test (e.g., a bang, bang, bang). Thus, the Rorschach now yields a variety of responses, which, properly understood, may well reveal something significant about Colin's personality. However, there is room for considerable disagreement about what constitutes "proper understanding," since many of those responses are not encountered in Rorschachs at later stages.

Authorities who are inclined to use the Rorschach with preschoolers clearly recognize the existence of major qualitative shifts in Rorschach performance of the kind leading to Colin's second protocol. In fact, it is the basis for their contention that the instrument begins to be appropriate for children at about the age of three or shortly thereafter.

Ames et al. (1952), for example, tested younger children primarily out of scientific curiosity. They acknowledge readily:

> At 2½ years as at 2 years, it does not seem that the Rorschach is a uniquely useful tool for determining intellectual and emotional characteristics of the child or for revealing the characteristic individuality of the child *or* of the age [p. 122].

In contrast, they believe children's responses at three are sufficiently complex and varied that judgments can be made about whether an individual's performance is above or below age level and a differentiated picture of the characteristics of the age can be offered.

Others express similar opinions in their own ways. Ford (1946), who did pilot studies with younger children, is convinced that only at three do children show sufficient interest in the test for the Rorschach to become an appropriate instrument for them. Klopfer, Fox, and Troup (1956) hold that the test can be administered to any child with a mental age of three or over. Likewise, Hemmendinger (1953), although interested in primitive Rorschach responses, begins his developmental study of the test with this age group.

What these authorities are responding to in children, and the reasons for asserting that a new developmental stage has been reached, can be appreciated by considering shifts in how children take the test and the nature of their protocols.

THE TEST PROCESS

In Stage II, the Rorschach can be administered in a form that bears some resemblance to that used with adults. Two-year-olds may or may not participate in testing as the spirit moves them; three-and-a-half-year-olds come to scheduled test sessions and produce protocols at that time. Two-year-olds perseverate and treat cards in such arbitrary ways that examiners often doubt that their subjects are responding to the inkblots at all; three-and-a-half-year-olds give responses of some kind *to the cards*. Above all, with two-year-olds, inquiry is a pointless exercise; with children a year or two older, it can be undertaken in at least a rudimentary form.

The test process in Stage II has its own distinct qualities. From the standpoint of examiners, the most significant of these qualities is the extraordinary effort required to administer the test in a form that even approximates that with older children and adults.

To test preschoolers it is necessary to compensate continuously for their limited understanding of the task, difficulty sustaining a set, low tolerance of frustration and anxiety, and preference for changing the test into a more interesting activity. Examiners must, in fact, accomplish two sets of divergent tasks. On one hand, they need not only to establish rapport with children, but also to work hard to provide children with support, encouragement, and assistance in dealing with anxiety, distractions, and other factors that interfere with the testing. On the other hand, examiners *must* provide a high degree of structure, working constantly to maintain the boundaries of the test and cope with children's efforts to avoid the task or transform it into something else.

Empathic responsiveness and assuring adherence to the "rules" of the test are, of course, important in work with subjects of all ages. With older subjects, however, except with the most profoundly disturbed patients, maintaining the structure of the test is seldom a major issue and the examiner's attunement to the subject chiefly affects the inquiry process, determining how good an understanding of the basis of test responses can be achieved. With children in Stage II, these qualities in examiners determine whether test protocols are obtained at all. Indeed, Klopfer and Margulies (1941) recommend work with this population as a means of honing testing skills, presumably on the grounds that if psychologists can test young children they can test anyone.

Perhaps the best testimony for the unique character of the test process in this second stage is the debate in the literature around whether to institute special test procedures. It is with regard to this period that consideration is given to such measures as: (1) restricting manipulation of cards in order to reduce distraction and decrease the play value of test material; (2) inquiring after each response or each card to reduce frustration, cope with distractibility and boredom, and compensate for memory problems; (3) limiting inquiry to maintain interest in the test and avoid excessive frustration; and (4) relying heavily on examiners' sensitivity to the shared context of the test situation for scoring responses where verbal indications of determinants are lacking. For our purposes, the significance of controversies around these procedures lies not in which position is correct, but in the existence of the controversies themselves. As has been seen, opposing positions on these issues are plausible strategies for addressing problems children experience with the test, and each choice among them has its own costs and benefits. In Stage III, children take the Rorschach in a different manner and these debates simply evaporate.

From the standpoint of children, two aspects of the test process in Stage II warrant particular attention. First, for young children the relationship with the examiner is primary and the test task is often only a peripheral concern. In part, these priorities are related to the Rorschach itself. As Halpern (1953, p. 7) notes, the requirements of the test are not clear to preschoolers and, for many, the task is not an especially appealing one. In part, the same is true of all tests. Young children do not come to do "tests"; they do not enter a situation they see defined by the objective requirements of such tasks. Rather, they are invited to play games or engage with the examiner in some activity that is far from clear. As a consequence, motives related to the relationship with the examiner—whether they involve wishes to play with a friendly adult or cope with an anxiety-filled encounter with a stranger—heavily influence how the child handles the test situation.

Recognizing this fact, skilled examiners know that to test preschoolers effectively they must do whatever they can to develop what each child will experience as a benign, supportive relationship (Ford, 1946, pp. 34–35). On their part, children are no less concerned with using the relationship for their own ends. While examiners "give tests," children bombard them with questions about every topic under the sun, take associations to any aspect of the tests as an occasion to tell stories or recount interesting events in their lives, change tests into games, or barter the "work" they are doing for a chance to play with toys around the room. In contrast to two-year-olds, who may simply stop the Rorschach to go off to play, three-and-a-half-year-olds can be kept at the task because of the relationship with the examiner. However, it is the interest derived from the capital examiners invest in that relationship that allows them to initiate and maintain the test process.

A second distinctive aspect of children's behavior during the test in this second stage is that they often do not treat the Rorschach as an objective task warranting serious consideration. To the contrary, Ames et al. (1952) note that, beginning at about the age of three and increasing over the next year, children engage in a good deal of silly behavior that can be seen in their language, their responses, and their attitudes toward the test. For example, the children in their sample gave responses such as "a gumba, gunga," "a broken bee bee bla," "a silly old moo coose," "a parade bee bee bee," and "a krozokus." Similarly, Allen (1954) notes that his son, a bright youngster who had experience earlier with the Rorschach, began giving silly responses at this time. In addition to perfectly adequate percepts, at three and a half, his protocol included such responses as a "sisser," a "piadigat," a "schniatz," and a "poopoohead"; three months later, he reported seeing a "red foomba" on Card II, "booms" on Cards VI and VII, a "soom" on Card VIII, and a "boonji" on Card IX; and, at four, although such responses diminished, he still managed to find two "boo-carriers" on Card VII. One cannot but be curious about the content categories to which such responses were assigned.

Similar behavior is also encountered in the inquiry process. Although it is often possible to obtain a clear idea of the location and determinants of some responses, at times percepts are described in such garbled or arbitrary ways that examiners have little confidence in their scoring. Describing work with a typical four-year-old, Klopfer, Spiegelman, and Fox (1956, pp. 27–28) note:

> frequently, the child may choose any of his favorite animals, point out one of its properties . . . and gleefully assign the rest of the blot material to the same concept. He merely *points* vaguely all over the card if the cruel examiner tries to pin him down as to the parts of the animals [pp. 27–28].

Hence, although children in Stage II are beginning to take the Rorschach in a recognizable form, there is reason to doubt that they do so with the dedication and seriousness so important a task undoubtedly warrants and older subjects are prepared to give it.

TEST PROTOCOLS

As has been seen, Rorschach protocols in Stage II differ significantly from those children produce earlier. Perseverative tendencies recede and different responses are given on most cards. Moreover, these responses can be scored as well because some inquiry is now possible. Hence, Rorschach records in this period are at least superficially similar to those obtained from older children.

Yet these protocols differ significantly from those of Stage III. Although many preschool test responses can be scored with a reasonable degree of assurance, others cannot. In some cases, examiners still wonder whether children are responding to the blot at all. The ability and willingness of children to participate in the inquiry process varies so markedly that examiners must either score many responses with question marks (Klopfer, Fox, and Troup, 1956) or rely on intuition (Ames et al., 1952). In addition, since investigators differ substantially in their administration and scoring of the test at this time, it is more difficult to compare findings across systems than with older groups. Consequently, although responses may be scored and tabulated in Stage II, the data are likely to look "soft" to any but the most committed advocates of preschool Rorschachs.

In spite of the differences in procedures across studies generalizations can be made about the salient characteristics of Stage II Rorschach protocols.

I. Number of Responses. Rorschach protocols in Stage I contain one to three distinct responses when perseveration is taken into consideration. In contrast, in Stage II, children produce one response, and even more, on each card.

The average number of responses reported for three- and four-year-olds varies with the population of children studied and the procedures used. At the low end of this range, Kay and Vorhaus (1943) obtain an average of 10 to 12 responses from these children; at the upper end, Ford (1946) and Meili-Dworetzski (1956) obtain 16 to 19 responses; and Ames et al. (1952) and Hemmendinger (1953) fall in the middle, reporting 13 to 15 responses. Because these figures still contain some perseverations, it is probably most reasonable to estimate children in this stage produce an average of 10 to 13 reponses. It is also likely that these lower figures are representative of the number of responses obtained under conditions comparable to the forms in which the Rorschach is commonly used with adults.

Six- and seven-year-old children, most of whom have reached Stage III, produce an average of 16 to 18 responses even when the test is administered using conservative procedures (Ames et al., 1952; Levitt and Truuma, 1972; Exner and Weiner, 1982).

II. Range of Responses. In Stage I, there is no range of responses. A single response is simply repeated. In Stage II a variety of responses begins to appear. In most studies about half of these responses are animals, although, through this period and into the next stage, there is a steady expansion in the variety of responses given and the content categories into which they fall.

III. Mode of Approach. The predominant response during Stage II is the whole response. Once again, because of variations in scoring techniques used with children who are often not clear about the basis of their responses, a range of scores are reported. Most investigators find that about half to two-thirds of the responses of three- and four-year-olds are W's with the remainder consisting primarily of large details. By six the percentage of W's is reduced by half, D responses predominate, and the number of small and rare details increase. For example, Hemmendinger (1953) notes that three- and four-year-olds in his study gave between 55% and 69% W responses, whereas with six-year-olds that figure fell to 30%; Kay and Vorhaus (1943) report a drop from 62%–71% to 46%; Ford (1946) from 37%–40% to 23%; and Meili-Dworetzki (1956) from about 46% to about 27%. The only major study yielding different trends is that of Ames et al. (1952), who describe little change in the mode of approach over these ages. However, their procedures may differ substantially from the others.

IV. Form Level. In spite of marked variations in how form level is measured, studies of preschool Rorschachs report significant changes between the stages. In Stage I, of course, form level is often so poor that it is hardly worth considering; in Stage II it begins to be relevant, although it is relatively poor; and, as children become older, it steadily improves. For example, Kay and Vorhaus (1943) report that their three- and four-year-olds gave 24%–34% W + responses in contrast to 50% by five-year-olds; conversely, what they describe as "crude," "arbitrary," "perseverative," and "pseudo-psychotic" W's fell from 76% to less than 50% over this period. Ford (1946) notes that her measures of F + % rose from 39%–57% among three- and four-year-olds to 66%–72% among six- and seven-year-olds. Hemmendinger (1953) finds his three- and four-year-olds gave only 17% to 25% "high" W and D responses whereas that figure had risen to 50%–60% with his seven-year-olds. Even using a considerably more generous scoring system, Ames et al. (1952) observe that F + % rose from 60%–67% for three- and four-year-olds to 81% for six-year-olds.

V. Confabulatory Whole Responses. Klopfer, Spiegelman, and Fox (1956) contend that the most salient aspect of the Rorschachs of three- to five-year-olds is that they are based on a confabulatory mode of concept formation. In such responses, which are epitomized by confabulatory whole (DW) responses, the subject generalizes from one detail to the whole card, but he is able to justify his response only in terms of the one clearly seen detail, and insists that the whole card is used when it is impossible to reconcile the concept with the shape of the whole blot [Klopfer et al., 1954, p. 64].

At first, Klopfer's assertion appears to run counter to the findings of other investigators, who place the incidence of DW responses among three- and four-year-olds at 10% (Hemmendinger, 1953) or even lower (Kay and Vorhaus, 1943). However, Klopfer, Spiegelman, and Fox (1956), in an effort to capture the process underlying responses, use a broader conception of the confabulatory responses, one in which a single aspect of the blot, including color, is overgeneralized and overrides all other constraints in dealing with the stimulus material. Defined in this manner, the concept may be viewed as an effort to encompass the crude and arbitrary W responses Kay and Vorhaus see as characteristic of the period and the Wv and W – responses emphasized by Hemmendinger. Their position is also consistent with Meili-Dworetzki's (1956) view of syncretistic perception as the dominant characteristic of the period and the stress Bohm (1958) and Meili-Dworetzki (1956) place on *pars pro toto* thinking in preschool Rorschachs.

VI. Confabulation. In characterizing this stage as confabulatory, Klopfer, Spiegelman, and Fox (1956) also make it clear that they are using the term in the broad sense emphasized by Rapaport, Gill, and Schafer (1946). Treated in this way, confabulations constitute a class of phenomena in which, instead of a balance being maintained between "perceptual" and "associative" aspects of the response process, the blot does little more than launch a subjective process that seems to take flight. Although some aspect of the card initiates the process, the subject is quickly caught up with ideas and fantasies that have little to do with the stimulus. This more elastic concept of confabulation covers many of the most extraordinary and, at the same time, most common aspects of the Rorschach performance of normal three- and four-year-olds.

The silly language highlighted by Ames et al. (1952) may be seen as a behavioral confabulatory response to the blot. For example, something about particular Rorschach cards may have started Allen's (1954) three-year-old son talking about "boonjis," "pink sissers," and "piadigats," but only the youngster at the time, and perhaps not even he, knew what. Certainly, the play with language quickly took precedence over dealing with the card.

Even more striking manifestations of confabulatory tendencies can be seen when children transform the Rorschach into a Children's Apperception Test (CAT). For example, Ames et al. (1952, pp. 152–153) note that four-year-olds are prone to give free rein to their "high unbridled imagination" and enjoy making up lively stories about the their percepts. In using the Rorschach for clinical purposes, Halpern (1953) encourages and exploits this inclination.

Similarly, children in this stage may enact fantasies with the blots that are so vivid Ames and her colleagues feel they exhibit "some confusion between reality and pictured items" (Ames et al., 1952, p. 127). For example, upon seeing bears on Card VIII, a youngster may exclaim "Ouch, they bit me!" or, seeing snow on Card VII, talk about making snowballs with it. Klopfer, Spiegelman, and Fox (1956) suggest that the "confused percepts and concepts" Ames describes as characteristic of three- and four-year-olds (e.g., "a fireplace with feet") are also confabulatory in nature.

Finally, children in this stage give that purest of confabulations, the response seemingly stimulated by no characteristics of the blot whatsoever. For example, describing three-and-a-half-year-olds, Ames et al. (1953, p. 140) note: "The child seems to feel perfect freedom to introduce objects and animals which do not actually exist in the blot." On Card X, for example, a youngster may refer to a cow that has walked onto and off of the card and thus is no longer there. Such responses pose interesting problems for those trying to determine location, not to mention score form level.

Each of the characteristics noted above is present in Stage II. However, three are especially important in differentiating it from prior and succeeding stages.

The number of responses is critical in distinguishing Stages I and II. Stage I protocols, in their purest form, contain one response that is perseverated. In Stage II, different responses are given to each card.

Stages II and III are best demarcated by the two types of confabulation. First, although differences exist about whether to characterize the process through which responses are formed in terms of syncretistic perception or confabulatory modes of thought, there appears to be agreement that children in Stage II are often responding primarily to one aspect of the blot—for example, a detail or color—or even an association to some aspect of the blot. This one aspect often appears to constitute the basis for the response. In the next stage, percepts are based on a process in which a number of features of the blot are integrated or the blot is analyzed so that parts that do not fit the response are not included in the percept. In effect, DW's become D's.

Second, in Stage II, confabulatory play is rampant—and absolutely normal. Examiners recognize it as an inescapable fact of life in working with three- and four-year-olds. In Stage III, confabulation may be present occasionally with normal children, but in milder and more subdued forms and in ways that no longer utterly color the test process.

CONFABULATORY COMBINATIONS

As children begin the transition from Stage II to Stage III, a number of changes can be seen in the manner in which they handle the Rorschach.

First, while testing children aged four-and-a-half to six is still not easy, problems encountered in the test process diminish. The location and determinants of percepts can now be determined more readily. For example, Klopfer, Fox, and Troup (1956) note that when testing children aged four and older they use few question marks in scoring, whereas these are common with younger children.

Second, there is a gradual increase in the number of responses and the number of large-detail responses relative to Whole responses. Hence, Hemmendinger (1953) contends by the age of five a new stage is reached in which children now notice and comment on parts.

Finally, Klopfer, Spiegelman, and Fox (1956) believe that a new stage is reached between ages four and five that can be defined in terms of "confabulatory combinations." Such combinations are seen in a broadening of confabulatory Whole responses in which now two details (e.g., the head and tail of a dog) are used as the basis for a response that still bears little resemblance to the blot. In contrast to the mature percepts of later stages, they argue, "the concept formation falls short in the way in which the specified elements are organized within a total concept. Not infrequently, the same blot areas may be used in a completely incompatible organization" (p. 28). They stress, however, that a transition is clearly under way. "The five-year-old child is normally expected to use confabulation and confabulatory combinations for at least half of his responses. The other half of his responses follow the pattern used for establishing minimum form-level requirements for the adult record" (p. 28).

Other investigators place less emphasis on confabulation by the fifth year, but take note of the changes Klopfer and his colleagues describe in their own ways. For example, Ames et al. (1952) suggest that by four and a half, most forms of confabulation begin to decline. However, they see this age as "the high point for the giving of extremely confused or unrelated concepts" (p. 168). These incongruous combinations are percepts in which elements are combined in an odd, seemingly idiosyncratic fashion. For example, children may see a fish with two heads, a person with several pairs of arms, or a dog with a head at each end.

From our standpoint, the phenomena Klopfer and Hemmendinger describe are characteristic of a transitional period rather than a separate stage. While reflecting significant changes in how children work, they nonetheless can be viewed as sophisticated variations of the principles underlying the main stage. For example, Hemmendinger (1953) acknowledges that although by age five his children do show more interest in details, "they are not markedly more mature in terms of quality of perception." Similarly, Klopfer's confabulatory combinations appear to be only a more complex variation of earlier confabulatory modes of "concept formation," whereas they are fundamentally different from the modes of thought characteristic of his next stage.

Stage III: "The Rorschach"

THE APPEARANCE OF A NEW STAGE

In one way or another, authorities on children's Rorschachs recognize a second major qualitative shift in test performance in the period between five and seven years of age.

Those who simply did not consider the Rorschach with younger children now become interested in the instrument. For example, Exner and Weiner (1982) and Levitt and Truuma (1970) begin presenting norms and tracing developmental trends at the age of five, although some (e.g., Weiner, personal communication) are skeptical about the validity of data on many five- and even six-year-olds.

Authorities who use the test with younger children register this shift in other ways. For example, Halpern (1953) recommends a different, more mature form of test administration when children reach school age. Loosli-Usteri (1952, p. xi) agrees with Ames's group that their work with "very young children offers an interest more scientific than diagnostic," but notes that their findings " will permit the application of the test as a diagnostic technique in any case for children from 5 to 6 years on." Similarly, Klopfer, Spiegelman, and Fox (1956) indicate that with children aged seven and older they are comfortable applying standard modes of interpreting Rorschach data rather than emphasizing the development of "concept formation" alone.

Perhaps most important, as children reach the ages of six and seven, divisions among experts about whether and how to use the Rorschach give way to a broad consensus about the suitability of the instrument as both a clinical and research tool. The reasons for this consensus are best appreciated by considering what it is like to test these children.

TESTING A SEVEN-YEAR-OLD

Not long after her seventh birthday, Mandy was referred for psychological testing because her parents were concerned that she had become increasingly unhappy and withdrawn over the preceding year. She often looked sad, cried easily, and was upset by trivial matters. Formerly a bright, lively, outgoing child, she now seemed inhibited. She functioned adequately in school, but apparently well below the level of her ability. She also insisted that "nobody liked her" in spite of her being popular with peers. There was no family history of depression, but her parents were convinced that, as the middle of five children, Mandy felt neglected and "lost in the shuffle." Yet when they gave her attention and tried to find out what was troubling her, she pulled away and appeared more unhappy and withdrawn than ever.

The psychiatrist who saw Mandy for a consultation noted her dysphoric moods and constriction, but also believed that she was a basically healthy youngster who could make good use of an expressive psychotherapy process or psychoanalysis. However, because she was quiet and uncommunicative with him as well, he requested testing. In addition to wanting information about her intelligence and academic abilities, he was interested in learning more about the reasons she seemed so unhappy and inhibited, in gaining reassurance that she in fact had the "ego strengths" he attributed to her and that more serious problems were not being missed, and in confirming his impression that she could benefit from an expressive therapy.

As part of the assessment, the psychologist administered the Rorschach on the second day of testing. Using the Rapaport system, he conducted the inquiry after each card. His interactions with Mandy around the first card afford a good sense of the test process with her.

Handed Card I, Mandy said immediately, "A bat. It looks like a bat." She briefly debated whether it looked more like a butterfly, but settled on a bat. She added, "It could be a person with a messy wall. That's all I see." She then put the card down.

Asked about the location of her percepts, she made it clear that the bat was the whole design, the person the central large detail, and the messy wall the two side details. With the card put away, the examiner asked what made it look like a bat and Mandy replied: "Well, the part that's long, the body. Also the wings, and it is black." The center looked like a person because it had two feet and hands and a dress. It was a woman. Asked about the wall, she said: "Well, 'cause it was black and all yucky." Suspecting shading played a role in her response, the examiner asked why it was "yucky." Mandy replied, "Because it's black," indicating through her manner that he really should have known that. To clarify the matter further, she added, "Someone was painting and they painted all over the wall." The woman, she noted, was cleaning the wall and yelling " 'cause the hands were up like that and the head was sort of tipped back like that." As she spoke, she imitated the gesture for the benefit of the examiner, whom, she seemed to feel, probably needed such visual aids. With this, they both proceeded to the second card.

As Mandy was responding to the first card and, even more, when later reviewing and analyzing her responses, the examiner made inferences about their bearing on the referral questions. For example, he noted a number of indications that Mandy was a bright girl with a capacity to organize her experience and make sense of her world. Her first response took account of the whole blot, incorporating a number of details into an acceptable percept. Her next involved detail responses, but integrated them in a unitary theme. The quality of her percepts in which form was dominant was good and she gave a well-perceived human movement response, which is often associated with an adaptive use of fantasy and a capacity to empathize with others.

These first responses also suggested that problematic issues might well be present. Two of her three percepts were influenced by the blackness of the card, a determinant often interpreted as a sign of struggles with dysphoric affects. In addition, the theme of the second response pointed to other conflicts. Someone had made a yucky mess and a woman, whom it was hard not to think of as a mother, was expressing her displeasure in no uncertain terms.

These issues, especially the first, had been noted by the psychiatrist in his interview with Mandy, but the test began to suggest a different perspective on her presenting problems. Although Mandy might be outwardly inhibited, her responses were not those of a timid, passive, compliant child. Rather, there were indications of feistiness. For example, the yucky mess on the wall was not the result of an inadvertent accident, but of a deliberate, mischievous act. As Mandy became involved in the Rorschach, she no longer acted inhibited. By her second response, she was ready to give free rein to her imagination and, in responding to the examiner's inquiries, she was prepared to take charge and let him know what was what. Furthermore, her readiness to share fantasies, reflect on her responses during the inquiry, and work cooperatively with the examiner boded well for the use she might make of an expressive therapy process.

Interpretations of the Rorschach, of course, are not based on a single card. They are reinforced, expanded, or modified as the rest of the cards are presented. In her 23 other responses on the test, for example, Mandy did not continue to give percepts that were primarily W's or organized combinations of D's. Her mode of approach, like most children her age, was predominantly to large details. She gave many popular responses (9), suggesting not only a capacity to see the world as others do, but also a propensity for overly conventional thinking. Her form level remained high, pointing to good reality testing, and her record contained no indicators of thought disorder. She gave only one other response involving achromatic color, diminishing the examiner's concerns about deeply entrenched depressive tendencies, and she gave four color responses (2FC, 2 CF), which he interpreted as signs of an openness to a range of other affects. She produced three other good human movement responses, some with themes involving cooperative activity (e.g., people washing clothes together). Finally, in addition to giving responses whose content centered on themes of messing and cleaning and vacillation between conventionality and rebelliousness, Mandy also seemed torn between expressing wishes to grow up and to regress and be taken care of. Whereas early in the testing she was a seven-year-old woman of the world who was ready to take charge of the process, by the middle she played at being an innocent little girl who saw cute little bunny rabbits and babies and who giggled and gushed about how pretty the color cards were.

On the basis of her responses to the Rorschach and other tests, the examiner concluded that Mandy was a youngster with a predominantly hysteroid character structure whose unhappiness and inhibition were rooted in conflicts around compliance and defiance, progressive and regressive wishes, and ambivalence around rivalry and identification with her mother. He concurred with the psychiatrist's assessment of Mandy's strengths and his impression that she would make good use of expressive psychotherapy. The latter conclusions, in particular, were amply confirmed by the course of her treatment. Not only did Mandy blossom with therapy, but also, when it was time to stop, the psychiatrist had more difficulty dealing with termination than did his patient.

What is most important about Mandy's case, however, is not the correctness of the interpretation of her Rorschach or how that interpretation was made. Even on the basis of the limited sample of Mandy's test responses and a partial discussion of the inference process, different clinicians experienced with the Rorschach will find some points with which they agree, others with which they would quibble, and still others that they may reject. What is essential is recognizing that both the interpretation of Mandy's responses and the disputes it can generate arise because her Rorschach is one that is familiar to all who utilize the test. They are now ready to apply to the material their preferred modes of analyzing the test and perhaps more than ready to argue with interpretations of others who approach that material in other ways. In short, with Mandy's Rorschach, we reach a point at which not only children but also those who give the test begin to act in customary and predictable ways.

THE TEST PROCESS

The manner in which Mandy handled the Rorschach illustrates two points that characterize the test process in Stage III. First, the child has a reasonable understanding of the Rorschach task. On Card I, for example, she offers a number of responses that are clearly to the inkblot. Second, in order to understand those responses, the examiner asks a number of questions to which the child responds with answers that allow those responses to be scored in conventional ways. For example, Mandy leaves no doubt that her first response is to the whole blot; she identifies a number of parts of the blot fitting her percept, thereby demonstrating that form is a major determinant of her response; and she indicates that achromatic color was also a consideration. Although the examiner thinks, not unreasonably, that shading may be a factor in her "messy wall" response, when he asks, she tells him that achromatic color again was the determinant. In addition, through her description of the person in her second response and her imitation of the action taking place, she makes it clear that a movement score is appropriate as well. In effect, epitomizing the child in Stage III, Mandy is able to give a number of varied responses to the inkblots, identify their location precisely, and answer questions in ways that permit them to be scored with a reasonable degree of assurance.

To be sure, the test process is by no means as easy with many school-age children. With five- and six-year-olds who are still making the transition into Stage III, minor modifications of procedures may still be necessary. For example, Exner and Weiner (1982), who favor conducting inquiry after all cards have been administered, recognize that some difficult youngsters in this age group may respond better to questioning after each card. However, they note most children of this age and certainly older ones can handle their standard procedures.

It is this fact, above all, that distinguishes Stage III. Examiners can now give the test in its most complex forms and expect that children will respond in ways comparable to those of older subjects. As a result, debates about whether to institute special procedures for administering and scoring the test disappear and those who had been reluctant to use the test with younger children now have confidence in the instrument. The change that has taken place is perhaps best illustrated in the work of Halpern. Whereas she recommends a host of modifications in technique in order to use the test with preschoolers, she notes: "Administration of the Rorschach to the school age child follows much the same procedure used with adults" (Halpern, 1952, p. 11). To be sure, establishing rapport and conducting inquiry still may require more effort with these children than with adolescents and adults. Yet the test process is nonetheless still fundamentally similar.

TEST PROTOCOLS AND THEIR INTERPRETATION

The preceding chapter discussed quantitative measures, such as number of responses and form level, on which the protocols of children in Stages II and III differ. However, these measures do not distinguish the stages well. For example, fluent, productive four-year-olds who are still clearly in Stage II may give more responses than cautious seven-year-olds whose handling of the test places them in Stage III. What differentiates the protocols in these stages are two factors that may not be immediately apparent in looking at test records, but which are of the utmost importance in their interpretation.

The first factor is the trust that can be placed in Rorschach scores. Because of the primitive nature of the inquiry process in Stage II, Rorschach data, especially scores, appear "soft." Young children may specify the location and determinants of some responses precisely, while leaving examiners puzzled about where and how other percepts were seen. Since it is often difficult to question them about their responses or to be sure of what their answers mean, those who use the test with preschoolers must either rely on intuition and subjective judgment or accept a high degree of indeterminacy in scoring many responses. As a consequence, some Rorschach experts so distrust these data that they are reluctant to consider the test at this stage, while even those who give it for "scientific" purposes are cautious about relying on it as a clinical instrument before children are of school age.

In contrast, for those who are committed to the Rorschach as a diagnostic test, the data in Stage III are trustworthy. For example, because Mandy was able to specify the location and determinants of her percepts on the first card, the examiner could score the responses with a high degree of confidence. Acting on this confidence, he was ready to interpret those responses and the psychogram summarizing their formal characteristics in his usual manner without qualms or second thoughts. Hence, the consensus about the appropriateness of the test for school-age children and its increasing application in clinical situations.

A second factor, the decrease in and changing meaning of confabulations, is equally important. The tendency toward confabulation does not disappear in the responses of normal seven-year-olds, but rather is transformed. For example, Mandy's image of a woman yelling in front of a messy wall embodies a vivid fantasy. Yet rather than the blot merely serving as a trigger for a fantasy that bears little relationship to it, "perceptual" and "associative" aspects of the response are well integrated. Mandy can point to the wall and the woman and tell why it looks as if she is yelling. Certainly there is as much justification for her description of the card as there is for suggesting it is a jack-o-lantern, animal face, or any other response typically described as having good form.

However, the blatant forms of confabulation so prevalent in the records of four-year-olds now disappear from those of normal children and become signs of psychopathology. For example, Klopfer, Spiegelman, and Fox (1956) assert:

If a seven-year-old child still gives responses based on any of the three steps of perseveration, confabulation, and confabulatory combination, we may assume that he functions below his age level. The reason for this may lie in mental retardation, emotional infantilism, or a temporary emotional disturbance [p. 28].

Similarly, Ames et al. (1952) observe:

Though contaminated responses appear to occur quite normally from 4½ through 5½ years of age, and confabulation responses from 4 through 7 years, their occurrence after these ages at least suggests immaturity if not the pathology which they would imply at later ages [p. 283].

Confabulation, which had been a common characteristic of the Rorschach responses of normal children, now becomes a "danger signal" indicative of possible psychopathology.

The significance of this shift in confabulatory responses goes far beyond changes in one scoring category on a psychogram. As has been seen, for some leading Rorschach authorities, confabulatory responses reflect a mode of concept formation that governs preschoolers' responses to the test as a whole. Insofar as this is true, scores for location and form level may be artifacts of this approach and have different meanings than are usually attributed to them. Hence, for Klopfer, for example, it is only once these primitive modes of approaching the test cease to be typical and become signs of immaturity or pathology that there is comfort in assuming that the test can be scored and analyzed in the same way with children and adults.

Because children reach Stage III does not mean that there will be no further signficant developmental changes in their Rorschachs as they grow older. Throughout middle childhood and adolescence, for example, form quality improves, movement responses increase, pure color and, later, CF responses decrease, and so forth (Levitt and Truuma, 1972; Exner and Weiner, 1982). However, from the beginning of Stage III on, it is assumed that the Rorschach is a reliable instrument and that scores on it register changes in children faithfully. Thus, for example, because they are now convinced that "Rorschach behavior means what it means regardless of the age of the subject," Exner and Weiner (1982, p. 14) assert that any clinician who understands the test is "fully prepared" to interpret the protocols of children as well as adults.

In short, as children reach this stage in the early school years, the Rorschach becomes "the Rorschach."

III

Psychosocial Aspects of the Rorschach Task

Formulating the Problem

SALIENT QUESTIONS

For those interested in children's Rorschachs, descriptions of stages in the mastery of the test stimulate a variety of questions. How are the curious phenomena encountered in each stage to be understood? How do children move from one stage to another? What can answers to these questions contribute to an understanding of the Rorschach task? And what implications do these answers have for clinical work with preschoolers and with profoundly disturbed older children who may take the Rorschach in similar ways?

One approach to problems of this kind begins with a consideration of a simpler question: What does it mean to say that a child has "taken the Rorschach?"

A PREHISTORY OF THE RORSCHACH

To appreciate what "taking the Rorschach" means, it may be helpful to try an exercise suggested by Vorhaus (1951) 40 years ago and, to the best of my knowledge, not undertaken again since. Let us imagine what children's responses to the test might be like *before* they reach the first stage of the model, that of perseverative reactions.

Were psychologists so inclined, they could administer the Rorschach to children soon after birth. Place an inkblot about 19 centimeters in front of a neonate in a quiet alert state, give the standard instructions, and a number of responses are likely to be forthcoming. The child may fixate on the card briefly and scan the contours of the figure, ignore the card, cry, or withdraw and go to sleep.

Repeat the procedure with a four-month-old, give the child a smile in the interest of establishing rapport, and different responses will be elicited. The baby may show some curiosity about the card, be more curious about the examiner, and offer a nice smile in return.

By 10 months, children will display a wider range of reactions. They may be puzzled by the examiner or fearful. Also, they may be more interested in the card, though chiefly in handling it, mouthing it, banging it, or dropping it on the floor.

By 18 months, reactions should be more varied. The card may be examined more carefully for a longer period of time. It may be manipulated, bent, or, if children are especially precocious and have a crayon handy, scribbled upon. In addition, if examiners are lucky, bright toddlers may even utter something vaguely resembling a "Rorschach response."

Six months later, more of these responses will be given as children begin to produce perseverative records.

Of course, we would not subject infants and toddlers to such foolishness. It makes little sense to "give" a test that will not be "taken." To be sure, in each case, inkblots could be presented, instructions repeated, and responses obtained that, whatever their other limitations, would be characteristic of the individual children and appropriate to their ages. Yet even the most enthusiastic advocate of preschool Rorschachs would accept only the very last of these responses, those that begin to be produced toward the end of the second year, as a first stage in children's Rorschachs. To have taken the Rorschach, subjects must have some understanding of the task expected of them and some capacity to cooperate with examiners in providing responses and participating in an inquiry process.

In effect, the Rorschach has a cognitive dimension, one that defines the test as an intellectual task with a particular meaning, and a psychosocial dimension, one that calls for a particular kind of interaction between tester and testee.

PERSPECTIVES ON THE DEVELOPMENTAL PROCESS

Explanations of how children master the Rorschach thus require consideration of two interrelated sets of developmental processes. On one hand, we need to investigate how children and examiners negotiate an interpersonal situation in which they will eventually work together on a common enterprise. On the other, we need to account for how children come to give the task a meaning that is within the range examiners will accept as constituting "the Rorschach."

For the purpose of analysis, these two processes will be examined in separate sections. The four chapters that follow will explore psychosocial aspects of children's Rorschach performance from a number of different perspectives: those of ego psychology, socialization and play, the "patient–examiner" relationship, and the developmental psychology of Heinz Werner (Werner, 1957, 1961; Werner and Kaplan, 1963). As will be seen, the perspectives are not mutually exclusive and each has distinct contributions to make to an understanding of how children take the Rorschach. In order to highlight psychosocial issues, the Rorschach task itself will be considered in only a general, schematic way. It will be viewed simply as one of a potentially broad class of intellectual tasks that preschool children initially find difficult, demanding, and sufficiently ambiguous that they cannot be sure of exactly what is expected of them. Specific cognitive aspects of the Rorschach will be explored in the section that follows these chapters.

An Ego-Psychological Perspective on Preschoolers' Handling of the Rorschach

EGO PSYCHOLOGY AND THE RORSCHACH SITUATION

Apart from Fox (1956), few have offered comprehensive explanations of the process through which children master the Rorschach. Yet if we consider interpretations of particular phenomena salient in that process and reasons advanced for modifying Rorschach technique with pre-schoolers, we can discern the outline of a theory that encompasses most of what has been written on the topic and offers a plausible account of how children move from one stage to another.

At the root of this theory is a recognition that the Rorschach is a psychosocial task to which children must adapt. To take the test in its typical form, subjects must meet with a person whom they have proba-bly never met before, doing so at a time and place of the other's choosing, and solve a cognitive problem that this person has defined and seems to expect to be handled in a particular way.

Negotiating this situation requires a variety of abilities. Subjects must be able to tolerate anxiety at meeting strangers; they must be able to accept a task set for them, even though it may mean subordinating their own desires to the wishes of another; and they must possess the interpersonal skills necessary to engage in a cooperative enterprise. They must have cognitive capacities that enable them to understand the problem posed by the Rorschach and devise strategies for its solution. In carrying out those strategies, they must be able to sustain attention, inhibit impulses that interfere with working in a goal-directed manner, and cope with affects such as fear, anxiety, boredom, frustration, or anger that can disrupt their work. Moreover, they must make use of these abilities across an entire test, one that involves not only producing responses to many different cards, but also explaining these responses so that a stranger can understand what they reveal. In doing so, children must deal with additional anxieties about the adequacy of their performance and about what the examiner and perhaps their parents, teachers, doctor, or others will make of their responses.

Since these skills are acquired only gradually in the course of childhood, the manner in which preschoolers handle the Rorschach is typically explained by referring to their level of cognitive development and their capacity to regulate affect and behavior. Writing at a time when ego psychology was at the peak of its popularity, Fox (1956) offered an explanation based chiefly on psychoanalytic concepts of ego development. Insofar as this type of explanation is presented in ordinary language and allowance is made for some differences in emphases, it can incorporate most published views of psychosocial aspects of early Rorschachs, including those of nonanalytic authors such as Ford (1946).

STAGE I PHENOMENA

In Stage I the skills necessary to cope with the Rorschach are present only in the most primitive form, if at all. As is obvious in descriptions of test behavior in this period, very young children have little capacity to deal with the kind of social situation in which the Rorschach is typically given. They are sufficiently troubled by meetings with strangers that the test is usually administered by parents and teachers or, at least, with a parent present. Even in these circumstances, the children cannot be counted upon to cooperate with the examiner and address themselves to the test. They may or may not do so according to "the spirit of the moment" (Klopfer and Margulies, 1941, p. 3) and, if they do begin to work with the examiner on the task, they may quit abruptly. For example, at the time of his first Rorschach, Colin was sufficiently lacking in refinement and social graces that he was not about to spend more than a few moments with his teacher on an activity he found boring when there were more exciting attractions across the playroom.

While taking note of problems with attention and impulsivity that interfere with young children registering the Rorschach task well, authorities agree that the major difficulty is cognitive. For example, Klopfer, Spiegelman, and Fox (1956, p. 26) note that the test situation is puzzling to many two- and three-year-olds and their responses chiefly reflect perplexity. Fox (1956) asserts that these children have trouble knowing how to deal with the inkblots themselves and offer responses that are not so much to the Rorschach card as the total test situation. So primitive are the cognitive operations involved that it has been repeatedly suggested that first responses are often little more than associations that "may or may not" be determined by features of the card (Klopfer and Margulies, 1941, p. 4; Ford, 1946, p. 36; Ames et al., 1952, p. 109). Needless to say, very young children lack the more sophisticated intellectual abilities necessary to reflect on their responses and participate in inquiry.

Most accounts of perseverations, the most prominent feature of early Rorschachs, follow Klopfer (Klopfer and Margulies, 1941; Klopfer, Spiegelman, and Fox, 1956) in characterizing the first response as a "magic wand" or "magic key" that is repeated as a way of negotiating the rest of the test. Yet although the term "magic" implies archaic mental operations and abandonment of "the reality principle," the explanations offered for these perseverations suggest that they are, in fact, an adaptive strategy immature egos adopt to cope with the problems the Rorschach poses for them.

Fox (1956, p. 52), for example, argues that perseveration "represents attempts at active mastery of a situation that is fraught with some anxiety." Faced with a bewildering task, he contends, children experience threats to self-esteem associated with recognition of inadequacy and fears of losing approval or love if they cannot do what is expected of them. To these concerns, others can be added as well, such as needs to cope with frustration and helplessness. In perseverating, children draw upon behavior that is well within their repertoire (e.g., they have long enjoyed repeating activities and stories) and offer responses to which examiners have already reacted with approval. Although acting as if perseverated responses are adequate may involve a substantial measure of avoidance and denial by the child, it is a defensive strategy that rapidly and effectively averts the anxieties attendant on grappling with the task in any other way. It is also a gambit well suited to handling examiners' demands. Responses are easily produced for each card, allowing potentially frustrating and upsetting social encounters to be finessed smoothly. From the examiner's standpoint, such maneuvers may leave something to be desired; from the child's, it is hard to conceive any other way of dealing with such a problematic situation as quickly and comfortably.

This strategy is not confined to preschoolers taking the Rorschach, but can be found in other populations in similar circumstances. In discussing the functional aspects of seemingly symptomatic behavior encountered in administering any psychological tests to mentally retarded children, Hirsch (1959) observes:

> *Perseveration*, while it reflects an inability to react spontaneously, flexibly, and creatively to new situations, nevertheless also represents an adaptive resolution. The child, in effect, consistently reacts with a response with which he has achieved some measure of success. He has received at least minimal approval implicit in the fact that the preceding task has apparently been successfully dealt with; that is, it has been removed and a new one put in its place. Hence, he continues to give the same response over and over, hoping that it will continue to see him through. Further, perseveration represents a relatively painless way of rather quickly "getting rid" of an onerous task (and frequently, too, of an onerous examiner) [p. 644].

The same explanation can be offered of the "mechanistic perseverations" of organically damaged adults on the Rorschach (Exner, 1978).

Each of the forms of modified perseverations in the transitional period at the end of this first stage may be seen to be based on growth in ego capacities. The substitution of refusals on some cards for perseverations reflects a greater degree of comfort in acknowledging limitations, an ability to inhibit an automatic response, and a more "realistic" way of grappling with the cognitive task. Production of a few nonperseverative responses reflects these qualities *and*, obviously, increasing intellectual skills.

The pattern of "perseverated logic" responses in which children now search cards for characteristics to justify their repetition of the initial response represents even more advanced ego functioning. Although the product, a perseverated response, remains the same, the process through which it is produced is far more sophisticated. Instead of automatic repititions of responses that are unrelated to Rorschach cards, children now give genuine responses to the inkblots. However, they can do so because they have defined the test not as one requiring production of different responses for each card, but rather as one in which they are to find some aspect of each blot that fits a concept they already have in mind. In an admirable way, these children master a difficult situation by transforming a problem they cannot solve into one that is within their abilities and, even, fun.

STAGE II PHENOMENA

In the fourth year of life, ego functions in normal children have matured to a degree that the Rorschach can be taken in a new way. One manifestation of these changes is an increased capacity to handle the social situation in which the Rorschach is given. Children are now able to work with an unfamiliar examiner and cooperate sufficiently to take the test in at least a rudimentary form.

Yet this advance is still modest. Although usually parents need not be present, examiners must often act less like testers than like surrogate parents. For example, Halpern (1953, p. 7) is even prepared to put an arm around children or invite them to sit on her lap while they work. Few other authorities go this far, but, as has been seen, many respond to the special needs of preschool children through significant modifications of the examiner's behavior and test procedures.

The reasons for these modifications are articulated well by Ford (1946, p. 32) in her discussion of conditions she deems "essential for maximum efficiency of the test." Because children rapidly lose interest in the test, she advises examiners to provide added encouragement when necessary to keep them at the task. Because young children are distractible, impulsive, and easily diverted by the play potential of Rorschach cards, she recommends intervening to bring them back to the task and help maintain their set. As a precautionary measure to help "improve attention" and "safeguard the goal of the test by reducing the possibilities for manipulation" (p. 33), she advocates not allowing cards to be turned. Because young children have difficulty understanding the task, she encourages flexibility in explaining and reminding them of procedures. Perhaps most significant, recognizing the emotional vulnerability of young children, she stresses the importance of examiners remaining attuned to their feelings and using subtle, nonverbal means "to create a feeling of security, adequacy, and general well-being." From the perspective of ego psychology, the problems Ford describes—distractibility, impulsivity, low frustration tolerance, struggles around managing affect, and difficulties sustaining goal-directed activity—could be lifted directly from a catalogue of "ego weaknesses." Her recommendations for dealing with these problems require that examiners function as "auxiliary egos" who act to compensate for these weaknesses in ways that allow children to manage the test situation.

As has been seen in the review of the literature on preschool Rorschachs, other authorities conceptualize issues in test administration in the same way. There is a broad consensus on the problems children of this age present, and even those who insist on adherence to standard forms of test administration recognize the need for some compensatory actions on the part of examiners to help children negotiate the test (Klopfer, Spiegelman, and Fox, 1956). What divides these authorities are preferred modes of providing this assistance and differences regarding the constraints their particular definition of the Rorschach places on how assistance may be offered.

There is also a consensus that the ego functions that most decisively shape Rorschachs in Stage II are cognitive ones. Although detailed discussion of the specific operations involved will be deferred until the next section, three general features of explanations based upon them should be noted here.

First, the movement beyond the perseverative Rorschach protocols of Stage I is attributed chiefly to growth of cognitive abilities. In accounting for the emergence of confabulatory approaches to the test at about the age of three, for example, Fox (1956) asserts:

> The child has undergone considerable development from the previous level of functioning. He now reacts discriminately to the cards themselves; moveover he is able to come to grips with some reality aspects of the blot, identifying a part of the blot and adequately relating it to a part of his concept or image. He apparently understands more clearly what is expected of him and copes with the expectation in a much more adequate manner [p. 93].

In short, children of age three produce different Rorschachs because they now have the capacity to deal with the task as they could not before.

Second, because this capacity is still limited relative to the demands of the task, many of the distinctive characteristics of Stage II protocols — for example, the number and range of responses, poor form level, and the prevalence of confabulated whole responses — are explained in terms of intellectual immaturity. For example, Meili-Dworetzki (1956) and Hemmindinger (1953) emphasize "syncretistic" perception; Fox (1956, p. 94) stresses "archaic thinking" and "the pars pro toto type of ideation"; Kay and Vorhaus (1943) note the high incidence of "crude," "arbitrary," and "pseudo psychotic" responses; and Ames et al. (1952, p. 140) refer to "immaturity of thinking and the confused perceptions and conceptions." Although focusing on different kinds of intellectual operations, the adjectives applied to them invariably connote "primitivity."

Third, the confabulatory nature of the content of characteristic Stage II responses is typically explained by invoking either preschool children's problems with "reality testing" or their indifference to distinctions between reality and fantasy. For example, Fox (1956, p. 93) suggests that "the boundary between levels of reality and unreality is still highly permeable." Because the child is easily caught up with affect and fantasy, "ideation is still largely governed by the pleasure principle, even though the reality principle has begun to operate in a significant way." Ames et al. (1952, p. 144) assert that their typical three-and-a-half-year-old is "highly imaginative" and "seems to confuse real and unreal in his play." The confabulated responses of the four-year-old, they assert, are the products of "high unbridled imagination" (p. 158). Similarly, Halpern (1960, p. 16) suggests that "the lack of good reality testing is one of the most conspicuous features" of the records of young children.

Accounts of the last distinctive aspect of Stage II Rorschach performance, children's handling of the inquiry process, focus on the same patterns of relative strengths and weaknesses of ego functions. On one hand, advances in cognitive development make it possible for children to begin to identify and share the determinants of their percepts. On the other, these advances are limited. Halpern (1953, p. 10) notes: "The difficulty in obtaining any inquiry from the child is accentuated by his inability to explain just why he made a particular interpretation." As has been seen, some who test preschoolers, such as Ames and her associates, try to compensate for these limitations by using their sensitivity to how children are dealing with Rorschach cards to intuit determinants of responses that the children cannot state explicitly. Others such as Klopfer accept those limitations and simply score responses with question marks.

The greater intellectual demands of the inquiry process both accentuate and are accentuated by preschoolers' problems with attention, impulsivity, tolerance of frustration and anxiety, and management of affect in general. Consequently, many of the recommendations for modifying administrative procedures concern altering the inquiry process in order to avoid exacerbating these problems. Halpern (1953, p. 10), for example, cautions against vigorous inquiry lest children become irritated and resistant. She also favors inquiry after each card and even after each response because of preschoolers' problems with memory and their impatience. Similarly, Ames et al. (1952, p. 27) combine the initial presentation of cards and inquiry to offset "restlessness and loss of interest." All who test these children emphasize the importance of titrating questioning to emotional states to avoid frustrating children or overtaxing their meager investment in the task.

In many respects, children's handling of inquiry in Stage II resembles their handling of responses in Stage I. Their appreciation of and commitment to the process is modest and their engagement with it erratic. They may or may not do the task, as the spirit moves them.

Avoidance, resistance, and regression are common. As a consequence, examiners often feel they get genuine answers to their questions on one response only to be led on a wild goose chase on the next.

STAGE III PHENOMENA

By the age of six or seven, normal children possess the abilities necessary to take the Rorschach in its standard form. They are able to meet with examiners they do not know and work together on the test they are given. They are able to understand the Rorschach task and produce responses comparable to those of older youngsters and adults. And they can answer questions about their responses in ways that raise no untoward questions about scoring and analysis.

Seven-year-olds, of course, do not take the test in exactly the same manner as adults. Maintaining rapport and remaining attuned to their handling of the task are still important with them. Nor are their Rorschachs identical to those of adults. With further ego development, protocols become richer and more sophisticated in a variety of ways. However, such assistance as need be offered with the test can be given within the framework of standard modes of test administration, and the responses produced are ones examiners are comfortable analyzing in the same ways they use with those of older subjects. Whatever abilities underlie the capacity to take the test are now assumed to be present in normal populations.

CONCLUSION

In sum, the most widely accepted explanation of children's mastery of the Rorschach, one associated with the perspective of ego psychology, contends that the capacity to take the test in its typical form requires a variety of adaptive skills that begin to appear in early childhood but are not well established until the early elementary school years. The process through which children come to be able to take the test is thus seen to be based on the maturation and development of cognitive abilities and capacities to regulate affect and behavior; the distinctive features of children's behavior and test responses in early stages of this process are viewed the products of an interaction of varying degrees of cognitive and emotional immaturity; and variations in the behavior of examiners in these stages are understood as efforts to cope with that immaturity in ways that allow children to manage the test as best they can.

Critical evaluations of this theory could stress the need for greater specificity with regard to particular ego functions, especially cognitive ones. Provision of means of measuring these functions are, no doubt, desirable as well. Yet, for the present purposes, what stands out about the theory is its promise. In its broad outline, it provides reasonable interpretations of salient phenomena at each stage of the developmental process and a plausible means of explaining movement from one stage to another.

11

Work and Play

DEFINITIONS OF THE SOCIAL SITUATION

In ego-psychological explanations of stages in early Rorschach performance, two of the three basic factors in the Rorschach equation, the test and the examiner, are constants. It is assumed that the Rorschach task is more or less the same for subjects at each stage and that all subjects are approached in sufficiently similar ways that protocols are not influenced unduly by the behavior of the examiner. Differences in test performance in each of the three stages are thus attributed to changes in the third factor, the subject.

Yet these stages can be seen from other perspectives. A different account of them becomes possible, for example, when they are viewed from the standpoint of changing definitions of the task.

At first glance, this idea appears odd. The Rorschach has a definition, one given it by Hermann Rorschach himself and maintained with only minor modifications by later systematizers of the test. Even those who introduce substantial changes in administrative procedures in working with young children try to remain as faithful to Rorschach's position as they believe circumstances allow. They present alterations in technique as temporary concessions to children's immaturity. But this definition of the task is that of examiners.

Children, were they so inclined, could raise interesting questions about the behavior of psychologists who approach what are advertised as "play" sessions convinced that they are entitled by virtue of their age, position, or social status to dictate the ground rules for the interaction to follow. Adults, of course, frequently act in this manner with children, and, given Rorschach examiners' commitments to providing clinical assistance or advancing science, they probably have a better right to do so than others. Nonetheless, it seems only fair that both parties to a social interchange be free to try to realize their own ends, that the definition of the situation be negotiated, and that, perhaps, disagreements even be resolved through some compromise. For examiners to insist on structuring the test situation in their own way can be taken to reflect a degree of egocentricity, if not outright rudeness. Moreover, for psychologists to engage in such bargaining with young children and expect their subjects to make most of the concessions—in this case, to expect that preschoolers will not impose their own definitions on an endeavor they find hard to understand and frustrating—is quite extraordinary. Certainly, children conduct very little of the rest of their lives in this manner.

Not much can be gained from trading accusations about whose behavior is more naïve and egocentric. However, if we do not give the claims of the examiner priority, psychosocial aspects of early Rorschachs can be approached from a new perspective. We can explore how both sets of participants in the test process negotiate the definition of the situation.

SOCIALIZATION AND PLAY

The principles governing the behavior of examiners in these negotiations are clear. Convinced that the Rorschach is a worthwhile task that human beings of a certain level of maturity should be able to accomplish, psychologists view their job as one of presenting the test in the prescribed way and assuring that subjects abide by its rules. In working with youngsters who lack that maturity, examiners provide the particular mixture of structure, education, and support they believe best suited to help children come as close to conforming to the rules of the task as possible. As these young subjects grow older, it is assumed, they will learn to take the test appropriately. From the standpoint of examiners, stages in the mastery of the Rorschach are steps in a socialization process.

The principles governing the behavior of preschoolers are quite different. As has been seen, for example, two- and three-year-olds give no indications that accomplishing the Rorschach in the prescribed manner weighs heavily on their minds.

The ends young children do seek to realize are apparent if we consider the test behavior that is most representative of them and unique to their age. A two-and-a-half-year-old is given a Rorschach card and the examiner must work hard to get her to look at the inkblot instead of spinning the card. A three-year-old spices his responses with large doses of silly language and behavior. A three-and-a-half-year-old decides to tell a story about a little man running about on Card X. Still another asserts he is being attacked by a monster on Card IV. Such behavior is hard to describe in Rorschach terms other than those implying significant pathology; it is rarely found in older subjects who do not exhibit retardation or serious emotional disturbances. Yet, when considered in the context of behavior ordinarily encountered with preschoolers, these actions are easily recognized. Children spend a significant part of their waking life playing and clearly they have not stopped upon entering the examiner's office.

Although "everybody" knows what play is, books and articles on the subject typically begin with the observation that the concept is notoriously difficult to define. A good dictionary will offer a dozen definitions and the psychological literature contains a plethora of more sophisticated ones linked to a host of different theories. Even the kinds of activities the term denotes are so diverse as to include the simple repetitive actions of infants shaking rattles, the enacted fantasies of youngsters pretending they are superheroes, and the organized social games of older children and adults. For the present purposes, the play of preschoolers taking the Rorschach can be defined in terms of three qualities that are prominent in common usage of the term and widely, if not universally, accepted in the psychological literature.

One primary characteristic of play, its affective and motivational aspect, is captured well in ordinary language when the activity is equated with "having fun" or "amusing oneself." Philosophers and psychologists frequently make the same point in more formal ways. For example, Spencer defines play as "an activity performed for the immediate gratification derived"; for Lazarus, it is "activity free, aimless, amusing, or diverting"; and for Allin, it is "activities which are accompanied by a state of comparative pleasure, exhilaration, power, and the feeling of self initiative" (Mitchell and Mason, 1948, pp. 86–87). Psychoanalysts initially treated play as an expression of the "pleasure principle" and, although other functions were later recognized, the close connection of the activity to wish fulfillment and the search for gratification has always been stressed (Waelder, 1933; Peller, 1954). The developmental literature emphasizes this pleasurable quality as well. Describing play across species, Garvey (1977, p. 3), observes: "Sheer exuberance is another seemingly universal characteristic of much playful behavior. The young of higher species frolic, frisk, gambol, cavort, engage in mock combat with every sign of pleasure and high spirits. . . ." Similarly, in articulating the concept in ways that can be applied to early child development, she notes that first among the "descriptive characteristics widely cited as critical to its definition" is simply that "play is pleasurable, enjoyable" (p. 4).

To be sure, because play assumes so many different forms, examples can be cited in which amusement is not evident. Psychoanalysts, in particular, have been sensitive to the roles of anxiety and conflict in it (Peller, 1954). Yet the idea of "fun" is so central to normative conceptions of the term that most people witnessing children playing in serious, driven, anxious, or troubled ways sense that the activity has ceased to be "play" and become something else, perhaps work. Similarly, insofar as pleasure is absent from a child's play, clinicians are prone to suspect something is awry.

A second quality often highlighted in philosophical and psychological definitions of play is spontaneity or freedom from external constraint (Mitchell and Mason, 1948). For example, Garvey (1977, p. 4) notes: "Play has no extrinsic goals. Its motivations are intrinsic and serve no other objectives. . . . Play is spontaneous and voluntary. It is freely chosen by the player." Similarly, Rubin, Fein, and Vandenberg (1983) observe:

> A feature that is almost unanimously acknowledged to be the hallmark of play is that it is an *intrinsically motivated* behavior neither governed by appetitive drives (Berlyne, 1960; Bruner, 1972; Garvey, 1977; Huizinga, 1955; Klinger, 1971; Koestler, 1964; Neuman, 1971; Schwartzman, 1978; Vandenberg, 1978; Weisler and McCall, 1976) nor compliance with social demands or inducements external to the behavior itself [p. 698].

In short, play is done for its own sake and, compared with other activities, enjoys a substantial degree of freedom from the immediate dictates of biology and society (Klinger, 1971; Singer, 1991).

Finally, play, or, more specifically, symbolic play of the kind encountered in preschoolers, has a cognitive aspect. In everyday language, play is a realm of "make believe," an activity in which, in its purest form, concerns about what is real are temporarily set aside in favor of indulgence in fantasy. Psychoanalytic theories, too, emphasize the role of fantasy in play and the relative independence of the activity from "the reality principle" (Waelder, 1933; Freud, 1908). In the most influential theoretical exposition of this view, Piaget (1951) conceives of symbolic play as an intellectual endeavor in which assimilatory modes of experience are predominant. Whereas most cognition involves a significant degree of "accommodation," efforts to adapt schemas and concepts to what is taken to be the demands of reality, in play those demands are suspended. "Reality" provides little more than material to be shaped according to the concepts and wishes of the subject. A stick ceases to be a stick and becomes a gun, a doll becomes a baby, a broom becomes a horse. Elaborating this concept, Fein (1987, p. 299) argues that pretend play is distinguished by such characteristics as "referential freedom, denotative license, sequential uncertainty, and self-mirroring," all of which in different ways reflect forms of cognition in which there is "independence from the immediate environment, actual experience, or the need to cast one's experience of life or self into a tidy story."

The wish to use the Rorschach situation to play in these ways does not necessarily bring children into conflict with examiners. To the contrary, there may be a convergence of interests that makes genuine testing possible. Most examiners would be pleased if their subjects, young and old, found the task enjoyable. Moreover, many would point out that the test lends itself to being treated in playful ways. After all, the Rorschach task involves a substantial degree of freedom from external constraints; subjects are encouraged to see the blots in any manner they choose. Most important, the Rorschach requires a predominantly assimilatory mode of mental functioning. Subjects *must* shape the ink-blots into percepts of their own choosing. Indeed, E. Schachtel (1966, p. 323) stresses that "a productive and rich test performance presupposes . . . the capacity for imaginative, intellectual play."

Yet, while the interests of young children and testers may at times overlap, they hardly coincide. For the Rorschach truly to be a form of play for children, examiners would have to permit them far greater latitude than is typically the case. After all, Card I might be a bat, but it might also be treated as an occasion for telling a story, a dumb game the child wishes to stop immediately, a toy for spinning, a Frisbee for sailing, a design for coloring, or a piece of cardboard that can be bent into interesting shapes.

Two factors save the Rorschach situation from degenerating into a battle of wills over who will do what with the examiner's equipment. First, as will be seen, maturing children engage in progressively more complex and social forms of play, notably games (Piaget, 1951). Thus, Rorschach examiners have some hope of interesting children in their games and getting subjects to "play by the rules." Second, examiners are able to obtain Rorschach responses from preschoolers—and safe-guard their cards—because, in addition to the wish to play, children exhibit another set of countervailing motivations that are more in ac-cord with examiners' interests. The striving to display competence and mastery (White, 1959; Lichtenberg, 1989), the capacity to recognize rules and the need to meet standards (Kagan, 1984; Emde, Johnson, and Easterbrooks, 1987), and the intellectual interest in imitation (Piaget, 1951) contribute to an at least sporadic readiness to "work" on tasks adults set for them. To be sure, even when in the presence of a "taskmas-ter" who exerts strong pressure to accomplish the Rorschach in a particu-lar way, preschoolers' attempts to meet the extrinsic requirements of the task and subordinate affective states to the necessity of "doing the job" are often short-lived. As with play, their conceptions of work and their readiness to do it change developmentally. However, the need to work operates as a force in the Rorschach situation from the first.

In sum, then, stages in children's handling of the Rorschach can be analyzed in terms of shifting definitions of the Rorschach situation negotiated by two sets of participants who operate according to differ-ent, though at times convergent, principles. For examiners, these nego-tiations are governed by efforts to get subjects to accomplish the Rorschach task in prescribed ways, although with younger subjects compromises are made in recognition of the amount and kind of work that can reasonably be expected. For children, the principles governing the bargaining are more complex, since they involve not only shifting balances in the readiness to work and the wish to play, but also develop-mental changes in each of these activities.

STAGE I: TOYS AND ASSOCIATIVE PLAY

To appreciate initial struggles around the definition of the Rorschach situation, let us return to the case of Colin that was used to illustrate Stage I Rorschachs and add to the earlier account of the child's behavior the interpreter's inferences about the test process (A. Schachtel, 1944).

As has been seen, the testing begins with a brief convergence of interests. The examiner offers to show Colin "some pictures" and Colin would like to see them. However, whereas his teacher wants the boy to come to a quiet room to work, Colin insists upon deciding where and when the activity will take place and, to secure his cooperation, the examiner agrees.

Schachtel suggests that Colin's interest in the first card is sufficient to offset any resistance he may feel to the task and he, in fact, quickly gives an initial response, "a mountain." However, because no inquiry is undertaken she can only speculate that his response is based on the upward slope of the top part of the inkblot. The examiner is obviously convinced that little is to be gained from such questioning since the child is neither willing nor able to engage in such work.

Presented with Card II, Colin asserts that it is a red mountain and immediately insists on going on to the next card. While acknowledging that this perseverative response may reflect boredom or a wish to get rid of the card, Schachtel's commitment to the test is such that she believes that adding the color "red" to his first response is of significance and indicates that Colin is genuinely grappling with the task. Others may have doubts about his involvement, since he gives the same response to the next eight inkblots. By the third card, even Schachtel is sure that Colin's interest in the test has waned and that his perseverative response reflects a wish to have done with the task as quickly as possible. By Card V, he is far more interested in two girls across the room who are singing and pretending that several chairs are a train and, within minutes of beginning the test, he goes off to play with them.

Over the next hour and a half, the examiner tries to entice Colin back to the test, a wish the boy complies with only when, while waiting to paint, he finds he has nothing better to do with his time. He then describes the next several cards as mountains, which may or may not reflect a minimal degree of compliance with the task the examiner has set for him. However, on Card VIII, he finds a way of changing the test into an activity more to his liking—propping the card in a crack in the desk and letting it drop through to the floor. The examiner, like Colin, finds this play funny. Perhaps because of this appreciation of the possibilities of the game, the two establish an implicit agreement that remains in force through the end of the test. Colin continues playing with the cards in this manner, while periodically allowing himself to be brought back to test task and rewarding the examiner with the now familiar response, "a mountain."

In her analysis of the last half of the test, Schachtel suggests ways in which characteristics of each of the five cards may have influenced Colin's behavior. For example, she hypothesizes that, in standing Card VIII on edge, he may have been representing a mountain. However, she also concedes that often Colin does not take the task very seriously. Others, such as Ford (1946), would argue that Colin's play at this point is chiefly determined by the manipulative possibilities of the card as an object rather than efforts to represent its content. Certainly by Card IX, Colin is far more interested in dropping the card through a crack in the table and playing with it with his feet than having it stand "like a mountain."

Colin's testing highlights three sets of characteristics that distinguish negotiations around the definition of the Rorschach situation in Stage I. First, although the examiner's goal throughout the testing is getting the child to take the test in ways in which it will be possible to obtain an interpretable record, what is most distinctive about the test administration at this stage is the generosity of the concessions she is prepared to make. Recognizing that very young children may be reluctant or even unable to do the work involved in taking the test, Colin's teacher is ready to give the test in as palatable a way as possible and alters test procedures substantially. For example, the test is described as "looking at pictures" to try to intrigue Colin; the boy can remain in the playroom in spite of noise and distractions; no effort at inquiry is made; he is allowed to leave the task after five cards in the hope that he can be lured back later; and he is permitted to use the last cards as toys as long he also gives some test responses. From the standpoint of the examiner, such compromises are far from ideal, but seem to be the best bargain that can be made at this time. At the least, they are sufficient to obtain a test protocol, which, as Schachtel demonstrates, can be subject to elaborate analyses in an effort to determine its meaning and make some inferences about Colin's personality.

Second, even with the concession examiners are prepared to make in Stage I, it is clear that children have little interest in doing the "work" involved in the test and engage in it only briefly in response to pressure. Rather, their chief interest is in play, and play of a kind for which examiners have little use—treating the Rorshach card as a toy (Ford, 1946). For example, Colin agrees to the Rorschach in the belief that looking at the examiner's pictures may be diverting and cooperates with the test process on Card I long enough to get an idea of the kind of game the examiner seems to want to play. Quickly discovering that the game is too hard and little fun, he perhaps works a bit on Card II, but by Card III is ready to stop the test altogether. Discovering that the girls across the room really know how to have a good time, he deserts the examiner to join them. Later, when bored, he yields to the examiner's entreaties to return to the "pictures," and works on them for two cards. Not until Card VIII does he find an answer that satisfies him regarding what the card could be—an object that can be manipulated in intriguing ways—and he succeeds in demonstrating this possibility to the examiner.

Finally, given these differences, the interactions of the two parties consist of a continual struggle around how the test situation is to be defined, which includes at best occasional periods of unstable compromise during which their interests run parallel. For example, a tenuous accommodation is reached only on the last cards of Colin's Rorschach when the examiner allows Colin to play with them in the manner he has chosen and in return Colin gives a response to each card until the test is completed.

Viewing this stage as one in which a child is only at the beginning of a socialization process that will make testing possible, examiners are inclined to interpret interactions chiefly in terms of children's ego weaknesses and limited psychosocial development. From the standpoint of children, however, these interactions can be seen differently. Uninterested in the work examiners wish done, they strive to transform the situation into a form of play that will be more fun, a goal Colin, for example, achieves with considerable success. Indeed, the behavior of both children and examiners can be interpreted as forms of associative and even parallel play (Parten, 1932; Millar, 1974). Although ostensibly engaged in an activity together, the two parties, in fact, are occupied with different, occasionally overlapping pursuits. Colin is concerned above all with the opportunities the Rorschach card affords as a toy; the examiner, being disposed to a more cerebral form of play, finds the situation of interest chiefly because it offers a chance for theorical speculation; and both seem reasonably pleased with the time spent together. Rorschach practitioners who take the test "seriously," of course, have little interest in such play and simply do not work with children of this age.

STAGE II: SYMBOLIC PLAY

In Stage II children and examiners enter into negotiations around the test situation differently and, as a consequence, interactions between them undergo marked changes.

Most examiners are still ready to make concessions on issues in test administration. As has been seen, debates about appropriate technique with preschoolers center on differing opinions regarding the nature and extent of the compromises that should be made. What is significant here, however, is not these differences of opinion, but rather two more general points. First, regardless of examiners' particular stances regarding modifications in technique, they find that, in contrast to Stage I, they need to concede less in their approach to children. The test process thus begins to resemble its standard form. Second, examiners get far more in return for the concessions they do make. Children now produce a distinct response on most cards and inquiry is possible in at least a rudimentary form.

At the same time, the socialization process that enables normal children to take the Rorschach in its typical form is far from complete.

While some inquiry into responses can be undertaken, the process is relatively circumscribed. Because of well-founded concerns about stimulating frustration and resistance, many examiners adopt self-imposed restraints on their questioning. Yet even psychologists who limit themselves in these ways are apt to encounter resistance. Preschoolers give perfectly satisfactory answers to questions about one response only to respond capriciously to those about the next.

More important, not just during inquiry, but at any point in the testing, preschoolers' attitudes may suddenly shift and examiners may find themselves confronted by the confabulatory behaviors and responses that are the hallmark of the stage. It is in this period that children are especially prone to talk and act silly, make up stories about cards, treat percepts as if they are real, or gleefully produce strange or fantastic percepts that lead some authorities to question their reality testing (Ames et al., 1974). As has been seen, for example, in his second Rorschach at the age of four, Colin offered several more or less reasonable percepts, but soon began giving responses such as "Peacocks. They are pulling something out of it and they are smack," or "A goal that pinches." He also engaged in playful fights with parts of cards (A. Schachtel, 1944). Other youngsters see "boonjis" and "pink sissers" (Allen, 1954), describe cows that have walked onto and off the cards, or claim to have been bitten by animals on Card VIII (Ames et al., 1974). Hence, examiners are especially sensitive to the fact that these children can now handle the Rorschach reasonably for periods of time, but are subject to abrupt regressions that disrupt the testing process and lead to peculiar responses.

If we approach these negotiations from the child's standpoint, they may be seen in a different light. To be sure, in Stage II, children have matured to a point where they can take the examiner's wishes more seriously and do some of the "work" the test requires. Yet this capacity for work is not the major factor altering their handling of the Rorschach. Play is still their overriding concern.

However, the kind of play in which children are most interested keeps changing with age. Piaget (1951) contends that interactive pretense play begins to become prominent during the latter part of the third year, is at its peak in the "preoperational" period, and declines with the increasing emphasis on concrete operational thought around the age of seven. Empirical studies are in accord with this timetable (Rubin, Maioni, and Hornung, 1976; Sanders and Harper, 1976; Emmerich, 1977; Rubin, Watson, and Jambor, 1978; Johnson and Eschler, 1981). For example, Rubin et al. (1983, p. 720) note: "In general, the research on *middle-class* children from *intact* families supports the notion that the proportion of pretense to all play forms increases with age, from 3 years until approximately 6 or 7 years." Similarly, it is in this period that dramatic play is a primary therapeutic modality.

The manner in which children handle the Rorschach is determined chiefly by this change in the nature of their play. Whereas in the preceding stage they prefer to treat the Rorschach card as a kind of toy to be manipulated, in Stage II they are increasingly interested in the opportunity the Rorschach task of "making inkblots into something" affords for symbolic play. This game the examiner invites them to play is sufficiently interesting to sustain them through the free-association aspects of the test. In contrast, children seldom experience inquiry as anything other than work. Consequently, questioning them about their responses can be undertaken in only a cursory fashion, frequently meets with resistance, and is easily disrupted.

The capacity for symbolic play is not merely important in Stage II; it is nothing less than a precondition for "doing" the Rorschach. As Rorschach (1921) recognized and Cattell (1951) and Exner (1986) stress, in order to take the Rorschach it is essential that subjects not be bound by reality. Rather than viewing the card as what it is, an inkblot, they must make it into something it is not—a bat, a pumpkin, a flying horse, or an animal face. In effect, children are able to produce Rorschach responses only when they can treat the test as a medium for symbolic play.

The concept of play has an especially important bearing upon what is the most distinctive feature of Stage II responses, the varied forms of confabulatory behavior such as the idiosyncratic language and actions, the extraordinary fabulized responses, or the readiness to act as if percepts are real. In particular, applications of the concept suggest the need for caution in interpreting such behaviors as indications of regression or lapses in reality testing.

To illustrate this point, let us consider an example in which there seem to be strong reasons for believing we are encountering regression and which authorities such as Ames would interpret as an indication of difficulties with reality testing. A child aged three and a half who has given a number of adequate responses to the preceding cards excitedly describes the two side figures on Card VIII as ferocious tigers that are attacking him. Asked about the percepts, he vehemently asserts not only that the tigers are real, but that they are about to attack the examiner as well. Additional questions lead to a more adamant insistence on the reality of the tigers and further graphic elaborations of their bloodthirsty ways.

From a broad normative perspective, such a response cannot be considered regressive. Far from reflecting a return to modes of behavior encountered with the Rorschach earlier, these types of responses are new ones that emerge regularly around the age of three and a half (Ames et al., 1974). As has been noted, the capacity for symbolic play underlying them is, in fact, the cognitive advance that makes it possible to take the test in a more mature fashion. The flamboyant nature of the particular confabulatory response results mainly from the child choosing to use this ability in one way rather than in the more careful, disciplined way the examiner would prefer. Instead of indicating abnormality, such confabulation is a manifestation of the dramatic pretense play that is characteristic of normal preschoolers (Rubin et al., 1983).

For similar reasons, although the child does insist vehemently that the tigers are real, what is involved is not necessarily a "lapse" in reality testing. The same child may insist with equal vigor that his tricycle is a fire engine, but there are no grounds for fear that he will confuse tricycles with fire engines should the need for the latter arise. What occurs as the child produces the tiger response is a shift in attitude. Earlier he had not so much been reality oriented—there is, after all, nothing real about describing inkblots as anything other than inkblots—as ready to accept the task set by the examiner. Now the child redefines the task in ways more to his liking and less to the examiner's.

Finally, while we can recognize that there is something "regressive" in the blatant fantasies about the tiger relative to the child's more "mature" handling of earlier responses on the test, even this seemingly infantile form of confabulation has important progressive aspects. When our three-and-a-half-year-old acts as if the tiger is real, he is engaging in play similar to that of Colin during the preceding stage when he left the testing to join friends who were pretending chairs were a train. However, in contrast to Colin, the child in Stage II does not discontinue the testing and abandon the relationship with the examiner. Instead, in a more sophisticated way, he transforms the test task and interaction in ways that allow him to complete the test without leaving the field.

In sum, then, in Stage II children are able to do somewhat more "work" with examiners than in the previous stage—and will do even more as the stage progresses. However, the major shift is a new interest in symbolic play and the convergence of that interest with the definition of the task of examiners. Instability in the Rorschach situation arises at two points, those at which task becomes work (notably, during inquiry) and those at which there are shifts in children's attitudes with regard to the particular kind of play in which they wish to indulge.

STAGE III: THE RORSCHACH AS A GAME

From the standpoint of examiners, Stage III is the point at which the socialization process is more or less complete. Children can now appreciate the task that is set for them and have both the cognitive and emotional capacities to do the work necessary to accomplish it.

From the standpoint of children, the situation can be seen in a complementary way. They now consent to doing the examiner's task; they recognize that it is to be done in some "accepted" ways; and the process, especially inquiry, may be experienced as nothing other than "work."

Yet described in this manner the developmental sequence seems dreary. Does a test that two-year-olds transform into toys and four-year-olds experience as an opportunity to exercise their rich imaginations end as an exercise in conformity? Has the promise of play disappeared in Stage III?

Clearly it has not. To the contrary, play is almost as important in this stage as in its predecessors. When examiners tell preschoolers that the Rorschach is "a game," they are not necessarily talking down to the children in an effort to make the test palatable. The Rorschach task in fact began as a children's game (Ellenberger, 1954) and, in important respects, remains one even if it is not described in those terms with older subjects and even if the seriousness of the clinical purposes for which it is used and the elaborate—some might say, ponderous—analyses to which it is subjected obscure that fact. As has been seen, play is a critical aspect of the task if subjects are to give any response to Rorschach cards other than the real one—"inkblot." The implicit, and at times explicit, suggestion that they see the blot as "something else" is nothing other than an invitation to play. Moreover, how subjects accept that invitation is a major determinant of their performance. As E. Schachtel (1966) observes, whether subjects experience the task as "work" or as an opportunity for imaginative play has an important influence on the length and richness of their test records.

What differentiates Stage III from its predecessors is, above all, the changing nature of the play. Developmental psychologists note that in the elementary school years there are significant shifts in how children play. First, by this time youngsters have moved from parallel and associative play to true, cooperative social play (Parten, 1932; Millar, 1968; Rubin et al., 1983). Second, as children mature, idiosyncratic, make-believe play may not decline as Piaget believed (Sutton-Smith, 1966; Bretherton, 1984; Singer, 1991), but it does become more private and gives way in the public domain to games and other forms of play in which accommodatory features are prominent (Piaget, 1951; Eifermann, 1971). In accord with these changes, children in Stage III approach the Rorschach in ways that suggest that the symbolic play of the preceding stage is now embedded in a social, rule-bound, gamelike context. The examiner, in effect, defines the game, invites the subject to play it, and, by and large, the subject does so "by the rules."

This appreciation and acceptance of "the rules of the game" can be seen in two ways. First, test performance is now more stable. The shifts in attitude of the preceding stage during which children suddenly alter the task and seem to be working on a different one of their own creation are no longer encountered with normal subjects. Second, there is a significant change in the nature of the inquiry process. Youngsters now not only grasp what examiners are asking of them, but often respond without questions about determinants even having to be asked.

One other aspect of symbolic play in Stage III Rorschachs warrants particular attention. The confabulatory processes so prominent in Stage II do not cease, but rather undergo transformation. For example, although children may no longer insist that a tiger on Card VIII is about to bite them, the tiger need not be an inert percept. It may be described as walking, climbing a mountain, or hunting for prey. The confabulatory tendencies of normal children in Stage II are now integrated into the percept. They are not allowed to divert subject from task of dealing with the blot, yet they provide the basis for fabulized and, above all, movement responses that enrich the Rorschach protocols of healthy adults.

Viewing fabulized responses in this light has important implications for our interpretation of them. In working with adults, we often act as if Rorschach stimuli yields only form responses and that movement or fantasy enrichment represents something subjects add to percept. For example, to draw upon Rapaport's view of the response process as one involving perceptual and association aspects (Rapaport, Gill, and Schafer, 1946), we act as if in characterizing Card II as stationary animals or human figures we remain close to perceptual aspects of the blot, whereas in describing these figures as playing patty-cake, drinking a toast, or fighting we have "added something."

While there are ways in which such an abstract, conceptual analysis can be justified, from a developmental perspective what is important is that in Stage III nothing is being added. There are no more grounds for saying Card II is a human being or an animal than for describing it as human or animal figures acting in some way. Anything other than describing the card as ink involves "reading something in." In fact, what may be said to occur with pure form responses in Stage III is that an absence of fabulized responses in records results from what individuals have learned to "read out" of their responses, that is, from closing off aspects of experience. Subjects who produce records of this kind may well have succeeded in making the Rorschach, and perhaps their lives, into enterprises that are largely work and devoid of play. Such may be the hazards of transforming the test into a truly social one in which there is a growing concern for how the audience will view the ways in which we approach the game.

Interpersonal Aspects of the Rorschach Situation

THE PATIENT–EXAMINER RELATIONSHIP

In addition to considering stages in the mastery of the Rorschach from the standpoints of the ego development of the subject and shifting definitions of the task, there is a third perspective from which they may be viewed, that of the relationship of the subject and the examiner.

The significance of the testing relationship has long been an area of interest and controversy in the Rorschach literature. As the major Rorschach systems evolved in the 1930s and 1940s, proponents of some accentuated "objective" aspects of the test that resembled the psychometric properties of other prominent assessment instruments. They emphasized scores, indexes, and normative tables and even advocated blind interpretation of protocols to assure that readings would not be contaminated by other sources of information such as impressions based on contact with the subject (Exner, 1969, 1986). In characterizing this attitude, E. Schachtel (1945) writes:

> By far the greater part of the literature and practice of personality testing seems to rest on the assumption that the way in which the subject experiences the test situation is irrelevant to the results of the tests, and therefore need not be considered in the evaluation of the results [p. 419].

Most Rorschach practitioners, of course, recognize that the relationship between the subject and examiner has some effect on the test results (Coffin, 1941; Lord, 1950; Gibby, Miller, and Walker, 1953; Masling, 1965; Exner, 1974). Yet, for those most concerned with the psychometric properties of the test, these effects are noise in the system that can be controlled and minimized through adherence to proper, standardized administrative procedures.

In contrast, other authorities stress the importance of the "patient-examiner" relationship in Rorschach interpretation. Drawing upon Sullivanian theory, E. Schachtel (1966, p. 269) contends that "since the Rorschach situation is constituted by two people and the perceptual object (inkblots), both these people will influence the situation and what happens in it." Because the social context of the testing is one in which the examiner plays the role of an authority figure and judge, he argues, patients' attitudes regarding dependency, competitiveness, and the adequacy of their performance are especially salient in shaping their subjective definitions of the test situation. These definitions, in turn, affect all aspects of Rorschach performance from the number of responses given and their determinants to whether the inquiry process is experienced as criticism and attack or support and reassurance.

Among the major Rorschach systems, interpersonal aspects of the test process are most heavily emphasized by Rapaport and his followers (Rapaport et al., 1946; Schafer, 1954; Schlesinger, 1973; Berg, 1986; Lerner, 1991). At the core of their position is the conviction that not only the Rorschach but all psychological tests should be viewed as forms of a standardized interview. Accordingly, they believe that the meaning of data can only be appreciated fully when evaluated in the context of the relationship within which the information was gathered.

Schafer offers the fullest exposition of this position in a long chapter, "Interpersonal Dynamics in the Test Situation," with which he began his *Psychoanalytic Interpretation in Rorschach Testing* (1954). He observes:

> The clinical testing situation has a complex psychological structure. It is not an impersonal getting-together of two people in order that one, with the help of a little "rapport," may obtain some "objective" test responses from the other. The psychiatric patient is in some acute or chronic life crisis. He cannot but bring many hopes, fears, assumptions, demands and expectations into the test situation. He cannot but respond to certain real as well as fantasied attributes of that situation. Being human and having to make a living—facts often ignored—the tester too brings hopes, fears, assumptions, demands and expectations into the test situation. He too responds personally and often intensely to what goes on—in reality and in

fantasy—in that situation, however well he may conceal his response from the patient, from himself, and from his colleagues [p. 6].

Rather than an evil to be striven against, this relationship, with its realistic and unrealistic aspects, is inevitable and, when recognized, "a gold mine of material for interpretation."

In analyzing the relationship, Schafer explores a wide range of influences upon what each party brings to it. On the part of examiners, for example, he notes social and historical factors that shape the role of tester that psychologists have carved for themselves, the more or less "objective" expectations they hold in playing that role, and the ways in which their personalities—especially their unconscious desires and defenses—affect the conduct of testing and interpretation of data. On the part of patients, he describes general attributes of the role of being a testee as well as the manner in which individual impulse-defense configurations shape perceptions of their relationship with the examiner and the test responses they offer. Assimilating the test situation to the model of a psychoanalytic process, Schafer emphasizes, above all, the manner in which Rorschach productions and their interpretation could be understood in light of the potent forces of transference and countertransference.

Differences of opinion regarding the significance of this patient-examiner relationship in Rorschach testing persist, and current approaches to test interpretation can be placed along a continuum with regard to it. At one end are "objective," quantitative approaches to the test that accept blind interpretation or its contemporary equivalent, computer-generated analyses based upon test scores alone. At the other are idiographic approaches that emphasize careful assessment of test responses in light of the ongoing dynamics of the testing relationship. Though most psychologists who give the Rorschach would place themselves somewhere toward the middle of this continuum, given the complex, often unarticulated ways in which interpretations are made, considerable variation undoubtedly exists in actual practice. One suspects that many advocates of the test, while acknowledging that the patient–examiner relationship plays some role in test responses, nonetheless "bracket" that relationship and base their analyses primarily on scores, ratios, and norms. In contrast, others, often those committed to psychoanalytic approaches to the test, make use of scores and indexes, but weigh the patient–examiner relationship and its influence on dramatic responses heavily in their interpretations.

Although the relative merits of different modes of interpreting adult protocols must be judged on other grounds, there can be little doubt that the relationship of subject and examiner has a critical bearing on how children respond to the Rorschach. Two aspects of that relationship are especially important in understanding early stages in children's handling of the test. On one hand, there are significant differences in the ways in which formal roles—those of tester and testee—operate in defining the framework for the testing; on the other, a number of factors serve to accentuate the role of subjective definitions of the situation with young children.

"OBJECTIVE" ASPECTS OF THE TESTING RELATIONSHIP WITH YOUNG CHILDREN

As Schachtel and Schafer stress, the Rorschach is typically given in a social context in which subject and examiner assume roles of tester and testee that are relatively clearly defined by accepted conventions. To be sure, there are some variations in these roles and the conventions defining them, depending upon the subject's age and the circumstances of the testing. For example, differences arise depending upon whether a patient is being evaluated for clinical purposes, a student is being seen in a school setting, or a volunteer is being tested as part of a research project. Yet in work with older children, adolescents, and adults, tester and testee have a reasonably clear appreciation that each is to play a particular role according to particular rules. At the least, subjects recognize that the examiner has license to define the task at hand and guide the testing according to established procedures and that they are to defer in these matters and abide by the ground rules of the test.

Among the most distinctive features of the initial stage in children's Rorschachs is the fact that these "objective" roles are simply not present. Two-year-olds neither know nor care what psychologists are supposed to do. They are chiefly interested in playing, not in being tested, and would have little interest in adhering to testing procedures even if they had some recognition of them. Accordingly, examiners modify the role they play, presenting the test as a form of play and altering its administration substantially (e.g., eliminating inquiry) in order to keep their subjects engaged.

In any case, at this stage the Rorschach is often not given by "testers," but rather by parents, preschool teachers, or other familiar figures. When young children are tested by psychologists whom they do not know, examiners go to considerable lengths to act like parental surrogates, preschool teachers, or benign playmates. For example, Bohm (1958, p. 309) cautions that even with older children too great a concern with acting like an examiner is likely to lead to "an unnatural, overanxious, and objectively misleading protocol." As noted, Halpern (1953) is prepared to have young children sit on her lap during the test, an invitation a caregiver might extend to the young, but one a psychologist would hardly extend to an older subject without risking unpleasant ethical and legal repercussions. In short, the tester–testee relationship is simply not operative with young children and, instead, the testing relationship is assimilated to others such as those of parent–child, preschooler–nursery teacher, or playmates.

The second stage is an intermediate one in which the testing relationship begins to change. Three- and four-year-olds are likely to be tested by stangers, albeit ones still trying hard to act like parental surrogates or benign preschool teachers. Children now have some sense that the Rorschach is governed by rules examiners are trying to enforce, although examiners continue to define the task as a playful one and often modify testing procedures in the interest of maintaining contact with their subjects. As seen in the preceding chapter, however, the relationship in this stage is fluid. At times, preschoolers accept the examiner's role and play the game according to the rules; at others they redefine the task and seek to get examiners to play their games and often, for tactical reasons, examiners may well accept roles assigned them for a while. Hence, though children in Stage II show some grasp of the formal roles that will later characterize the test situation, their appreciation of those roles is limited and their acceptance of them sporadic.

Only in Stage III do subject and examiner maintain their established, socially defined roles throughout the course of the testing. Examiners can now adhere to typical modes of test administration, and children, except those exhibiting significant psychopathology, play the part assigned them appropriately. There are variations in how roles are defined. For example, children are inclined to view the relationship as more like that of student and teacher than patient and examiner. Yet the roles nonetheless allow for standarized administration and provide a stable framework within which test responses can be obtained and interpreted in customary ways.

The stability of this framework allows some Rorschach practitioners simply to take it for granted, act as if the patient–examiner relationship is a constant, and focus chiefly upon test results in their interpretations. For others such as Schachtel and Schafer the formal roles are like those in a play in which different actors offer their own distinctive readings of the script. Yet even for these approaches to Rorschach interpretation, it is the more or less invariant nature of the role that allows an appreciation of variations in how it is enacted.

"SUBJECTIVE" ASPECTS OF THE TESTING RELATIONSHIP WITH CHILDREN

Those who favor clinical approaches to Rorschach interpretation are concerned less with the formal social roles in the test situation than with the "subjective definition" patients give the testing relationship based upon their own "hopes, fears, assumptions, demands and expectations" (Schafer, 1954, p. 6). For a variety of reasons, these subjective factors play a more prominent role in testing children than in working with adults.

One reason is that children are less bound by conventional social roles in the testing situation. Such roles dictate much of our behavior, guiding it in routine directions and often obscuring what is unique and distinctive. In contrast, as the hold of conventions diminishes, subjects, of necessity, respond in more personal, individualized ways. For example, in offering a rationale for psychoanalytic technique, Eissler (1965) argues that the use of the couch, the absence of face-to-face contact, and the limited responsiveness of the analyst are valuable because they markedly reduce the cues that govern ordinary social behavior and thereby maximize the role of what the analysand brings to the process. In an analogous manner, the less appreciation children have of formal roles in the test situation (i.e., the less sense they have of how they are supposed to behave), the greater the leeway for imposing their own definitions on the situation.

A second, more obvious reason that subjective definitions of the testing situation heavily influence early stages of Rorschach performance is simply that children are children and the younger they are, the more likely they are to act like young children. Preschoolers express their wishes, fears, hopes, and aspirations directly; they act in less guarded and frequently less controlled ways than they will when they are older; and, as parents know to their amusement and consternation, children at this age make little distinction between what is public and what is private. As has been seen repeatedly, in taking the Rorschach they impose their own definitions on the testing relationship quite forcefully, and many recommendations regarding modifications of administrative procedures with them are ways of coping with these tendencies.

Subjective aspects of the test process are also heightened for examiners working with preschoolers. Being adults, examiners do recognize formal roles guiding their conduct of tests. Yet with young children the rules of testing are less fixed and more open to adaptation. In trying to administer the Rorschach, examiners make a myriad of decisions shaped by their ways of experiencing the children with whom they are working and their own personalities.

These decisions are usually discussed under the rubric of "establishing rapport," a process typically described as a precondition for testing children. For example, stressing the importance of developing "natural affective contact," Bohm (1958) asserts:

> In no test situation do the "scientific" findings depend as much on the Examiner and his contact, or lack of it, as in investigations of children. In some instances, one may have to postpone the test to another time. Or if rapport cannot be established at all, one may have to refer the child to some other Examiner in whom the child may have more confidence [pp. 309–310].

Rapport is, of course, important in testing subjects of all ages. Yet with adults, it affects the richness of records and the quality of the inquiry process; with young children, as Bohm notes, it determines whether testing can be conducted at all.

Discussions of rapport, not only in the Rorschach literature but in that on all tests for children, are often abstract and general in nature. By acting in a warm, responsive, interested manner, it is suggested, examiners put children at ease and create a relaxed, nonthreatening working relationship that diminishes resistance to the tests and allows subjects to perform in an optimal manner on them. Treating rapport as a relatively uniform state, test manuals accord it some recognition, while nonetheless emphasizing standardization in test administration and focusing attention on test results obtained under such circumstances.

Manuals do occasionally acknowledge that the situation is more complex and that the behavior of examiners in establishing this kind of testing relationship is extraordinarily varied (Leichtman, 1995). For example, in describing "the importance of rapport" in the administration of the Stanford-Binet, Terman and Merrill (1960) observe:

> To elicit the subject's best efforts and maintain both high motivation and optimal performance level throughout the test session are the *sine qua non* of good testing, but the means by which these ends are accomplished are so varied as to defy specific formulation. The address which puts one child at ease with a strange adult may belittle or even antagonize another. The competent examiner, like the good clinician, must be able to sense the needs of the subject so that he can help him to accept and adjust to the testing situation. Sympathetic, understanding relationships with children are achieved in the most diverse ways and no armory of technical skills is a satisfactory substitute for this kind of interpersonal know-how [pp. 50–51].

This process can be appreciated best if we consider how examiners actually work with children.

For example, a highly anxious three-and-a-half-year-old has difficulty separating from his mother and clings to her desperately when invited to accompany the examiner to the office. To set the boy at ease, the examiner brings a teddy bear to the waiting room and, after period of conversation with the bear, who also proves to be a very shy creature, the child takes its paw and leads it to the office. Although enjoying the examiner's attention, the boy remains skittish through early tests and quickly withdraws when puzzled or upset by items. Sensing that the Rorschach will be especially hard for him, the examiner brings out the bear, who has some pictures to show his friend. While occasionally bewildered by the bear's inkblots, the child gives responses to each, answers the bear's questions about them, and is especially helpful when the poor animal cannot figure out how to see particular percepts on a card.

In contrast, a four-year-old child who has been through a string of foster homes has no difficulty separating from her social worker in the waiting room. She treats the unfamiliar examiner as if he were an old friend and rapidly enters into a relationship in which she acts like an extraordinarily needy two-year-old. The child's hunger for care and nurturance make her a cooperative test subject as long as the examiner acts like a benevolent caregiver.

A third child is initially frightened of the examiner but is quickly reassured and behaves like a dependent, good little girl eager to win praise from a parent.

A fourth remains frightened throughout, and the examiner strives to be a soothing figure, constantly attuned to the necessity of providing reassurance, managing the youngster's anxiety, and countering her readiness to see him as threatening and dangerous.

A fifth is stubborn, oppositional, and provocative. Struggling to cope with annoyance at a child acting like a spoiled brat, the examiner tries to balance the need to humor the youngster with maintaining the structure of the test, lest the situation degenerate into either a battle of wills or a farce.

Another child, a budding femme fatale, flounces into the office with rings on her fingers and bows in her hair. Eliciting Rorschach responses is easy, since she needs only an appreciative audience and an appropriate stage in order to try to demonstrate how bright and charming she can be. However, her performance becomes strained at any point she doubts she is being charming enough and she becomes anxious and regresses when she feels that she has been too successful and seductive.

Although many more examples might be offered, they are hardly needed to see that children enter the test ready to enact roles that are central to their identities, roles embodying a mixture of wishes and fears, impulses and defenses, talents and limitations, and identifications with parents and efforts to win their love. To make affective contact with subjects, examiners must be sensitive to these roles and conduct testing in ways that are consonant with them. Doing so does not require carefully planned strategies, but making innumerable small decisions on a moment-by-moment basis that feel like the right way to conduct testing with a particular child. Often what feels "right" is a rhythm of testing, a tone of voice used in asking questions, a posture, an expression, or other nonverbal cues that make up so much of our communication with one another. Effective testing is done so smoothly and naturally that examiners are usually not conscious of playing a role. Frequently, it is only when reflecting back on the nature of the interaction at the end of a session that they begin to recognize and articulate what they have been doing intuitively. Whether they are aware of doing so or not, however, it is the capacity of examiners to adopt, in their own individual ways, roles complementary to those of their subjects that are essential to "establishing rapport."

The overriding importance for both children and examiners of subjective definitions of the testing relationship in early stages of the mastery of the Rorschach can be appreciated if we consider a hypothetical diagnostic situation. Assume that an experienced clinician is asked to offer an assessment of a child based solely on information gathered from administering the Rorschach, information that includes not only test responses but also the manner in which the child and examiner behave in the course of taking the test. How would that diagnostic impression be formed at each stage?

In Stage I, the examiner might well be inclined to balk at the task. Perseverative Rorschachs after all consist of little more than a single response whose basis is unclear that is repeated across ten cards. There is little point in developing a psychogram or even scoring the test, since almost nothing in formal scores will differentiate one child from another.

Yet, as can be seen in the examples of different testing relationships, experienced clinicians could offer numerous inferences about a child based upon the test process. Whether and how children separate from parents, their behavior with examiners, the roles they enact with them, and the manner in which examiners use themselves in making contact with children and helping them negotiate the task all provide insights into children's personalities and ways of working with them. At this point, the Rorschach truly resembles a clinical interview; it is less a distinctive projective test than part of the kind of play session a clinician might use in a consultation with a child.

In Stage II, the situation changes to some degree. Because children offer responses to the inkblots and allow some inquiry, they produce scorable records from which some inferences can be made. However, the test data are sparse; determinants of responses may be unclear; and the consistency of children's engagement with the task is open to question. Hence, authorities on the Rorschach begin to describe warning signs or "danger signals," but are cautious in their clinical use of the test (Ames et al., 1974).

At the same time, as children move through the preschool years, they interact with examiners in more revealing ways than they did earlier. They are freer to play in the test situation than younger children; their play is richer and more dramatic; and they are readier to cast examiners in particular roles. However unfortunate such behavior may be from the standpoint of eliciting valid and reliable test records, it provides a rich source of clinical data. Hence, at times the Rorschach now resembles the test it will later become and at times it resembles a play-therapy session.

Only with Stage III are clinicians likely to feel that children's test responses may take precedence over observations of their behavior and their relationship with the examiner. Now the formal roles of tester and testee are operative, and consistent records that can be scored confidently are obtained. Those who choose to do so can begin to base their interpretations on those records alone with some degree of confidence. Others such as Schafer and Schachtel insist that subjective definitions of the test situation remain important, yet they must use considerable ingenuity in defending their position because of the prominence of the test data itself and the subtle manner in which the effects of the testing relationship are incorporated in responses.

In effect, in the first stages subjective definitions of the test situation are so striking they overshadow the test data. Indeed, initially the definition of the test situation and, above all, the subject–examiner relationship are the projective test as much as the inkblots themselves. Only in the final stage does the test become sufficiently prominent that decisions about whether or not and how to consider that relationship in interpretations become meaningful.

13

The Rorschach Situation
and the Orthogenetic
Principle

THE ORTHOGENETIC PRINCIPLE

A fourth perspective on the Rorschach situation, one that encompasses aspects of the others, is afforded by the work of Heinz Werner (Werner, 1957, 1961; Werner and Kaplan, 1963).

Werner bases his comparative psychology of mental development on the assumption that organismic development, whether biological or mental, follows a systematic, orderly sequence governed by a central regulative principle. This "orthogenetic principle" states that "wherever development occurs it proceeds from a state of relative globality and lack of differentiation to a state of increasing differentiation, articulation, and hierarchic integration" (Werner, 1957, p. 126).

In elaborating upon the concept, Werner (1961) describes a number of properties that distinguish relatively primitive states from mature ones. First, early stages of mental development are *syncretic* in the sense that "mental functions and phenomena, which would appear distinct from each other in a mature state of consciousness, are merged without differentiation" (p. 53); in later stages, these functions are *discrete*. Second, the formal structure of states of consciousness is initially *diffuse*. Parts are indistinct and structures are relatively uniform and homogeneous. Later structures will be *articulated*. Third, as structures become more complex, there is increasing *hierarchization*. Parts are subordinated to wholes and central regulation of functions is increased. Fourth, primitive structures and functions tend to be *rigid;* when they are more articulated and organized, they become *flexible*. Finally, primitive states are *labile* or subject to rapid, unpredictable shifts; with increasing organization and flexibility, later states are *stable*.

The application of this developmental perspective to psychosocial aspects of the mastery of the Rorschach is illustrated in Figure 1. The three stages in the process are represented by a series of concentric circles; the basic components of the Rorschach situation—the subject, the examiner, and the task—by radii trisecting the circles; and the

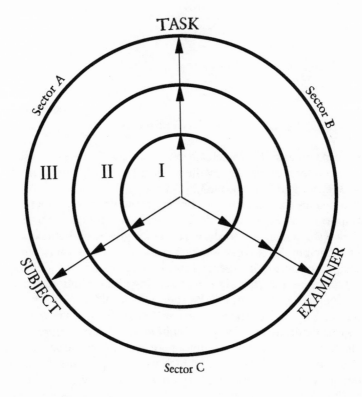

Figure 1. Diagram of developmental change in the components of the Rorschach situation.

degree of articulation and hierachic organization of these components by the distance from the center of the circles. The increasing distance between the radii from stage to stage suggests the manner in which each becomes distinct and functions as a more clearly defined, independent constituent of the test situation in the course of development.

The processes depicted by the figure can best be appreciated if we consider separately the progressive changes in the relationships of each set of components of the test situation, relationships represented by the three sectors of the diagram.

THE SUBJECT AND THE TASK

The aspect of the Rorschach situation that has received the most attention is the relationship of the subject and the task (Sector A).

The salient aspects of this relationship in early Rorschachs are exemplified well by Colin's first Rorschach. As has been noted, at age three the boy seemed to have only a vague idea of what the test was about and his handling of it was determined chiefly by "the spirit of the moment." Initially, Colin gave a response that the examiner felt, but could not be sure, was to the blot itself; soon, however, he gave only perseverated responses that make it hard to believe that he was still engaged in that exercise. At one moment Colin seemed to cooperate with at least a rudimentary form of the Rorschach task; at another, he ignored the task altogether and went off to play; at yet another, he redefined the task, making the Rorschach card into a toy; finally, he seemed to be doing two things at once—responding to the examiner's requests and playing with his toy.

In Wernerian terms, the initial experience of the test situation is global and diffuse. Colin has, at best, only a vague sense of what the task may be and acts in ways suggesting that he recognizes little difference between doing it and simply acting on his wishes, needs, or anxieties. His actions often seem to express different and even contradictory intentions. It may be difficult to tell whether he is responding to the Rorschach task in some way, avoiding it, or doing both simultaneously. There is little subordination of means to ends in the child's behavior. Colin simply does one thing and then another that may be quite unrelated. As a consequence, the situation is at once rigid—the product after all is a perseverated response that does not change from card to card—and extraordinarily labile, as the child's definition of the situation and behavior change abruptly from moment to moment.

In Stage II, children have some recognition that the Rorschach task has a distinct form. For example, they give responses to the blots themselves. Yet their handling of the test and attitudes toward it still change rapidly with shifts in their wishes and affective states. At one point, they are taking "the Rorschach"; at another, they make up stories that start to transform the test into a CAT; and at another, the test becomes, at least temporarily, a play situation. Thus, although the test begins to have a meaning that is independent of children's emotional states, the situation is still unstable and the task subject to abrupt redefinition.

With Stage III there is a clear differentiation of task and subject. The Rorschach is now recognized as an exercise with its own set of rules and, except in rare circumstances, children adapt flexibly to the test, adhering to its rules regardless of their wishes or moods at the time. As a consequence, the task has a meaning that remains stable over time and can be scored and interpreted accordingly.

The subject, it should be stressed, does not disappear from the Rorschach equation at this point. Just as the test is becoming more differentiated, so, too, are children's personalities. With increasing intellectual and creative abilities come an expansion in the range and diversity of the products of those abilities. In the case of the Rorschach, as personal needs are subordinated to "doing *the* test," children produce richer, fuller records. Because their motives, defenses, talents, and conflicts enter into the creation of responses, these records provide the basis for far more detailed and comprehensive interpretations of personality characteristics than was possible earlier. Hence, as the task and subject become increasingly independent, more rather than less of the individuality of the subject is revealed.

THE EXAMINER AND THE TASK

An analogous developmental process can be seen with regard to the relationship of the examiner and the Rorschach (Sector B).

For young children in Stage I, there is little distinction between the task and the examiner's wishes or demands upon them. They experience the test chiefly as "something the examiner wants them to do." In commenting on early Rorschachs, for example, Fox (1956, pp. 89–90) observes: "It seems apparent that the child does not respond to the inkblots themselves, but to the total testing situation." Because the most salient aspect of that situation for the child is the examiner, he notes, children are concerned primarily with acting in ways that win approval or avoid the adult's displeasure.

This close identification of the test with the tester provides one explanation of perseverative protocols. Fox suggests that the perseverated response is an answer young children feel has been approved by the examiner and that it is repeated for this reason. As often, one suspects, responses are perverated for a different reason. Experiencing the test, especially its continuation after the first response, as a demand that they work on a task they hardly understand and have little wish to do, children find perseveration a "magic wand" whose chief function is pacifying the examiner while moving on to some other less noxious activity. In either case, there is little separation between "the test" and the expectations of the examiner.

In Stage II, as preschoolers gain a growing appreciation of the task itself, the Rorschach begins to be seen as a form of play to be indulged in for its own sake. Yet from the first, it is play *with the examiner*. More important, it may also be experienced as a form of work that examiners set for them. As noted, at times children comply with these expectations and at others resist them, especially during the inquiry process. Again, in both cases, the test is closely identified with the tester.

In these early stages it is not just for the child that there is less differentiation between the examiner and the task than will later be the case. As has been seen, in working with young children examiners are prepared to make substantial modifications in how they present the test, conduct inquiry, and score responses based on their judgments about what the situation warrants. The same examiner may vary the way the test is given from one child to another, and even greater variations are present from one examiner to another. Hence, the test at these stages has a less stable, less uniform definition—indeed, there is less agreement about what constitutes "the Rorschach." In practice, what the test is depends heavily upon who is giving it.

Once again, it is in the third stage that this situation changes. Now it is clearly recognized that the task has a meaning apart from the examiner's wishes and preferences. The test consists of a set of procedures that determine the behavior of the examiner as much as that of the subject as formal roles of tester and testee are assumed. The stability this change introduces allows the assumption of standardized administration and scoring upon which the elaborate edifice of Rorschach interpretation is based.

Examiners do not cease to be a factor in the Rorschach at this point. Their personalities still subtly affect even the presentation of the test. For example, Goodman (1979) found that "warmer," more experienced examiners elicit more human responses. Because inquiry is open ended, their personalities can have an even greater effect on it. And, obviously, differences among examiners have a profound impact on interpretation. It is at this point, for example, that analyses of the role of countertransference in test administration and interpretation are germane (Schafer, 1954). Thus, although in Stage III the Rorschach becomes a more sophisticated tool whose use is governed by particular rules, the reports it is used to create, for better and for worse, are more influenced by the skills and personalities of those who wield it than ever before.

THE SUBJECT AND THE EXAMINER

Finally, the relationship between the subject and examiner (Sector C) undergoes a similar developmental progression. This process can best be appreciated through a consideration of how the test is administered and interpreted.

In Stage I, there is a relative lack of differentiation of subject and examiner. As has been seen in Chapter 10, in addition to administering the test, examiners function as "auxiliary egos" for young children. On the basis of careful attunement to the child's state, the examiner intervenes subtly to help cope with problems with attention and concentration, impulsivity, management of affective states, and cognitive difficulties in appreciating the nature of the task. While the test response is still the child's, in these respects at least, it is a joint product.

The lack of differentiation of subject and examiner can also be seen in problems with the inquiry process. Although inquiry is not typically undertaken because two-year-olds have little concept of what it means to "explain" their responses to another person, even if they had the means to do so, they would be puzzled by the task. A response looks like what it is and questions about why it looks that way are unnecessary. Others must see the same thing. As Ames et al. (1952) observe, should examiners raise questions about responses that in any way suggest doubt about the percept, young children frequently simply agree with what they take to be the adult's view, assuming their own responses were wrong. In both cases, they experience little distinction between their views and others'.

A similar lack of distance between child and examiner characterizes the interpretive process. Working with responses that differ significantly from those ordinarily obtained on the Rorschach and lacking data from inquiry, examiners must put themselves in the child's position and rely heavily upon their intuitive understanding of how the child is responding to the inkblots in order to draw any significant conclusions from the test. In these circumstances, how much of the assessment is truly a reflection of the child and how much is a manifestation of the examiner's overactive imagination is open to question. For example, in commenting on Schachtel's discussion of Colin's initial Rorschachs, Beck (1944a) notes that her interpretation is highly subjective and that there are often no clear grounds for distinguishing between characteristics of the boy and her "free associations." While Beck's observation is true, it is also true that without relying on the intimate attunement of the examiner to the child and intuitions about the response process derived from that contact, no interpretation is possible at this time.

In Stage II, again, the situation begins to change. Children are better able to negotiate the test, although examiners still function as auxiliary egos and modify test administration to some degree to assist them. Inquiry can now be undertaken because children are capable of making some effort to explain their responses to another, but that capacity is modest. Many are still puzzled and some exasperated that examiners cannot see what is clearly before them on the blot; inquiry is abbreviated because of the strain and frustration children experience with it; and examiners often rely heavily on their intuitive understanding of the situation in scoring responses. For example, Ames et al. (1974) score records of young children during the testing because they often base those scores on clues such as movements, expressions, and inflections that quickly evaporate once the interpersonal context in which the response is given changes. As was the case with interpretations in Stage I, questions can be raised about these scoring procedures (Klopfer, Spiegelman, and Fox, 1956), yet, given the child's limited tolerance of inquiry, scoring may at times be difficult and even impossible without them.

With the third stage, a clear differentiation of subject and examiner in the Rorschach situation is apparent in the manner in which the test is taken. Children now handle the Rorschach task on their own. They require little assistance with attending or offering responses to the inkblots. They also recognize that they and others perceive the cards differently and that explanation of the location and determinants of their percepts may be necessary. With these changes, the dangers of confounding what subjects and examiners bring to the testing is markedly reduced and scoring decisions can be made with far greater confidence.

At the same time, as the relationship between subject and examiner becomes clearer and more distinct, it has a new and more potent influence on test productions. Perhaps the best documented and most striking manifestation of this change lies not in the responses subjects give to the tests, but in the ones they do not give. For all of their sensitivity to the examiner in the process of defining the Rorschach in Stage II, normal preschoolers blithely produce odd, confabulated responses that speak to an indifference or, more often, a lack of awareness of what others will think about them. In contrast, in Stage III, subjects are extremely sensitive to how their productions will be seen and tailor them accordingly. The fantastic imaginative productions of the preceding stage give way to percepts that conform to "realistic" standards and children become more critical of their responses (Ames et al., 1974). Considerations of social desirability and censorship now become key factors in determining which of their many potential responses to cards subjects will share (Exner, Armbruster, and Mittman, 1978; Exner, 1986).

The subject–examiner relationship also enters into the constitution of responses themselves to a greater degree than ever before. As E. Schachtel (1966) stresses, for mature subjects, the Rorschach task is not merely one of deciding what inkblots "might be." Even by the elementary school years, children recognize that their answers reveal aspects of themselves and judge their responses accordingly. They also clearly appreciate that what they communicate will be used by examiners to make decisions about them. Consequently, impressions subjects wish to convey about themselves (and ones they wish to suppress), experiences of the examiner, and concerns about the outcome of the testing can now play the kind of roles in the formulation and sharing of responses described by Schafer (1954) and Schachtel (1966).

In sum, as the three basic components of the Rorschach situation operate in distinct, differentiated, yet integrated ways in Stage III, the test becomes more stable and complex and it is possible to undertake the variety of types of sophisticated analyses for which the Rorschach is noted.

IV

Cognitive Aspects of the Rorschach Task

The Perception Hypothesis

RORSCHACH THEORY AND PRESCHOOL RORSCHACHS

From the standpoint of Rorschach theory, cognitive aspects of children's mastery of the test are far more important than psychosocial ones. Explorations of the latter issues in the preceding chapters, after all, treat the Rorschach merely as one of a class of tests children find puzzling and only gradually learn to manage. What makes the task distinctive is largely ignored. In contrast, explanations of cognitive aspects of early Rorschach performance require examination of the specific processes involved in formulating an answer to the question of what an inkblot might be.

At this point, the problem of preschool Rorschachs coincides with what has been described as the central problem in Rorschach theory, that of defining the nature of the Rorschach task. Presumably the phenomena encountered in early Rorschachs can be explained in terms of primitive forms of the psychological processes required for accomplishing that task and the movement through stages of mastering the test explained in terms of developmental changes in those processes.

Here, however, we can begin to sense the challenge preschool Rorschachs pose for Rorschach theory. Rorschach (1921) and most of his principal followers began with the assumption stated in the subtitle of his monograph, namely, that their diagnostic test is one "based on perception." Yet even a superficial consideration of early stages of children's Rorschach performance suggests two problems that call this assumption into question.

The first concerns the means by which children move from one stage to another. Theories of perceptual development can provide a reasonable account of some changes that occur across children's Rorschachs in the preschool years, such as the gradual improvement in form level. Yet it is far from clear how they can explain the most significant changes, the dramatic, qualitative shifts in Rorschach performance that differentiate one period from another. Insofar as these transformations do not appear to be correlated with any major milestones in perceptual development, theories of perception do not readily supply a mechanism for children's movement across stages.

A second and more important problem lies in accounting for central features of preschool Rorschach protocols. Perhaps the most striking characteristic of early Rorschach responses is how little they appear to be based on perception. In the perseverative protocols of Stage I, many initial responses do not seem related to the inkblot at all and certainly subsequent responses consist of repetitions of the first regardless of the stimuli. The confabulatory protocols of Stage II are often based on a confabulatory Whole (DW) process in which the stimulus plays a limited role and on a readiness to launch into associations and fantasies that quickly leave the inkblot behind in any case. So far do these early protocols depart from anything that can be explained by perceptual development that Klopfer, Speigelman, and Fox (1956) contend the first Rorschach stages are based on different modes of concept formation. Only in Stage III do Rorschach responses consistently appear to be products of perceptual processes.

To be sure, these points fail to do justice to the complexity of perceptual theories of the Rorschach and to specific arguments that can be advanced on their behalf. Nonetheless, the problems do suggest that such arguments should be weighed carefully, for the issues involved go beyond young children's Rorschachs alone. To the extent theories of the Rorschach as a perceptual task cannot account for salient aspects of the developmental process through which the test is mastered, there are grounds for doubting their adequacy and looking for alternatives to them.

THE BASIC PERCEPTION HYPOTHESIS

It is not hard to appreciate why Rorschach theorists conceive of their test as a perceptual one. The nature of the task seems self-evident in descriptions of the test process.

Consider the following sequence. The subject is given an inkblot to look at and the examiner says, "What might this be?" "What does it look like to you?" or "What do you see?" After a few seconds, the subject responds that it "looks like" a bat, mask, animal face, or jack-o-lantern. Later, the examiner returns to the response, and gives instructions such as those recommended by Exner (1986):

> I want you to help me *see* what you *saw*. I'm going to read what you said, and then I want you to show me where on the blot you *saw* it and what there is there that makes it *look like* that, so that I can *see* it too. I'd like to *see* it like you did [p. 72; italics mine].

On the basis of answers to these questions, the examiner scores and analyzes the "percepts." From beginning to end the language and actions of the subject and examiner imply that the task is perceptual.

A major impetus to Rorschach's research was his dissatisfaction with earlier treatments of inkblot tests that, he believed, failed to deal sufficiently with their "perceptual aspects" (Exner, 1969). It was this point, above all others, around which his work was oriented. He and major proponents of the test such as Rapaport (Rapaport, Gill, and Schafer, 1946), E. Schachtel (1966), and Exner (Exner and Weiner, 1982; Exner, 1986), insofar as they articulate their views of the processes underlying Rorschach responses, emphasize a complex form of perception, alone or in combination with other operations. However, regardless of the additional operations they propose, most agree with Rorschach's basic assumption about its core component.

Part of the reason for this insistence is that the perception hypothesis provides the theoretical foundation for Rorschach interpretation. It is the assumption that the test reveals habitual modes of seeing and experiencing the world that links test data and inferences about personality characteristics. This linkage is spelled out most clearly by experimentalists seeking to operationalize Rorschach theories in order to test them. For example, Mooney (1962) asserts:

> If the clinician were to make explicit the premises underlying the utilization of the Rorschach test and express them as a syllogism, it would assume a form such as: The Rorschach is a perceptual task; personality traits are known to determine, in part, perceptual processes; therefore, from a consideration of the operation of perceptual processes revealed in the Rorschach, the clinician can obtain useful information about an individual's personality structure [p. 18].

Similarly, Zubin et al. (1965) write:

Stated more generally, the hypothesis which underlies the Rorschach experiment is that the perception of inkblots parallels perception in the everyday world and that the unstructured character of the inkblots themselves permits us to observe those features of the perceptual process which are due to the observer's own habitual modes and ingrained patterns of subjective organization [p. 253].

In effect, diagnostic use of the test rests upon claims that it reveals critical aspects of what the subject brings to the perceptual experience, characteristics that are held to reflect enduring personality traits and behavioral dispositions.

Nowhere is this linkage, and the insistence on the perceptual nature of the task, clearer than in interpretations of the most important of Rorschach determinants, form. In articulating Rorschach's generally accepted conception of the processes underlying the production of good form responses, for example, Beck (1951) stresses: (1) "the ability to center the attention, making possible clear perception"; (2) "possession of clear mental pictures *(Engramme)*"; (3) "power to bring these clear memory pictures into consciousness"; and (4) "ability to select from among the memory pictures . . . the one most nearly resembling the stimulus" (p. 106). In effect, good form depends upon good perception and a capacity for matching perceptual images. This assumption, in turn, provides the basis for the interpretation of high form level as "indicative of the ability to perceive things conventionally and respond to them in a manner relatively free of affective domination" (Exner, 1969, p. 234). Conversely, low form level is treated as a measure of poor reality testing that reflects either limitations in the intellectual abilities required to deal with the perceptual task or the intrusion of pathological influences that result in distorted perceptions.

The assumption that the Rorschach is a perceptual task is not confined to its proponents. Sharing it, some academic perception theorists criticize advocates of the Rorschach for not paying sufficient attention to the manner in which theories of perception bear on the response process. Noting that Rorschach theorists "have rarely attempted a strictly perceptual analysis of what happens when a subject looks at a card and produces his responses," Michael Wertheimer (1957) emphasizes the importance of taking the Gestalt principles articulated by his father into account. "Any percept," he notes, "is organized according to the autochthonous principles, and Rorschach responses are no exception" (p. 209). He also suggests that the "New Look" movement in perception theory (Bruner, 1951; Witkin et al., 1954), a group of researchers contending that personality and motivational variables have an important bearing on perceptual organization, is clearly relevant to Rorschach theory. Bruner (1948), a leading member of this group, insists that because the Rorschach is a perceptual task, its interpretation must be subordinate to a general theory of perception. He acknowledges, however, that perception theory at the time neglected personality dynamics and that much could be gained from a "coalescence" of research in the two areas. Werner and Wapner (1956) suggest ways in which these new perceptual theories bear on the handling of the Rorschach task as well.

Until recently, then, the preponderant view of both Rorschach theorists and academics has been that the test is chiefly perceptual (Blatt, 1990).

THE PERCEPTION HYPOTHESIS AND PRESCHOOL RORSCHACHS

There have been few systematic efforts to apply principles of perceptual development to children's Rorschachs. The most noteworthy are those of Meili-Dworetzki (1956), who bases her work on Gestalt psychology, and the theories of Claparède and Piaget, and Hemmendinger (1953), who bases his on Werner's developmental psychology.

The two offer similar accounts of "the development of perception in the Rorschach" (Meili-Dworetzki, 1956). Both propose stages organized chiefly around the handling of location and form, although Meili-Dworetzki makes interesting observations about other Rorschach determinants as well. Both postulate a developmental progression from an initial stage of global, syncretistic modes of perception to later stages involving progressively more differentiated, flexible, and integrated ones. And both advance roughly the same timetable.

There are some differences between their stages and those proposed here. They begin with this second stage and carry their analyses beyond the third through later childhood and adolescence. Nonetheless, the degree of overlap is substantial and a perceptual explanation of stages in the mastery of the test can be extracted from their work with relative ease.

For example, though Meili-Dworetzki starts her research with subjects who are beyond the stage of purely perseverative protocols, she does discuss the topic. Perseverations, she suggests, arise because "young children manifest little eagerness or attention and often display a great deal of agitation in handling the cards" (p. 119). The questionable nature of children's initial responses to inkblots and their subsequent repetition of these responses are thus products of difficulties attending to the blots and of emotional struggles that interfere with their dealing with the test at all.

As children grapple with the blots in a more serious fashion in Stage II, both Meili-Dworetzki and Hemmendinger contend that the most distinctive feature of their protocols is the predominance of crude wholes of relatively poor form. These responses are attributed to perception "best described qualitatively as immature, inflexible, undifferentiated" (Hemmendinger, 1953, p. 168) or "a general and confused perception of the whole" (Meili-Dworetzki, 1956, p. 112). In this primitive, global mode of perception a single feature of the blot often determines the image and there is a lack of capacity to effectively coordinate details within it. Hemmendinger (1953) notes that as children approach school age they do give more detail responses, but these "are not markedly more mature in terms of the quality of perception" (p. 168). Meili-Dworetzki also suggests that the "arbitrary" whole responses and gross confabulations encountered in the period reflect a flight from the perceptual task as consequence "complete inattention or embarrassment" (p. 121).

In the five- to eight-year-old period, as children move into Stage III, both researchers observe a steady increase in D responses and an improvement in form level. Meili-Dworetzki (1956) explains these change in terms of an increasing capacity for perceptual differentiation or "distinct and analytic perception of the parts" (p. 112). In later childhood and adolescence, perceptual capacities develop further, allowing for complex, well-articulated responses in which there is "synthetic recomposition of the whole with an awareness of parts."

These analyses present a refined form of the theory many Rorschach practitioners would advance to explain stages in preschool Rorschachs. At first, lacking the capacities to attend to and make sense of Rorschach stimuli, children can do little more than repeat an initial vaguely perceived response or a response that covers an incapacity to deal with the perceptual task at all. Later, they display a rudimentary capacity to deal with the task, producing chiefly global responses of poor form that reflect their still-limited perceptual abilities. Also, because of the difficulty inhibiting other psychological processes that interfere with perception and because of wishes to escape the Rorschach task itself, they are prone to engage in extraneous behavior that results in confabulatory responses having little to do with the inkblots. Finally, as their capacities to attend to, analyze, and later synthesize visual figures develop, children are able to offer varied percepts of predominantly good form.

A CRITIQUE OF THE BASIC PERCEPTION HYPOTHESIS

Although on the surface this view of changes in children's Rorschachs as a manifestation of perceptual development has much to recommend it, young children's Rorschachs pose a major problem for the perception hypothesis in its basic form. To appreciate this problem, let us imagine that a group of irate preschoolers, tired of hearing aspersions cast upon their capacities, hires a team of aggressive young lawyers to file a class action suit charging the Rorschach guild with slander and misrepresentation. At the heart of the children's case are contentions that their perceptual abilities are perfectly adequate to deal with inkblots, that examiners encourage them to bring these abilities to bear on the Rorschach task, and that, when they do so, their responses are analyzed in ways that penalize them for doing exactly as they have been instructed, and interpreted in a manner that denigrates not only their perceptual abilities but also their character in general.

Plaintiff's Exhibit I (Figure 2) might well be a variation of an exercise used by Exner in his Rorschach Workshops. Card I could simply be placed next to several images commonly encountered by children that examiners believe make a "good fit" with the blot, for example, a butterfly or a jack-o-lantern. Inspecting the exhibit, not only a lay jury, but even those of us long familiar with the Rorschach are likely to be surprised by how little resemblance there is between the card and these pictures. Certainly the plaintiff's lawyers could argue with telling effect that for children to look at Card I and not "see" a butterfly or jack-o-lantern—indeed, for them to not see much of anything—is hardly a sign of defective perception. To the contrary, preschoolers know what butterflies and pumpkins look like and are not about to mistake a diffuse inkblot for them.

To cast the problem in Rorschach terms, were the test chiefly a perceptual one, an appropriate scoring system would treat percepts such as "an inkblot," "paint," or "a smudge of dirt" as F + responses. For "a bat" or "a butterfly" to be scored anything other than F − would depend heavily on the generosity or lax standards of the scorer.

Were Exhibit I not enough, the plaintiffs' lawyers could put a number of expert witnesses on the stand to buttress their case. Experimental psychologists might be called to testify that Rorschach theory bears little relationship to the kinds of processes they study. For example, Gibson (1956) contends:

> Although the reactions of a person to an inkblot are said to be indicative of an act of *perception*, this usage goes against the commonsense meaning of the term. From a strictly psychophysical and toughminded standpoint, certainly, Rorschach reactions have very little to do with perception [p. 203].

Figure 2. Exhibit I. (Card I of the Rorschach is reproduced here with the permission of Hans Huber Publishers, Bern, Switzerland.)

At best, he suggests the test may be a diagnostically useful "perceptual game played with pictures of low fidelity" (p. 296). Mooney (1962) could add that Rorschach categories were chosen because of hopes that they would distinguish clinical groups, not because of any grounding in theories of perception. The test's scoring system, he notes, bears only "a tenuous relation to dimensions of perception" (p. 24). On the basis of his analysis of the Rorschach literature from an experimental standpoint, Zubin (1956) would assert that perceptual aspects of the Rorschach task are so thoroughly confounded with a host of nonperceptual variables that it is difficult even to develop empirical tests of them and that such studies as have been done provide little support for perceptual hypotheses. Given this situation, he concludes, it is best "to minimize the perceptual approach" and to regard "the technique as a systematic interview behind the veil of inkblots" (p. 191).

To be sure, the defendants' attorneys could counter these opinions with those of other academic experts who stress perceptual aspects of the Rorschach (Brosin and Fromm, 1942; Bruner, 1948; Klein and Arnheim, 1953; Werner and Wapner, 1956; Wertheimer, 1957). What would be devastating to their defense, however, would be testimony from preeminent Rorschach authorities.

For example, Exner (1986), following the lead of Cattell (1951), would acknowledge that the Rorschach is, in fact, based on "misperception." When children insist that a Rorschach card is "a bunch of ink," they are absolutely right. "In reality," he observes, "those children gave the only truly correct answer. The stimulus is only an inkblot!" He goes on to note, "But if that correct answer is delivered as the *first* response, it is *not* accepted. Instead, the examiner encourages some other identification" (p. 29). The test, he asserts, rests on a requirement that the subject "misidentify" the stimuli.

Elaborating these points specifically with regard to the testing of children, Weiner (1986) could add:

> In a literal sense, there is only one correct response to the administration directions: "An inkblot!" But this is not an acceptable response. Instead subjects are required to misperceive the blot—to see it as something that it is not [p. 143].

In the face of such testimony, psychologists contending that the Rorschach is a "perceptual" task in the sense the term is commonly understood would have to base their hope of escaping a financially debilitating settlement on the fact that most preschoolers prefer lots of small coins to paper money.

Rorschach Perception
Hypotheses

PERCEPTION HYPOTHESES IN RORSCHACH THEORY

Confronted with our hypothetical suit, the Rorschach community might well charge the children's lawyers with deliberately misrepresenting their position and suggest that the many unpleasant jokes made about the legal profession are richly deserved. More to the point, the test's defenders would accuse the author of setting up a straw man. And they would do so with considerable justification.

The limitations of the basic perception hypothesis have not been ignored. Not only have they been stated explicitly by contemporary proponents of the test such as Exner, but they were recognized and fully acknowleged by Rorschach at the outset of his work. Given this acknowledgment, however, questions arise of why and in what sense he and his followers claim the test is a "perceptual" one.

The basis of their claim is, of course, that perception is a far more complex mental activity than envisaged in popular conceptions of the term. Working with Bleuler's concept of apperception, Rorschach (1921, p. 17) contended that perception is an interpretive process that combines sensation, memory, and association. Subjects register sensations or groups of sensations, organize them into images on the basis of past experience, and attribute meaning to these images by associating them with analogous memory engrams. In ordinary perception, this "associative integration of engrams (memory-pictures) with recent complexes of sensations" occurs in so natural and spontaneous a manner that subjects have no realization of the degree of interpretive activity involved. The task seems to consist of no more than recognizing objects or pictures. In contrast, with "chance forms," that is, inkblots, the "complex of sensations" and "memory pictures" are not "perfectly identical." Subjects must work to establish a fit and, in so doing, become conscious of the "associative-assimilative" process. By requiring this work, the Rorschach task thus highlights the integrative activity of the subject in perception.

Rorschach is aware that the intellectual demands of the task are too great for some subjects. Lacking the necessary capacities, the retarded, the brain-injured, and the profoundly psychotic may do little more than try to identify pictures. They cannot pass "a kind of threshold beyond which perception (assimilation without consciousness of assimilative effort) becomes interpretation (perception with consciousness of assimilative effort)" (p. 17). Yet, even recognizing this threshold, he concludes, perception and interpretation lie on a continuum along which "there is no sharp delineation, but a gradual shifting of emphasis." In this sense, "interpretation may be called a special kind of perception" and "there is, therefore, no doubt that this experiment can be called a test of perceptive power of the subject" (p. 18).

A quarter of a century later, Rapaport (Rapaport, Gill, and Schafer, 1946) initiated one of the most influential inquiries into the "psychological processes underlying Rorschach responses" by reiterating central aspects of Rorschach's position. Noting the potential of relatively unstructured stimuli to highlight the form-giving nature of perception, he observes:

> These considerations may prompt the examiner to see in the subject's reactions to the Rorschach inkblots a perceptual organizing process which has a fundamental continuity with perception in everyday life. However, while everyday perceptions allow conventions, specific memories, and familiarities to obscure the active nature of the perceptual process, the Rorschach inkblots bring the active organizing aspect of perception into the foreground and provide the examiner with a treasure of insight into hidden aspects of an individual's adjustment or maladjustment [p. 90].

To this point, Rapaport's position differs from Rorschach's only in his use of Gestalt psychology to offer a more sophisticated conception of the principles of perceptual organization than was available to his predecessor.

Rapaport's treatment of the response process departs from Rorschach's on two points. First, he argues that the association process does not consist simply of matching stimulus patterns to memory engrams. "Response-content," he insists (p. 91), "is not given in the inkblot." Rather, "salient perceptual features" or "partial impressions" initiate associations or ideas that enter into shaping the percept far more extensively than in Rorschach's concept of apperception. In this regard, the Rorschach is similar to an association test. Second, Rapaport proposes an intricate "cogwheeling" model of the integration of perceptual and associative aspects of response formation. An initial process of perceptual organization gives rise to an associative process in which that organization is elaborated, which in turn leads to further perceptual judgments in which the "potentialities and limitations of the inkblot act as a regulating reality for the association process itself" (pp. 93–94). Thus, while Rapaport attributes a larger role to associative processes, perception also becomes more important in that it now affects responses decisively in two ways, first originating the response process and later serving as its final arbiter.

Working from a phenomenological perspective, E. Schachtel (1966) proposes a conception of the response process that begins at a similar point. He notes:

> Whether one agrees with Bleuler's and Rorschach's concept of perception or not, it is clear that the processes of perceiving the inkblot, of associating remembered ideas and images and trying to integrate them with inkblots (i.e., to restructure the perception of the inkblot in the light of these images), and conversely, to try out these images for "fit" (congruence) with the inkblot play a decisive role in the typical "normal" Rorschach response. These are essentially the same processes that Rorschach had in mind when he came to the conclusion that the responses to his blots are based on perception [p. 13].

Schachtel's own contribution to Rorschach theory lies in adding components to this model. Going beyond the idea that the perceptual qualities of the blot serve to limit the associative process, he notes that subjects hone responses and judge them according to their "goodness of fit." Also, sensitive to the interpersonal context of the testing, they decide which among the responses acceptable to them they will share. Thus, he stresses, in addition to perception and association, the core aspects of Rorschach's theory, the response process includes judgment and communication as well.

Recently, approaching the problem from an empirical standpoint, Exner (1986) advanced another variation on these basic themes. He, too, accepts that the task is initially a perceptual one, translating Rorschach's ideas about apperception into a contemporary language of "encoding the stimulus field" and "classification of the field and/or its parts" (p. 34). Yet, while convinced that Rorschach is "correct in his basic hypotheses," Exner also believes that the process is "considerably more complex" and that "numerous operations occur before a response is actually delivered, and they occur within a time frame that few recognized during the early days of the development of the test" (p. 28). On the basis of experimentation, he demonstrates that in a short time subjects can generate many more percepts than they reveal and concludes that, following the initial formation of percepts, subjects discard some for reasons of economy, withhold others because of censorship, and select among the rest on the basis of styles, traits, and psychological states activated by the demands of the task.

In sum, then, preeminent Rorschach theorists typically start their accounts of the response process with Rorschach's basic assumption that, at its core, his test involves a complex form of perception in which interpretive aspects of the process are heightened. Where they differ from Rorschach is in a growing appreciation of additional processes that shape percepts and determine which among them are shared.

MODIFIED PERCEPTION HYPOTHESES AND PRESCHOOL RORSCHACHS

Explanations of preschool Rorschachs from the standpoint of these perception hypotheses are similar in many respects to those outlined in the preceding chapter. Insofar as perceptual aspects of the Rorschach task are core components of Rorschach theories, concepts of perceptual development will be central to their treatment of early stages in the mastery of the test. Moreover, because Meili-Dworetzki and Hemmendinger base their work on Gestalt psychology, Piaget, and Werner, their developmental perspectives on the test are, in fact, oriented around concepts of perception as an active, organizing process similar to those with which major Rorschach theorists work. The more elaborate Rorschach "perception" theories can, however, expand and deepen these explanations of early stages in performance on the test.

The perseverative protocols children first produce on the test, for example, are still seen as a result of the perceptual task being too difficult for young subjects, but too difficult in a particular way. Very young children approach the test in the same manner Rorschach (1921) ascribes to other subjects who have problems with the test because of limited intelligence or extreme psychopathology. As he notes:

> These subjects do not interpret pictures, they name them. They may be astonished that someone else is able to see something different in them. We deal in these cases not with an interpretation but with perception in the strict sense of the word [p. 17].

Fully capable of perception "as recognition," young children know that an inkblot is an inkblot and that it is not a decent picture of a bat or jack-o-lantern. Yet, precisely because they are fixed on this type of perception, they have difficulty seeing inkblots "as something else" when there is not clear congruence between the stimuli and the image of the object. In Rorschach's terms, they have not passed the "threshold" that separates "perception without consciousness of assimilative effort" from "perception with consciousness of assimilative effort." It is the move to perception as interpretation that may be seen as distinguishing subsequent stages from this initial one.

In a similar manner, the protocols characteristic of older preschoolers can be explained by accepting the descriptions of limitations in perceptual processes relative to the Rorschach task noted in the preceding chapter and supplementing them with a consideration of additional processes in accounting for the prominence of confabulatory phenomena. Although it is not hard to adapt the theories of Schachtel and Exner for these purposes, Rapaport's "cogwheeling" model readily lends itself to explaining three distinguishing characteristics of Stage II protocols.

First, the DW nature of responses may be treated as a consequence of a premature shift from perception to association. Rather than struggling to integrate a variety of aspects of the perceptual stimuli, preschoolers jump from a registration of one characteristic of the blot to associations that result in a response that may accord poorly with the blot as a whole.

Second, not only is there a rapid shift to associations, but the associative process may run wild. The blot stimulates a series of ideas and fantasies that take precedence over the Rorschach task the examiner sets for the child. Hence, the confabulatory quality of Stage II responses.

Finally, preschoolers have little ability and even less inclination to undertake the third aspect of Rapaport's response process, returning to the perceptual aspects of the task to assess and revise percepts. Young children are, in fact, unaware that there is such a step to be taken.

In Stage III, each aspect of the response process becomes increasingly sophisticated and coordinated with the others. Growing perceptual abilities allow subjects to combine more parts of the stimulus field appropriately; associative processes are more disciplined and integrated with perceptual ones; perceptual judgments are brought to bear in evaluating responses; and personal and social judgments enter more fully into what subjects accept and communicate. Thus, the assumption that such processes are present now provides a normative framework for interpreting the adequacy of test responses.

A Critique of the Expanded
Perception Hypotheses

METHODOLOGICAL ISSUES

Although the perception hypotheses advanced by leading Rorschach theorists provide more sophisticated conceptions of the test task and richer explanations of young children's handling of it than the basic perception hypothesis, they face problems of their own. Not the least of these problems are methodological ones. Imagine, for example, what it would be like to describe "the Rorschach experiment" to an academic psychologist who knows nothing of the test, but is ready to give serious consideration to any technique that promises to reveal the manner in which personality variables enter into perception.

We would, of course, explain that our procedure consists of three steps. First, subjects are presented with the Rorschach stimuli and asked what the inkblots might be. Second, if "determinants" of "percepts" cannot be inferred from the initial responses, one or two brief, nondirective questions are asked to elicit them. Third, using the information obtained in this manner, we code responses according to location, content, and a few determinant categories (notably, form, color, shading, and "movement"), tabulate these scores, and compare various sums and ratios with normative data. These comparisons, along with qualitative analyses of individual responses, provide the basis for broad inferences about subjects' perceptual styles and personality characteristics.

Unhappily, as is so often the case in dialogues with academics, the ensuing discussion is likely to degenerate into an increasingly unpleasant discourse on method. Our colleague might well begin by observing condescendingly that we have little idea of the complexity of the issues with which we are grappling. In rigorously controlled, laboratory conditions, specifying how a multiplicity of aspects of a stimulus field affects perceptual processes is fraught with difficulty; in the more complicated, less controlled Rorschach situation, problems in delineating specific contributions to those processes increase severalfold. For example, Zubin, Eron, and Schumer (1965) note:

> In analyzing the so-called perceptual response in the Rorschach situation, we need to determine the different levels of influence which bring about the final "percept." It is difficult enough to attempt this task in "real" perception, that is, perception of objects in space. It is all the more difficult to accomplish this analysis with pictures (pictorial space), and virtually impossible in "Rorschach space" [pp. 259–260].

Were we reluctant to accept the opinions of such unsympathetic experimental critics, our companion could point out that the interplay of cognitive, associative, and interpersonal constituents of the response process described by Rapaport, Schachtel, and Exner should alone be sufficient to shake our confidence in how well we can truly disentangle perceptual contributions to it with the best of methods.

Far from being among the best methods for investigating perceptual processes, he might add, the means by which Rorschach examiners seek to detect "determinants" are hopelessly inadequate. First, examiners must rely on that least valued of psychological methodologies, reports of "untrained introspectionists" — and, at times, untrained introspectionists whose sanity is in doubt (Levin, 1953; Mooney, 1962). Second, far from engaging in focused, detailed inquiries into subjects' responses, seldom do examiners ask more than a question or two, and even these are distinguished by how little clue they give subjects about what is sought. Third, even were more extensive inquiries conducted with mature, rational subjects, trust in the information obtained would still rest on the shaky assumptions that subjects know and are able to articulate, in a consistent and reliable way, the bases of what they perceive. For example, if subjects "see" Card VI as an animal skin, note the shape, and make no reference to shading, can we, in fact, assume that the latter quality plays little role in determining their percept?

Would they be as likely to give the same response if the inkblot were a solid color? Probably not. As Baughman (1959) has demonstrated, many more perceptual factors enter into the formation of responses than those stated by subjects and used in scoring "determinants."

Finally, given the richness of perceptual stimuli, our colleague might note, Rorschach scoring categories are surprisingly limited. Location and content scores are good enough, but can a handful of determinant scores suffice? Consider, for example, some of the qualities noted by E. Schachtel (1966) that elude such scoring:

> They may be designated as directness versus diffusion; focused or un-focused; smoothness, evenness versus raggedness, jaggedness; fluid versus angular lines; openness versus closedness; shelter versus oppression; pointedness versus roundedness; completeness versus incompleteness; viable space versus crowdedness and collision. . . . There are other qualities (e.g., of color or shading or texture) that are also significant. For example: softness versus hardness (of texture); dryness versus wetness; smoothness (pleasant tone) versus sliminess (unpleasant tone); warmth versus coldness (of color or of texture); lightness versus darkness [p. 41].

Moreover, whereas ordinarily perception is shaped by the interaction of many variables, Rorschach percepts are typically scored with only a single determinant. Sometimes two determinants may be specified, but seldom more. As a means of representing influences on perception, such a coding system is remarkable for the amount of information it loses.

In short, insofar as we present the Rorschach as a test of perception, critics of its methodology would stress the discrepancy between the complexity of the problem and the naïveté of the techniques through which it is addressed.

THE "PERCEPTUAL CONTINUUM" AND DISCONTINUITIES

The elasticity of their concepts of perception pose a second set of problems for traditional Rorschach theories. In trying to capture what proponents of the test mean in describing it as a "perceptual task," Mooney (1962) observes that "perception" is defined:

> simply as the behavioral process which falls between dependence upon stimuli (sensation) and independence of stimuli (conceptualization or thinking) whereby the individual represents reality to himself. The range of behavior patterns that are included under the label "perception" are not

considered to cluster around some point midway between pure sensation and cognitive activity, but rather to extend to both extremes of this imaginary continuum [p. 19].

At the least, this position runs the risk of allowing theorists to slide too casually from one meaning of the term to another, obscuring differences in the processes involved. Nowhere is this problem greater than with regard to the critical discontinuity that marks the starting point of true mastery of the test.

As Rorschach (1921, p. 17) recognizes at the outset of his work, the decisive step in taking his test lies in the shift from treating the task as one of perception without awareness of the necessity of engaging in an "associative-assimilative" process to one of readily engaging in such a process. Nonetheless, in spite of the seeming radical differences between "ordinary perception" and "perception as interpretation," he believes that there is an underlying continuity between the two sets of processes. All perception, he contends, involves interpretation, but associative or intellectual capacities must pass a certain "threshold" before subjects are able to attribute meaning to "chance forms." It is as this threshold is passed that what appears to be a different form of perception arises.

There are, however, strong grounds for believing that the changes involved in being able to take the test do not involve simply a quantitative increase in intellectual capacities bearing upon perception, but rather involve qualitatively different forms of intellectual activity. Exner (1986) and Weiner (1986) recognize this distinction implicitly when they describe the Rorschach as based on "misperception" or "misidentification." Clearly they do not mean to imply that some error or deficiency is involved in producing responses. Rather, their dramatic choice of terms is intended to emphasize the point that fundamental differences separate "perception as recognition" from "perception as interpretation."

Rorschach's (1921) exposition of his perception theory provides a starting point for understanding the nature of these differences. He begins that discussion by observing: "Almost all subjects regard the experiment as a test of imagination. This conception is so general that it becomes, practically, a condition of the experiment" (p. 16). To be sure, he goes on to assert his belief that it is "unnecessary to consider imagination a prerequisite" for the test and that the results are similar "whether one encourages the subject to give free rein to his imagination or not." Nonetheless, there remains the question of why the supposedly mistaken belief that the Rorschach is a test of imagination should be "a condition of the experiment."

The reason can be seen if we consider what the test would be like if subjects did not hold this belief. Rorschach, in fact, describes these subjects a few paragraphs later: They are ones who do not interpret pictures, but rather name them. The function of the assumption that the test is one of imagination is that it introduces a different attitude toward the Rorschach stimuli. They are not pictures to be recognized, but stimulus material to be seen "as something else."

An appreciation of the importance of this shift in attitude can be seen in a variety of ways in the Rorschach literature. For example, in discussing administration, Piotrowski (1950) recommends:

> As most subjects regard it as a test of imagination, the purpose of the examination may be described by saying, "Well, I'd like you to see what you can say about this, what kind of imagination you have. All sorts of things can be seen in clouds and in this too" or something to that effect [p. 544].

The intent of these instructions, as Exner (1969, p. 125) observes, is to introduce an "instructional set," an attitude intended to move subjects away from viewing it as a task of perceptual recognition.

Most proponents of the test are convinced that Piotrowski's instructions are neither necessary nor desirable, because almost all mature subjects approach the test appropriately without them. However, efforts to discourage one set of attitudes toward the test and induce another are common in work with young children. For example, Ames et al. (1974) stress that care should be taken to avoid mentioning the word "pictures" in explaining the test to them. Similarly, while not favoring the strategy themselves, Klopfer, Fox, and Troup (1956, p. 14) acknowledge that many who administer the test to preschoolers try "to impress on the child that the blots are 'not really pictures.'" Yet even when instructions of this kind are not initially given, as Weiner (1986, p. 143) notes, if children respond to standard directions with the only correct answer ("an inkblot"), it is not accepted. Instead, they are "required to misperceive the blot—to see it as something it is not." In effect, the critical factor in the initial stage of mastering the test is adoption of a particular attitude toward the task.

The point that should be stressed regarding this attitude is that although it affects how "perception" is undertaken, it is cognitive in nature. It is based on a decision not to view Rorschach stimuli as "perceptual" in the ordinary sense of the term, but rather to see them "as something else." From a developmental standpoint, the growth of perceptual capacities as they are commonly understood is not essential to this process. To the contrary, subjects must take stimuli they now recognize to be one thing and deliberately treat them differently. For the present, we can leave open the questions of whether this process is based on imagination or association or something else. What is clear is that the decisive step that must be taken by subjects in order to do the Rorschach is one in which the hold of perception in dealing with the inkblots is broken. This is not a step along a "perceptual continuum," but rather one off that continuum that allows the Rorschach task to be approached in a fundamentally different way.

THE "PERCEPTUAL CONTINUUM" AND THE RESPONSE PROCESS

The elasticity of Rorschach concepts of perception are also problematic in that they obscure differences among theories of the response process and inhibit questions of how "perceptual" that process is.

In Rorschach's theory, both the description of the test as one of perception and the notion of a continuum are justified. He assumes that all perception is apperceptive and involves interpretation. In ordinary perception, the stimulus is well defined for the subject and heavily determines the resultant percept. Indeed, because the sensory input is so clear and the processes by which it is formed so routine and automatized, the active, organizing character of perceptual activity goes unnoticed. In contrast, the "chance forms" of the Rorschach experiment create a situation similar to a favorite example of Rorschach theorists taken from Gestalt psychology, that of a figure only beginning to emerge from a fog. In such circumstances, the ambiguous nature of the stimulus makes seemingly "simple" recognition impossible and necessitates a sharp increase in interpretive efforts of the subject, thereby highlighting this aspect of perception.

As has been seen, although typically beginning with Rorschach's ideas about the perceptual nature of the test, later theorists subtly changed his conception of the task, increasingly emphasizing other aspects of the response process. For example, Rapaport, Gill, and Schafer (1946) contend that initial perceptual impressions quickly give rise to associations that become a determining force in shaping the treatment of perceptual material. Indeed, insofar as it is the association that "affects a more or less intensive organization of the inkblot" (p. 93), perceptual aspects of the blot appear to serve chiefly as raw material to be shaped in a manner similar to the ways in which sculptors or painters might work with different media. The confabulations characteristic of preschool Rorschachs attest to how powerful this aspect of the response process may be and require reintroducing "perception" as a corrective device in the last phase of the response process. Certainly in Rapaport's account cognitive and judgmental elements play as prominent a role in the formation of responses as perceptual ones.

While perhaps not going as far as Rapaport, E. Schachtel (1966) and Exner (1986) also heavily stress the role of processes such as association, judgment, and communication in shaping responses or, at least, determining which responses are shared. This shift in emphasis can be seen in Exner's definition of the test as a "perceptual-cognitive" one whose critical feature is "problem-solving" (Exner, 1982, p. 3).

Although undoubtedly correct in stressing cognitive aspects of the Rorschach response process, the "perceptual-cognitive" definition of the task can obscure differences among theories about what kind of perceptual-cognitive task it is and, even more, the fact that theories are not specific on this point.

PERCEPTION HYPOTHESES AND THE PROBLEM OF FORM LEVEL

One of the seeming strengths of perception hypotheses is that they provide theoretical links between performance on the Rorschach and inferences about personality characteristics. How subjects perceive the world, it is assumed, reflects significant aspects of their personality. Yet this assumption is not easily translated into viable theories regarding specific determinants. Nowhere are these problems more striking than in the case of the phenomenon perceptual theories seem best suited to explain, form level.

In offering a rationale for inferences about the meaning of form level, even positions defining the Rorschach as a "perceptual-cognitive" task tend to slide back along the continuum and stress perceptual aspects of the test. As has been seen, Rorschach theorists typically base their arguments about the relationship of form level and reality testing on the concept of "perceptual accuracy" or the "goodness of fit" between the Rorschach percept and memory engrams of objects.

Yet insofar as they rely on this criterion, their positions face the same problem that confronts the basic perception hypothesis. Card I does not in fact bear much resemblance to a picture of a bat or jack-o-lantern. By the standards of ordinary perception, even F + responses are not very accurate. At best, judgments of form level based upon them can be only relative ones in which F + responses involve a poor fit, weak form responses an even worse fit, and F – responses an atrocious mismatch. But to treat the problem of form in this way obviously fails to do justice to the process of creating Rorschach responses. When shown an F + response, even unsophisticated observers recognize intuitively that it is not a poorly realized depiction of an object, but an aesthetic achievement. Criteria for making such judgments must exist, but they are not "accuracy of fit" according to some concrete physical resemblance.

The difficulties posed by the theoretical rationale offered for the concept of form level and the lack of accord between Rorschach percepts and ordinary perception are at the root of one of the most significant problems in the Rorschach literature. Kimball (1950) highlights this problem in her review of the efforts of Rorschach systematizers to apply their concepts of form level in practice. After citing definitions of good form in terms of "clearly visualized forms," "form accuracy," "congruence with the inkblot," and "correspondence of the response with 'reality,' " she observes:

> Inspection of these definitions of form-level would lead to the assumption that there exists a fair amount of agreement among Rorschach examiners, first with respect to the "perceptual reality of the inkblot" with which the response is to be compared, and second, concerning whether or not any given response corresponds closely with this reality.
>
> When the form-level scores which have been published by different authors are compared, however, no such agreement is apparent. In many cases the same response has been scored F + (good or accurate form) by one author, and F – (poor or inaccurate form) by another [p. 140].

As Korchin (1960) notes, although Rorschach theorists assert that form level reflects perceptual accuracy or fit with "reality," they disagree radically about what these concepts mean and how such matters should be assessed.

Two different types of criteria have been advanced for determining form level (Kimball, 1950; Korchin, 1960; Exner, 1969). From the standpoint of perception hypotheses, the simpler and more straightforward one is based on examiners' judgments of how closely a subject's percept resembles the object it is meant to represent. Although Klopfer and his colleagues (Klopfer et al., 1954) have made some efforts to refine criteria for such judgments, ultimately they rest upon the examiners' capacity to see a subject's percept and evaluate its adequacy.

Recognizing differences between the products of ordinary perception and Rorschach percepts, other theorists such as Beck, Exner, Hertz, and Rorschach himself distrust the subjectivity seemingly inherent in these judgments and favor a quantitative standard for determination of form level based on the frequency of occurrence of responses. For them, good form responses are ones that are given often by normal subjects and that differentiate this population from pathological groups.

Yet these criteria suggest a discomfort with, if not abandonment of, the perceptual "goodness of fit" standard. For example, expressing the rationale for this approach in its most extreme form, Beck et al. (1950) assert:

> Our assumption is that since there is no accuracy, or reality at all within these originally chance ink blots—therefore the forms which these normal people perceive in them are the absolute accuracy or reality that obtains in the blots [p. 263].

In practice, if not in theory, proponents of statistical criteria for form level have moved a long way from the perception hypothesis.

To be sure, there are ways of effecting at least a degree of reconciliation among these positions. It can be argued that judgments of form level are based on perception whether they are made by individual examiners or large samples of normal subjects, and that differences among systems regarding criteria are heuristic ones based upon the methodological preferences of Rorschach practitioners. It can be noted that, for all of the differences among systems, most use mixed criteria. For example, Rapaport, who favors a qualitative approach, makes use of statistical norms, whereas Rorschach and others who advocate quantitative approaches make qualitative judgments as well. Even Beck has formulated his position in less extreme forms and relies on more qualitative judgments in determining form level than his theoretical statement suggests (Kinder et al., 1982). Indeed, examiners can hardly do otherwise, since without such judgments they cannot deal with the most impressive Rorschach phenomenon, original responses of good form. Although such responses are clearly significant intellectual achievements, there can be no normative basis for judging them. Finally, it can also be pointed out that for all their differences, there is a substantial degree of agreement across systems regarding particular responses that are good and poor.

For our purposes, it is not important either to choose among contending positions in these debates or to find ways of reconciling their conflicts. What is significant is what the debates themselves reveal. In particular, they highlight (1) the manner in which the concept of a perceptual continuum allows theorists to shift casually from one definition of perception to another in their work; (2) the pull of the "perceptual" pole of that continuum in their theorizing about the Rorschach as a "perceptual-cognitive" task; and (3) the problem this emphasis poses as such ideas are translated into practice. At the least, these debates suggest ways in which the elasticity in the definition of perception allows the concept to be invoked to imply a solution to problems in Rorschach theory that are far from settled. Thus, for example, even the question of what makes a good response "good" is still open.

PERCEPTION HYPOTHESES AND RORSCHACH INTERPRETATION

Most Rorschach practitioners base their interpretations of protocols not only on the premise that the way in which subjects perceive the world reflects critical aspects of their personality, but also on assumptions that an emphasis on specific aspects of perception—form, color, shading, movement—is associated with distinctive personality characteristics and types of pathology. Such assumptions are, however, more articles of faith than principles with solid theoretical grounding or empirical support. Indeed, when they are examined closely, it is surprising how little attention has been given to articulating their theoretical foundations.

In his initial monograph, Rorschach (1921) does not spell out the conceptual underpinnings of his scoring system, but rather justifies it on the basis of its capacity to differentiate clinical populations. Following this pattern, later scoring systems are, for the most part, elaborations of Rorschach's categories, and research supporting them consists chiefly of efforts to demonstrate how scores and patterns of scores can be used to predict differences in groups of subjects. To be sure, a rationale for Rorschach scores is, at least, implicit in Rorschach's monograph and is elaborated in a few subsequent works by others. Yet these publications are only a minuscule fraction of the Rorschach literature. Only a handful of works are devoted to examining the theoretical basis for most categories, and the two books that give the most sustained attention to the issue did not appear until forty years after Rorschach proposed his system (Rickers-Ovsiankina, 1960; E. Schachtel, 1966).

Although differing in their particulars, most theories that have been advanced about the meaning of determinants have a common form that derives from Rorschach's view that perception involves not only the registration of stimuli, but also a complex organizational process through which stimuli are formed into images and the attribution of meaning to these images on the basis of memory and association. From the standpoint of perception hypotheses, the first two aspects of the process—the registration and organization of stimuli—are critical and each plays a role in theories about the meaning of determinants.

One set of assumptions underlying Rorschach interpretations centers on a presumed linkage between sensitivity to different kinds of perceptual stimuli and types of psychological dispositions. Rorschach's scoring system assumes that each "determinant" is based on an emphasis on some aspect of perception. In the case of form, color, and shading, these roots are evident, although Rorschach contends, and most of his followers concur, that even movement responses have their origins in kinesthetic sensations stimulated by the inkblots. In addition, probably on the bases of phenomenological analyses, Rorschach suggests (and his followers concur) that sensitivity to at least some kinds of stimuli are associated with different facets of psychological experience. In particular, like artists and interior decorators, they believe that there is an inherent connection between the experience of color and affect. Consequently, they hold that the more color plays a role in Rorschach responses, the more the subject is open to and swayed by affective experience. Conversely, the absence of color responses is linked to emotional constriction. Perhaps the most striking example of stimulus-based interpretations of determinants is that of achromatic color, which holds that a responsiveness to dark colors, with their heavy, somber overtones, is related to a proneness to dysphoric mood.

Theories centering on differential sensitivities to stimuli, however, play a secondary role in Rorschach interpretation in part because of limits to their explanatory power. Although they provide some basis for the interpretation of color and achromatic color responses, for example, there is no readily apparent link between a predisposition to register kinesthetic sensations and interpretations of movement responses such as their presumed association with a capacity for "inner creation" (Rorschach, 1964). Moreover, stimulus-based theories can support only a portion of the interpretations made of color responses. For example, Rorschach (1964) ascribed eight characteristics to subjects in whose records color is predominant: "stereotyped intelligence, more reproductive ability, more 'outward' life, labile affective reactions, more adaptable to reality, more extensive than intensive rapport, restless, labile motility, skill and adroitness" (p. 78). Of these attributes, the color-affect association affords an explanation of only labile affective reactions and, perhaps, restless, labile motility.

In explaining the meaning of determinants, Rorschach theorists focus primarily on central processes. Interested, above all, in perception as an apperceptive process, Rorschach contends that the unique feature of his test is that it highlights the active, organizing processes subjects bring to bear in interpreting perceptual experience. Theories about these processes lie at the core of most interpretations of Rorschach determinants.

The meanings attributed to form responses provide a good illustration of the nature of such theories. Articulating the basic assumption underlying them, E. Schachtel (1966, p. 87) notes that there is a long philosophical tradition supporting the idea that form is the fundamental ordering principle through which human beings make sense of the universe. In giving form to experience, what is required is both careful attention to stimuli and an active intellectual operation through which structure is discerned in or imposed on them. Working on these premises, Rorschach (1964) interprets the capacity to produce good form as reflecting two characteristics: capacities to attend and concentrate that allow for clear appreciation of stimuli, and intellectual capacities that allow stimuli to be organized into accurate and sophisticated forms. Taken together, such characteristics are associated with disciplined, reality-oriented thinking. Other major Rorschach theorists interpret form along similar lines. For example, Rapaport (Rapaport, Gill, and Schafer, 1946) contends that good form responses reflect a capacity for formal reasoning and adherence to the demands of reality, and Beck (1944b, 1945) asserts that they indicate intellectual, conscious control and respect for reality.

Interpretations of the specific qualities of form in Rorschach protocols involve, for the most part, variations on these themes. Production of poor, unsophisticated forms are associated with low intelligence, whereas complex, well-integrated forms are seen as reflective of high intelligence. A preponderance of ordinary, uncomplicated, "popular" forms is associated with adequate, conventional thinking, whereas original forms are associated with unconventionality, whether due to creativity or madness. Good form level is taken as evidence of good reality testing; the production of peculiar, distorted forms as signs of disturbances in reality testing. Protocols that emphasize pure form to the exclusions of other determinants are held to be indicative of an emphasis on intellect to the exclusion of fantasy and emotion. And so forth.

Major theories about the use of color in Rorschach responses stress central organizing processes as well. Although accepting the hypothesized linkage of color and affect, Rickers-Ovsiankina (1943), E. Schachtel (1966), and Shapiro (1960) stress that, in contrast to form, the experience of color is a more passive process. Color has an immediacy; it impinges upon or affects subjects directly. For these theorists and for Rorschach himself, the overriding issue in interpreting color responses is the attitude subjects take toward this kind of experience as reflected in the relationship of color and form. Pure color responses are seen as reflecting a passive attitude toward life whereby individuals are readily affected by events impinging upon them, easily swayed by emotion, and at the mercy of feelings. These assumptions provide a basis for ascribing to subjects with significant numbers of C responses characteristics such as impulsivity, emotional lability, and an alloplastic character style. In contrast, responses in which form predominates over color are taken as indications of a capacity to control emotion and experience it in well-modulated ways. In these theories it is not so much the registration of stimuli as the attitude or stance subjects take toward them that provides the explanatory link between modes of handling the inkblots and inferences about personality and pathology.

The same emphasis is present even with regard to interpretations that seem most closely tied to the nature of the stimuli, responses to dark, achromatic color. For example, E. Schachtel (1966) notes:

> We can observe that depressive patients seem to look for those factors in the environment which fit into their depressive mood and sometimes seem almost disappointed when something good happens to them, as if it interfered with a wish to prove how dark everything is [pp. 246–247].

For them, he argues, accentuation of achromatic responses is a way of calling attention to their "black mood" and the "blackness of the environment." They do not just react to a stimulus property of cards, but use it as a way of representing and communicating their experience.

Interpretations of movement responses stress central processes so heavily that they seem to move beyond the domain of perception altogether. In advancing theories to support Rorschach's belief that such responses reflect a capacity for "inner creation," fantasy, and empathy, Furrer (1925), Binder (1932), and E. Schachtel (1966) do posit a sequence that begins with inkblots stimulating kinesthetic sensations and arousing drives that press for action. However, what is essential in their theories is that these sensations and desires do *not* give rise to action. Rather, overt responses are inhibited and wishes sublimated and translated into symbolic forms. It is both the inhibition of overt action and the capacity to express intentions through representations that provide the explanation of character traits such as introversion, a capacity to use fantasy adaptively, and creativity.

This account, of course, hardly does justice to the richness and complexity of interpretations of Rorschach determinants. It does not acknowledge sufficiently the diverse inferences that are made about individual determinants. For example, a preponderance of complex, well-organized form responses may reflect not only intellectual capacities but also motivational variables such as ambition. It gives little attention to the manner in which Rorschach interpretation involves inferences based on the interaction of scores of different determinants. And it gives no attention to theories of such determinants as animal movement and inanimate movement that center on assumptions about associational as opposed to perceptual processes.

Yet in assessing the role of perception in the explanation of Rorschach determinants, appreciation of such complexities only reinforces the points made about the general form of Rorschach interpretation. As they are taken into consideration, perceptual processes involving the registration of stimuli play an even more modest role in Rorschach interpretation relative to cognitive, motivational, and attitudinal variables. It is the assumption that these variables enter into modes or styles of interpreting perceptual stimuli that lie at the core of theories of the meaning of determinants, and it is the assumption that these perceptual styles or attitudes are, in turn, aspects of more general modes of experiencing and acting upon the world that provide the bridge that allows inferences to be made about personality functioning in general from responses to the Rorschach.

In evaluating the viability of perception hypotheses and whether they are necessary to Rorschach interpretation, a number of points should be highlighted. First, as has been seen, Rorschach categories were not derived from well-recognized principles in the psychology of perception. Rather, they were proposed initially on intuitive grounds and defended on the basis of their capacity to distinguish diagnostic groups. Efforts to explain the meaning of particular determinants in terms of theories involving perceptual processes have been confined to a handful of publications, and these usually seek to offer justifications of scoring procedures that are already presupposed. More often, principles of interpretation rest simply on claims about their clinical utility. As a consequence, Zubin et al. (1965) contend, "With few major exceptions, this theory has little implication beyond the clinic or Rorschach interpretation, and fails to interact or mesh with non-Rorschach research or theory" (pp. 178–179).

Second, even theories advanced to justify Rorschach scores raise questions about the perceptual basis of those explanations. Although aspects of those theories related to the registration of stimuli clearly fall under the rubric of perception, they are subordinate to an overriding concern with central processes that are assumed to shape the "interpretation" of stimuli. Although the concept of a perceptual continuum is used to rationalize treating the latter processes as "perceptual," so heavily do some of these theories stress cognitive variables that the term "perception" subtly changes meaning and becomes synonymous with "understanding," "representing," or "experiencing the world." As has been seen, for example, achromatic color responses are viewed not simply as a reaction to the darkness of the stimuli, but as an active effort to represent and communicate aspects of one's experience. More important, explanations of movement responses stress a transformational process whereby urges initiated by perceptual stimuli are inhibited and translated into symbolic activities. At such points, interpretation of Rorschach determinants appear to have strayed beyond the borders of a "perceptual continuum" into that domain Mooney (1962, p. 19) describes as "conceptualization or thinking."

Third, although Rorschach defended his view of his test on empirical grounds and considerable research has been done to buttress his contentions, little of that research will support a conception of the test as primarily one of perception as opposed to another process such as cognition, imagination, or symbolization. There is a dearth of research seeking to validate interpretations of the meaning of determinants independent of the test itself. Consequently, Mooney (1962, p. 20) notes that there is "no clear-cut linkage between perceptual task variables and Rorschach categories." By and large, research on the test has followed Rorschach's lead, trying to support principles of interpretation by showing how scores differentiate clinical groups. However, even if the adequacy of this research is granted, it cannot establish the perception hypotheses in a definitive way. Insofar as other theories of the test as one chiefly of imagination, cognition, or symbolization use the same scoring system and invoke the same central processes, Rorschach research cannot be used to support one hypothesis in preference to another.

17

Alternatives to the
Perception Hypotheses

THEORIES WITH NONPERCEPTUAL EMPHASES

In the three quarters of a century since Rorschach initiated his research, a number of theories have been advanced that elevate facets of the response process other than perception to a central position in explanations of the test. As seen in the preceding chapters, Rorschach (1964) began his theoretical discussion of the test by arguing that it is not one of imagination as had been believed (Dearborn, 1898; Whipple, 1910). Yet he conceded that most subjects believe it to be one of imagination and, in spite of his views, authorities such as Piotrowski (1950, 1957) and E. Schachtel (1966) make a place for the concept in their theories of the test.

In the late 1930s, other conceptions of the Rorschach were advanced in the context of theories about the then new concept of "projective techniques." Initially it was implied that such tasks tap processes related to the psychoanalytic defense of projection, one involving attribution of aspects of the self to others. However, the term quickly took on a different and broader meaning. In a seminal paper on the topic, Frank (1939) treats the Rorschach as one of a class of instruments that provide "plastic" media (e.g., objects, materials, experiences) that subjects are required to organize in ways of their own choosing. In such conditions, he posits, individuals "project" upon materials their ways of giving meaning to experience, thereby revealing essential aspects of their personalities. While no less a psychoanalytic authority than Rapaport (Rapaport, Schafer, and Gill, 1946) dismisses the idea that the Rorschach is based on a reality-distorting defensive process, he is sympathetic to Frank's concept of projection. Such tests, he suggests, do serve as a kind of lens through which aspects of psychological structure are projected onto a screen or as a catalyst for the expression of personality (p. 7).

Another conception of the test stressed associative processes. Going far beyond Rorschach's view of associations as a constituent of apperception and Rapaport's "cogwheel" model of the response process, Lindzey (1961) classifies the Rorschach as an "association technique." With instruments of this kind, he notes that

> the subject is set to respond to some stimulus presented by the examiner with the first word, image, or percept that occurs to him. Such devices minimize ideation and emphasize immediacy. The subject is not to reflect or reason but rather to respond with whatever concept or word, however unreasonable, first rises to consciousness [p. 51].

In effect, the Rorschach is like the Word Association Test except that the stimulus is a design rather than a word.

Yet another conception of the test treats it as a specialized clinical interview. As has been seen, Schafer (1952) and E. Schachtel (1945, 1966) stress the influence of the interpersonal context on test responses. Similarly, Rapaport views all psychological tests from the perspective of standardized interviews and, in part for this reason, adds to established Rorschach scores additional ones for "deviant verbalizations" that are taken to indicate the presence of disordered thinking (Rapaport, Gill, and Schafer, 1946). For these theorists, however, recognition that the Rorschach is embedded in a clinical situation expands and supplements views of the test as basically a perceptual task. In contrast, frustrated with confusion around the perception hypotheses and problems in testing them experimentally, Zubin (1956, p. 191) proposes "eliminating perceptual factors upon which Rorschach based his theory" and "regarding the Rorschach technique as a systematic interview behind the veil of ink-blots." By treating protocols in this way, he suggests, dimensions of personality can be elicited through the use of content analysis methods alone.

LIMITATIONS OF ALTERNATE THEORIES

Although each of these alternatives to Rorschach's position deals with important aspects of his test, none has posed a serious challenge to the general acceptance of some form of the perception hypothesis within the Rorschach community. For most adherents of the test, these challengers, in spite of their marked differences from one another, share two common failings.

Their most significant defect is that they do not appreciate, as Rorschach did, that the essence of the test lies in how subjects grapple with concrete visual stimuli. Though imagination may play a role in responses, it is how subjects "read" stimuli, not what they "read into" them, that is central to most analyses of Rorschach protocols. Though projection as a defense may influence the responses of some subjects, it is not present with other subjects and certainly not a necessary condition for the formation of responses. To the contrary, such a reality-distorting process is significant because of the way it interferes with the execution of a task that requires subjects to make the best sense possible of the stimuli (Rapaport, Gill, and Schafer, 1946; E. Schachtel, 1966). Even the broader conception of projection, namely, that in which the test is a medium upon which subjects are free to impose meanings in any way they choose, downplays the fact that examiners make judgments about responses in terms of standards of how "accurately" or "realistically" that medium has been used (E. Schachtel, 1966).

Conceptions of the test as an association technique are even more problematic in this regard. For example, Rapaport (Rapaport, Gill, and Schafer, 1946), who highlights features which the Rorschach shares with association tests, would reject the elevation of this aspect to preeminence because positions such as Lindzey's neglect the fact that subjects must first organize visual stimuli in some way before associating to them. Equally important, like E. Schachtel (1966), Rapaport would stress that Lindzey is mistaken in describing the Rorschach task as one of offering uncritically the first association that comes to mind. Rather, as emphasized in the third stage of Rapaport's model, the test calls for subjects to assess the fit of the association with the percept.

Finally, even Rorschach theorists who emphasize the role of the interpersonal context in response process are likely to find Zubin's approach nihilistic. In the face of difficulties in making sense of perceptual aspects of the Rorschach, he seems to give up and retreat to a mode of analysis that is indifferent to the situation to which it is applied. If the Rorschach is to be treated as simply a disguised clinical interview, why even bother to give the test? Zubin's content analyses can be done with the text of any clinical interaction.

Those who use the Rorschach are loath to reject perception hypotheses in favor of these alternatives for a second set of reasons. Perception theories provide not only a general theoretical link between the test and hypotheses about personality, but also a rationale for specific ways of scoring responses and interpreting these scores as signs of particular personality characteristics (E. Schachtel, 1966). In contrast, other theories typically only allude to the relationship between the Rorschach and personality traits in abstract ways; they do not provide a basis for Rorschach scoring systems; and, indeed, their advocates may eschew interpretation of location and determinants in favor of content analyses. While serious questions have been raised about the validity of interpretations of Rorschach scores (Zubin, Eron, and Schumer, 1965), generations of Rorschach practitioners have nonetheless found them useful and can point to a substantial body of data in their support (Exner, 1986, 1991). Theories that bear little relationship to standard practice are unlikely to gain much following within this group.

In sum, then, perception hypotheses continue to receive widespread support because, however imperfect, they come closer to capturing the essence of the test as experienced by subjects and examiners than do their competitors, and they provide a theoretical rationale for established forms of test interpretation. To be viable, other theories of the test must be able at least to incorporate perceptual components of the Rorschach task and offer a theoretical foundation for standard forms of practice.

18

The Rorschach and
Representation: I. The
Nature of Projective Tests

THE RORSCHACH AND REPRESENTATIONAL THOUGHT

Consideration of the timetable of stages through which the Rorschach is mastered can point us in the direction of a viable alternative to perceptual theories of the test. As has been seen, there are three major periods of transition as children move from one stage in their handling of the Rorschach to another. Roughly between 18 months and two years of age, they first give some primitive responses to the inkblots; between the ages of three and three and a half, they begin to produce diverse confabulatory protocols; and between the ages of five and seven, they start to take the test in a standard way.

If a group of child psychologists was told that marked changes occur in performance on some unspecified mental test at these times, few would think the task a perceptual one. Rather, many, if not most, might note that the first of the transitions coincides with the epochal change in children's thinking Piaget describes as the shift from sensori-motor intelligence to representational thought and that the last transition comes as children move from preoperational thought to the stage of concrete operations (Piaget, 1967; Piaget and Inhelder, 1969). And, though fewer would comment on the middle transition, one to which Piaget has given less attention (Flavell, 1963), the period is that in which he and others note a dramatic upsurge in children's symbolic play (see Chapter 9).

Given this correlation, it is reasonable to follow the lead of Blatt (1990) and ask whether the Rorschach task is not one that centers on representational thought and, if so, what kind of symbolic representation is involved.

THE NATURE OF "OBJECTIVE" AND "PROJECTIVE" TESTS

The question Frank (1939) raises about the nature of projective tests is a good starting point for this inquiry. As noted in the preceding chapter, Frank argues that two critical attributes distinguish these tests from "objective" ones: They make use of plastic media, that is, materials that can be shaped in a wide variety of ways, and they set open-ended tasks that encourage and, indeed, require individuals to "project" meanings onto that material. Offering their own increasingly sophisticated analyses of the problem in the decades following publication of Frank's paper, leading experts on psychological testing have reiterated his main points and noted additional properties differentiating projective and objective instruments (White, 1944; Rapaport et al., 1946; Cronbach, 1949; Goodenough, 1950; Ainsworth, 1954; Anastasi, 1955; Monroe, 1955). Summarizing these efforts, Lindzey (1961, p. 41) observes that among the features attributed to typical projective tests are:

(a) ambiguity or lack of structure of the stimulus material, (b) encouragement of a holistic treatment of personality, (c) lack of awareness on the part of the subject as to the purpose of the test, (d) wide individual latitude in responding to the test, (e) measurement of an unlimited number of variables and their interrelationships, (f) reasonable brevity, (g) removal from everyday behavior and habitual response [p. 41].

In seeking to highlight the essential defining characteristic of these tests, however, we may be better served by adopting a naïve rather than sophisticated approach to the problem. To this end, let us imagine that standard psychological tests are not clinical instruments at all, but academic tests given to students rather late in their schooling. We can then ask what kind of skills and knowledge are required to do well on these exams and in what classes would these skills be developed and this knowledge acquired.

In the case of objective instruments such as those of intelligence and achievement, the answers are clear. The tests focus on abilities required to perceive and represent the world accurately and act upon it efficaciously. For example, they assess judgment, reasoning, concept formation, mathematics, and analysis and synthesis of spatial relations. They are concerned with abilities necessary to gather, retain, and share information about the world. For example, they measure perception, attention, concentration, memory, vocabulary, reading, and spelling. And they assess familiarity with organized bodies of knowledge about aspects of the world. Thus, the WISC-III (Wechsler, 1991) includes questions about astronomy ("In what direction does the sun set?"), anatomy and physiology ("How many ears do you have?" "What does the stomach do?"), geography ("On what continent is Brazil?"), history ("Who was Christopher Columbus?"), political science ("What are the advantages of having senators and congressmen?"), and social customs and mores ("What is the thing to do if a boy/girl who is much smaller than you starts to fight with you?"). The term "objective" applies to such tests not only because of the ways in which they have been constructed and their techniques for interpreting data, but also because they focus on skills and information necessary to deal effectively with the physical and social environment. In a loose sense, "objective" tests are concerned with the methods and modes of thought of the sciences, both pure and applied (Cassirer, 1944).

What of projective tests? Were we to recommend a course of study to help students do well on these exams, it would not consist of the same classes we would advise for objective tests. Rather, we would propose a curriculum in the creative arts. With the Human Figure Drawing, Kinetic Family Drawings, or the House–Tree–Person tests, we are, after all, commissioning sketches of various subjects. With the Thematic Apperception Test, the Children's Apperception Test, the Sentence Completion Test, and related instruments, we require the production of short stories—at times very short stories—around particular themes. Even the Early Memories Test (Mayman, 1968) qualifies as a projective instrument because it is not treated as a means of acquiring data to write a case history, but rather as fragments of an autobiography or even "creatively constructed fantasies about the past" (Bruhn, 1990, p. 5). In effect, with the quintessential projective tests, we are dealing with the methods and modes of representation of the arts (Cassirer, 1944).

This fact was recognized from the first by Frank (1939), who includes among projective techniques activities such as painting, sculpting, and the creation of drama in play. In labeling these tests "projective," however, he may have diverted attention from their primary characteristic. The tests require subjects to produce some form of art and, for all of the complex and varied methods by which these productions are interpreted, their analyses consist of efforts to infer from the form and content of symbolic representations aspects of the personalities of their creators. Above all, these are "expressive" tests, tests that examine the formation of artistic representations.

THE RORSCHACH: PERCEPTION EXPERIMENT OR EXERCISE IN VISUAL REPRESENTATION?

Returning to the Rorschach, we can ask: Are we dealing with a test of this kind – that is, with a form of artistic representation – or with a form of perception as that term is ordinarily understood?

Consider another exercise. Insofar as the Rorschach "experiment" centers upon making sense of what are commonly described as "ambiguous stimuli," we can devise a number of perception experiments that approximate it. For example, to observe how subjects form perceptions of objects when stimulus cues are reduced, we can simulate a figure gradually emerging from a fog or present objects tachistoscopically; we can construct stimuli consisting of multiple overlapping figures that can be perceived in different ways; or we can adopt Meili-Dworetzki's (1956) analogue for the Rorschach, ambiguous figures that can be organized as parts or wholes. Taken individually or in combination, do these experiments truly approximate the Rorschach? Or does the test, in fact, more resemble one of artistic expression such as the Human Figure Drawing Test?

On the surface, the Rorschach appears closer to our perception experiments. The stimuli are similar, certainly far more similar than is the case with the materials of the Human Figure Drawing, which consist of nothing more than a pencil and a blank sheet of paper. Moreover, the perception experiments clearly deal with processes involved in the creation of Rorschach responses. They allow us to study principles of perceptual organization, figure–ground relationships, and the analysis and synthesis of spatial relations. They can also be used to study differences in these processes across varied populations and age groups.

Yet, while examining processes that play a role in Rorschach responses, such experiments miss the essence of the test. As E. Schachtel (1966) observes:

> In everyday perception of a dimly seen or unfamiliar object, the perceiver knows that he is confronted with a real object and, furthermore, the context of the situation together with the visible features of the object furnish many clues as to what kind of object it is likely to be or, at least, to what class of objects it might belong [p. 17].

Our experiments are tests of visual recognition. There are real objects or designs to be perceived; there are clear-cut standards of accuracy; the initial range of the subject's associations is limited; and, as more information is provided about the objects in the experiments, that range narrows until objects are perceived correctly. In contrast, E. Schachtel (1966, p. 17) notes, "Most testees are aware that inkblots might resemble anything." As a consequence, there are no external constraints on their associations—in principle, they may choose to make the inkblot into anything—and interpretations of the test are ultimately based on analyses of those choices.

Although the materials used in the Rorschach and Human Figure Drawings are dissimilar and although their tasks differ, the tests are alike in critical respects. Both provide media that can be shaped in an extraordinary variety of ways; both offer wide latitude to the subject in how those media are used; and both base their analyses on the choices subjects make. We could, in fact, set up a scoring system for drawings that is analogous to that for the Rorschach. Though location scores would not apply because of the nature of the task, analyses of the form quality of drawings would be in order (e.g., are the forms good or poor, popular or original, complex and well organized or simple and diffuse). Similarly, consideration of movement would be appropriate as would the use of color, achromatic color, and shading if we provided subjects with a suitable array of materials. The content category for the Human Figure Drawing is obviously set, but in obtaining associations, we would learn a great deal from an analysis of themes chosen within those constraints. Despite differences in appearance, the Rorschach is closer in spirit to a test of this kind than to a perception experiment.

In short, the Rorschach can be seen as a test that explores the creation of a particular type of artistic representation. The inkblot is a medium and the task facing the subject is to make it into something (Willock, 1992). Like sculptors carving designs out of marble using eye, hand, and chisel, Rorschach subjects engage in a similar process using the eye as their tool.

The Rorschach and Representation: II. The Symbol Situation

THE SYMBOL SITUATION

As Leonard Cirillo argued in a series of unpublished lectures at Clark University in the early 1970s, the model of the formation of symbols proposed by Werner and Kaplan (1963) offers a potent way of conceptualizing the Rorschach as a representational task that allows disparate views of the nature of the test to be integrated within a single theory. In accord with most contemporary concepts of representation (Goodman, 1978; Perner, 1991; Olson and Campbell, 1993; Pratt and Garton, 1993), Werner and Kaplan treat it as an intentional act in which a symbolic vehicle is used to depict or, in some other manner, stand for an object or concept. Describing the structure of such acts, they note:

> The situation in which symbolic activity occurs may basically be viewed in terms of four principal (generic) components: two persons—an *addressor* and an *addressee*—, the object of reference or the *referent*, and the *symbolic vehicle* employed in referential representation [p. 40].

The relationship of these factors can be captured in a simple diagram (Figure 3) with the addressor or self and addressee or other along one axis and the symbolic vehicle and referent on the other. The vertical axis

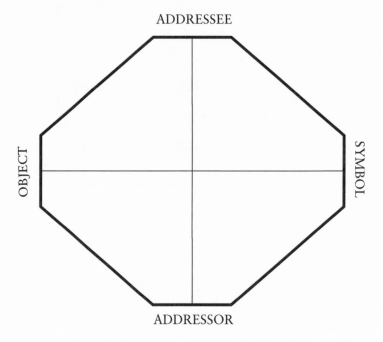

Figure 3. Components of the Symbol Situation.

reflects the fact that all symbolic activity or representation is a form of communication, even if the audience is often an internal one; the horizontal axis reflects that communication presupposes something to be communicated and a means of doing so.

As responses to the Rorschach are examined in terms of the components on each axis, it becomes clear why the instrument has been described variously as a perceptual task, an associational process, a test of imagination, and a form of communication. At the same time, consideration of the nature of these components and their relationship to one another reveals why each can be understood fully only as constituent parts of a representational act.

PERCEPTION AND ASSOCIATION/VEHICLE AND REFERENT

Throughout the history of the Rorschach, efforts to define the test have been bedeviled by the paradox that it is and is not a perceptual task.

Those who would deny that the test is perceptual must confront the fact that subjects experience it in precisely such a manner. Asked what an inkblot "looks like," they reply that they "see" an animal face or a human figure.

The belief that the task is perceptual is based on a number of considerations. First, the response process is typically initiated by attention to perceptual qualities of the inkblots. Subjects process stimulus material and then try to develop ideas of what it "might be." Second, these ideas often appear largely determined by the stimulus. For example, because of the structure of Card V, it is hard for subjects to look at the blot and not "see" a bat, bird, or butterfly. Third, even responses that are not popular ones are usually experienced as arising in a natural, spontaneous manner *from the stimuli*, not from efforts to impose form on the material consciously and deliberately. And, finally, responses are formed so rapidly that they are experienced as seen rather than constructed.

Yet those who would define the task as chiefly perceptual face no less formidable problems. The process of producing Rorschach responses differs significantly from "perception" as the term is ordinarily defined. Acknowledging this fact, Rorschach himself distinguished between "perception as recognition" and "perception as interpretation," though he linked the two through his concept of a perceptual continuum. A half century later, highlighting the distinction, Exner (1978) defined the Rorschach task as one of "misperception."

Counterinstances or alternative explanations can be found for each of the qualities that contribute to making the Rorschach task appear to be perceptual. Although subjects almost always begin to formulate responses by considering perceptual aspects of the inkblots, they need not do so. By adopting the strategy of "perseverated logic" that Ford (1946) notes in preschoolers, subjects can assume that each of the cards is a bat or butterfly and find ways of making successive blots fit that image. Then, too, while many responses of older children and adults appear heavily determined by the stimulus material, others do not. Subjects labor hard to respond to some cards and clearly experience a sense of effort in imposing a form on the medium. Moreover, the spontaneous, unpremeditated quality of the typical response process is characteristic not only of perception, but also of a host of creative processes as well. Thus, sculptors may try to carve out designs they feel are inherent in their material and writers may seek to let stories write themselves. Even the rapidity with which responses can be formed is not testimony to their being "perceptual." On one hand, forming Rorschach percepts takes considerably longer than ordinary tasks of perceptual recognition; on the other, many mental processes (e.g., solving an arithmetic problem, "seeing" the solution to a dilemma, finding the right way of expressing oneself, coming up with an idea for a painting) can occur rapidly.

Approaching the Rorschach as a task of visual representation allows for an appreciation of senses in which the test is and is not perceptual. Because inkblots are visual media, perception must play a role in any task involving them. The Rorschach is obviously not a test that can be given to the blind. A natural first step in the response process is thus that which Exner (1986, p. 234) describes as "the input or encoding of the stimulus field," that is, attending to the cards, scanning them, and becoming aware of such characteristics as figure–ground relations, shapes, colors, textures, and the like. To this extent, the Rorschach is indeed a perceptual task and the kinds of analyses offered by Brosnin and Fromm (1942), Klein and Arnheim (1953), Meili-Dworetski (1956), E. Schachtel (1966), and others do have a bearing on how it is undertaken.

In a representational theory of the Rorschach, the role of perception in the response process is closer to that posited by Rapaport than that of Rorschach. Whereas Rorschach (1921) suggests that the organization of stimulus material proceeds to a point where images are formed that can be compared with memory engrams of other images, Rapaport (Rapaport, Gill, and Schafer, 1946) argues that associational processes come into play sooner and have a larger role in the organization of the image. For example, some aspect of the card stimulates an idea of what it might be that then determines how the rest of blot is treated. Perhaps a contour or detail reminds the subject of a muzzle or a head, leading to the thought that the design might be a dog. Looking at the card with this thought in mind, the subject then "sees" that other areas might be the body and legs if the dog is pictured as standing at a particular angle and if a section that could be a second tail is excluded or ignored. For Rapaport, the process is not one of forming images and then making associations, but rather of associations actively shaping the percept. In addition, as has been noted, he also stresses that perception plays a role in the final stage of the process as subjects assess the adequacy of the emergent image.

There are, however, important differences between traditional positions such as Rapaport's and a representational theory. The former portray the formation of Rorschach percepts as if it consisted primarily of an interaction, albeit a complex interaction, of perceptual and associational processes to which judgments about the quality of percepts and about what to share with examiners are added. In contrast, the latter theory stresses that Rorschach responses cannot be explained satisfactorily as a process of perception, association, or their interaction, even if they are supplemented with decisions about the adequacy of percepts and their suitability for communication. Something more is involved, something that incorporates, but utterly transforms, perception and association. That something is an intention to use the stimulus to represent an object or a concept. Insofar as this intention is operative in approaching the Rorschach, perception becomes different from perception and association different from association. The processes are now components of a superordinate system that determines their functions and the manner in which they are coordinated—and they can be understood only as such.

Consider the role of perception in the Rorschach response process. As has been stressed in the preceding chapters, it is not perception in the ordinary sense of the term. With the exception of perhaps a few blatantly psychotic individuals, those with extraordinary intellectual impairments, and the very young, subjects never doubt that they are seeing an inkblot. The Rorschach involves no misperception. Rather, subjects approach the inkblot knowing that they are being asked to make it into something, to treat it as a symbolic vehicle. It is the implicit recognition that how cards are to be seen is governed by a representational intention that is the basis for Rorschach's observation that subjects believe the test is one of imagination. Consequently, when subjects look at inkblots, they do so searching for contours, colors, textures, or physiognomic properties that will suggest what the medium can be molded into. These are perceptual processes defined by their role in a representational act.

In a similar fashion, Rorschach responses involve associations to the visual stimuli, but not just associations. For example, although Lindzey (1961) likens the Rorschach to the Word Association Test, the two are different in critical respects. In the latter task, a word is presented, the subject responds quickly with another that comes to mind, and that is it. From the subject's standpoint, the process is relatively passive. In the case of the Rorschach, the association occurs in a context set by the representation task. Presented with visual stimuli, the subject actively searches for what it could be shaped into. What emerges is not any association, but an idea that arises from an effort to find a referent.

Moreover, as Rapaport stresses, the process is not over at this point. Rather, the thought of what the blot might be plays a major role in shaping the stimulus material as the subject explores whether and how it can fit that idea. The choice of the referent enters into decisions about the boundaries of the image and guides efforts to bring it sharply into focus. At this point, there is a kind of "cogwheeling" of the two processes, but this interaction is governed by the intention to coordinate them in order to achieve the goal of creating an appropriate representation. In effect, each of the processes involved in formulating Rorschach responses operates as part of a system and can be understood only in terms of the manner in which it subserves the functions of that system.

ADDRESSOR–ADDRESSEE: THE INTERPERSONAL CONTEXT

Werner and Kaplan (1963) stress that an appreciation of the roles of the vehicle and referent are necessary, but not sufficient, for an adequate characterization of the process of symbolization. That process begins and, in important respects always remains, social. Shaping material provided by inkblots into representations of objects and concepts, for example, takes place in an interpersonal context that influences not only the definition of the test situation and the general manner in which the Rorschach task is approached, as noted in earlier chapters, but also representations themselves. Just as artists' needs, wishes, and intentions and the character of their real and imagined audiences affect the form and content of their work, so, too, do such factors enter into Rorschach images.

Individuals who take the test as part of clinical evaluations are usually acutely aware that their responses will reveal things about themselves and their difficulties and that examiners will scrutinize their productions carefully in order to offer assessments of their personality and make recommendations that may have a profound effect on their future. In such circumstances, the Rorschach is experienced as a form of communication and, as such, cannot but be affected by what subjects wish to communicate and by their experience of their audience.

These influences can be illustrated by the responses of Sarah, a fifteen-year-old girl who was referred for evaluation after she made a serious suicidal gesture. The older of two children in a family in which there had been chronic marital conflict, Sarah had served as a buffer and mediator between her parents before her hospitalization.

As the Rorschach began, she stared at Card I for almost 40 seconds before stating: "It looks like a butterfly that's been torn up on the sides." Twenty seconds later she added, "Looks like Siamese twins and something is pulling them apart. That's all I can see." On the inquiry, she indicated that the butterfly was the whole figure and, when asked about it being torn up, she noted: "It was just disfigured and uneven. It just looks like a mess." The second response also referred to the whole card, with the center detail being the twins, because "It looks like it had two heads and arms and feet at the bottom and the hands were reaching up and it was like something was pulling them apart and they didn't want to go or something." Struggling to articulate what was pulling them apart, the side details, she added:

It looks like a lot of force. I couldn't see what it was. Just that they were being pulled apart. It was just so mixed up in the middle. It wasn't moving apart, it was being pulled. . . . It looks torn out of shape. I don't know whether it's pulling them apart physically or some other way. Like it's splitting up their feelings or something weird like that. . . . It's like its pulling something away from them. . . . Feelings, any feelings. It's just taking them all away.

As she spoke, she appeared increasingly troubled and the examiner felt that she was desperately in need of help.

Much of the rest of Sarah's Rorschach consisted of variations on these themes of being crippled and disfigured, experiencing intense pressures threatening a dissolution of self, and facing terrible consequences as a result of the disruption of symbiotic relationships or of being torn apart by external forces. For example, on Card III, she saw two people holding down a smashed, injured butterfly, while another, smaller one floated away. She described Card V as a man who was also a butterfly whose wings were too heavy for him to fly. Card VI was "a person with really broad shoulders and his head has been pulled out at the neck and it's exploding at the sides." Card VII was two women who were "stuck together" at the waist. On inquiry, she noted: "Each separate one is splitting apart . . . and they are blaming each other for it. Like the other one is blamed as the reason for it." Little clinical sophistication is required to recognize that such responses, coming from a youngster being evaluated in the midst of a crisis, reflect efforts to convey a sense of being profoundly damaged by family conflicts, hopelessness about being able to negotiate adolescent struggles around separation and individuation, and fears of decompensation.

To be sure, what most subjects seek to communicate about themselves through the Rorschach is less transparent and more clouded by conflicts about what they wish known. Also, how they experience themselves and want to be experienced by others may influence the form as much as the content of responses. Yet, though manifested in subtle ways, such influences are no less present in all Rorschach responses. As they form inkblots into images, subjects may strive to show that they are brilliant and creative or hide the fact that they are not, that they are sane or that they are crazy, that they are cautious or daring, imaginative or realistic, conventional or bohemian, stubbornly independent or compliant, and so forth. In the Rorschach, as in most communication, through everything we say and do, most of us try both to display and to hide things about ourselves.

Similarly, the experience of the audience, the addressee, has a major impact on test productions. Its influence can be illustrated by a personal example in which the same percept was handled in radically different ways on two occasions in response to two different audiences.

In my second year of college, I was required, like other students in the introductory psychology class, to "donate" a number of hours to the department. Many of my classmates participated in experiments, the college sophomore having replaced the white rat as the preferred laboratory animal at the time. I was part of a group sent to the clinic to give fledgling testers practice as they learned projective instruments. Apart from the fact that I was tested by a pretty female graduate student who was not a great deal older than I was, I remember only one thing about this initial encounter with the Rorschach. Card X, I was pleased to report, looked rather like two giant blue crabs stalking down the Champs Elysées intent on devouring the Eiffel Tower.

A dozen years later I took the Rorschach a second time when applying to a psychoanalytic institute. Again only a few memories remain of the test, which was administered by a respected senior colleague. One was my surprise at discovering how much giving Rorschach responses is an intuitive process in which experience with the test and knowledge of interpretive procedures had less influence than I would have expected. Another is that Card X still looked rather like giant crabs with designs on the Eiffel Tower. I do not recall the response I gave instead, but am reasonably sure it did not involve inappropriate use of color, odd combinations of ideas, or marked confabulation.

Given only the initial crab response and asked to speculate about its diagnostic significance, Rorschach experts would, no doubt, have a variety of reactions. Some of a Freudian persuasion might suggest that the circumstances of the testing had a significant impact on the percept, hypothesizing that a mixture of arousal and anxiety in a late adolescent in the presence of an older woman contributed to the choice of the image of an internationally recognized phallic symbol being attacked by crustaceans with prominent pincers. Most who administer the test would be more concerned about the formal qualities of the response. Noting the arbitrary use of color, the confabulatory combination, and the extent to which fantasy was read into the blot, many might wonder about the presence of a borderline personality disorder with narcissistic features, if not the possibility of psychotic tendencies.

Though some of my colleagues today would argue that this diagnosis is not far off the mark, considered in its original context the response is open to other interpretations. For example, it was given in the early 1960s when cartoons and science fiction movies about resurrected prehistoric monsters or giant radioactive insects wreaking havoc on major cities constituted a common, if unwholesome, staple of the undergraduate cultural diet. The response was produced in a university setting in which not only were the costs of appearing crazy minimal, but the prospect of appearing normal, or worse, conventional, constituted a threat to self-esteem. In addition, the response may have been a facetious expression of resentment at being required to serve as guinea pig by the psychology department and, no doubt, it was an opportunity to make a show of rebellion against repressive social institutions, a stance coming into vogue in the period. However, the percept was probably most influenced by the relationship with the examiner. It was, I suspect, above all a misguided attempt to impress an attractive young woman with my wit and erudition. In the absence of data from the rest of the test, such interpretations remain only speculation. Perhaps the only inferences that can be made with assurance from the response are that its creator displayed an abysmal ignorance of Parisian geography and was, quite literally, sophomoric.

Explanations of why the blue crab response did not appear in the second Rorschach protocol are not hard to fathom. The response was now less salient; quite possibly it would not even have come to mind had it not been for the memory of the earlier testing. Although it did come to mind, a dozen years of experience had produced a level of maturity that, while insufficient to eliminate sophomoric tendencies, was at least enough for me to keep them under wraps rather than display them proudly. Wishes to appear unconventional and creative were still present, but now tempered by desires not to appear infantile or insane. More important, even if time had produced less maturity than may be desirable, the circumstances of the testing were sufficient to induce a serious approach to the test. The examiner was no longer a young woman whose interest I hoped to elicit through clever responses, but an experienced older colleague whose good opinion mattered to me and whose analysis of the test would have an effect on my career. At the least, the situation encouraged a tempering of narcissistic displays and regressive excursions and induced a more responsible attitude toward the test. Without the rest of the protocol, the presence of this attitude is hard to document, although I did gain entree into an institution that, at the time, was particularly concerned with screening out candidates who exhibited marked borderline tendencies and an excess of pathological narcissism.

The effects of the audience on Rorschach productions are, of course, enormously varied. If examiners are experienced as treacherous enemies out to trip subjects up, for example, responses are tailored one way; if they are seen as saviors who might come to the rescue if only they knew the subjects' desperate plight, responses are shaped differently. The experience of the audience may shift in the midst of the test. For example, a borderline patient with narcissistic tendencies may begin with elaborate flamboyant percepts, seeking to impress an audience with his brilliance, only to give constricted, guarded responses as the examiner is seen in a more paranoid way when the subject runs into difficulty or reveals more than he intends.

Perhaps most significant, there are in fact multiple addressees for responses, one being an internal audience. Symbolization and representation are ways in which we learn about ourselves. Indeed, a strong case can be made that what we call the conscious mind is based on a capacity to represent thoughts and feelings in ways that can then be reflected on (Stern, 1985). In commenting on her Rorschach responses after the test, for example, Sarah emphasized her surprise at now realizing how bad she felt and used the experience to articulate the conflicts that had led to her hospitalization. More often, subjects are concerned with hiding conflicts and pain from themselves and others. Psychodynamic approaches to Rorschach interpretation often focus on defensive efforts to control what is revealed or sequences in which self-revelation is followed by renewed efforts at constriction and control (Schafer, 1954).

REPRESENTATION AND EARLIER THEORIES OF THE RORSCHACH

Among the attractive features of a representational conception of the Rorschach is its capacity to incorporate earlier theories in a way that appreciates their contributions to understanding the response process, while avoiding their limitations.

In this theory, perception plays a prominent role in the response process, but "perception" in this case is a process whose form and function are determined by its role in a representational act. From the first, subjects look at inkblots as visual media that are to be shaped into images. It is this intention that, in part, accounts for why the task is experienced as one of imagination.

Association plays an equally significant role in the formation of responses, but again it is association governed by an overriding intention. The subject actively tries to formulate ideas about what the visual stimuli can be made into, and once potential referents come to mind they guide the process of trying to shape the medium to fit them. Both the extraordinary freedom the Rorschach task gives subjects in choosing referents and the role these ideas then play in the formation of additional images are other reasons the task is experienced as one of imagination.

The addressor–addressee axis of the symbol situation allows other features of theories of the response process to be incorporated naturally. For example, Zubin's (1956, p. 191) seemingly extreme proposal that the Rorschach be treated as a "systematic interview behind the veil of inkblots" and interpreted on the basis of content analysis methods is one that simply confines itself to this dimension alone. Those aspects of the response process described by E. Schachtel (1966) as judgment and communication and by Exner (1986) as ranking responses and discarding through censorship are located along this axis. As has been stressed (see Chapter 12), this feature of the model allows for a full appreciation of the work of Rapaport, Schafer, E. Schachtel, and others who treat testing as a form of standardized interview and analyze the Rorschach in terms of transference–countertransference paradigms. Finally, when the audience is viewed as an internal one, psychodynamic conceptions of the role of intrapsychic processes such as defenses can be encompassed by conceiving of them as factors shaping communication within an internal system of representation.

The Rorschach and Representation: III. Conceptualizing Primary Aspects of the Test

RORSCHACH STIMULI: AMBIGUOUS OR PLASTIC?

The superiority of a representational conception of the Rorschach over perceptual ones can be seen if we consider the four major aspects of the test: its stimuli, task, scoring, and interpretation.

Of these features, the Rorschach stimuli are the most distinctive. But what is there about inkblots that is of such value that they provide the basis of one of the most widely used psychological tests of the last half century?

The traditional reply, that Rorschach cards are ambiguous or unstructured stimuli, is quite simply wrong in critical respects. The cards are readily recognizable as inkblots, each of which has its own unique structure. Schafer (1954) notes:

They have definite, easily perceivable shapes, colors, textures, and configurations. In other words, if we did not leave patients on their own, but instead simply asked them direct, detailed questions about these properties of the blots, they would manifest little individual variability of response, except perhaps in style of verbalization [p. 114].

In describing the Rorschach situation as unstructured or ambiguous, he suggests, we are referring not so much to the stimuli as to their relationship to the task set for the subject. Because inkblots do not bear a clear resemblance to objects, when asking subjects "What might this be?" we do not get uniform answers determined chiefly by the stimulus material.

Yet the value of inkblots does not lie chiefly in this negative quality, that is, that their unfamiliarity forces subjects to make choices. Rather, it resides in the rich variety of choices they afford. Each blot, with its distinct structure, colors, and shading, provides material that can be formed into hundreds of responses. As Schafer (1954, p. 115) observes, in describing blots as "unstructured," we mean that they are "plastic" rather than "unclear or elusive." In our terms, they are an unusually rich medium that can be formed into an extraordinary variety of representations.

The overriding importance of this property of inkblots can be illustrated through two examples. One is the distinction Piotrowski (1981) makes between "good" Rorschach cards and poorer ones. Although, like the ten commandments, each Rorschach card is good in its own way, some are better than others. For example, if only a single blot could be given, few who use the test would prefer Card V to Card I. The reason, Piotrowski argues, is that good cards produce a maximum of individual variation in responses. Because of its complex shape, open spaces, and shading, Card I can be molded into more varied responses than Card V, which is simpler and bears a sufficient resemblance to images of birds, bats, and butterflies that it yields a high percentage of these popular responses. In his form-quality tables, Exner (1986) lists two-thirds more responses for the former card than the latter. In effect, Piotrowski's judgments of the quality of cards, and no doubt those of others who use the test, are based on their quality as a medium.

The best demonstration that plasticity is the essential feature of Rorschach cards can be seen in a fortuitous accident that had a profound influence on the nature of the test. Although Rorschach's research was done with solid blots, Ellenberger (1954) notes that when *Psychodiagnostics* was published,

> the printing of the cards was more than unsatisfactory. The cards were reduced in size, the colors changed and the original uniformity of the black areas was reproduced in a variety of shades, delineating all kinds of vague forms. The printer probably did not expect congratulations for his slovenly work, but as soon as Rorschach had seen the proofs he was seized by a renewed enthusiasm, and understood at once the new possibilities the prints offered [p. 206].

Far from being outraged that the integrity of his experiment was violated, Rorschach appreciated immediately that shading enriched the test by further increasing the creative possibilities the cards afforded. If, as Frank (1939) contends, plasticity of material is one of the chief properties of projective tests, it is precisely Rorschach's sensitivity to this quality of his stimuli that accounts for the prominence of his test among such instruments.

THE RORSCHACH TASK

The Rorschach task is also more amenable to interpretation as a test of visual representation than of perception. As E. Schachtel (1966) observes, in ordinary perception there is an object to be perceived and the main question is how it comes to be grasped in more or less veridical ways. In seeking to answer such a question, we would not be inclined to search for the chief "determinant" of the percept. Recognition is usually based on form perception, although other attributes contribute as well, with the percept being codetermined by information from a variety of sources. For example, a Rorschach card is perceived as an inkblot of a particular kind because of its form *and* its color *and* its shading. Moreover, if the Rorschach is a perceptual task, a question we would be inclined to ask is: If it were not an inkblot, which of the myriad of whole responses given to any card does it really look most like? Indeed, not only might we ask such a question, which Rorschach theorists do not, but we would assume that it could be answered reasonably.

The Rorschach, however, is a task of a different order. We assume that a number of utterly different meanings can be assigned to the same stimulus array, that these meanings can be attributed in a variety of ways, and that it is reasonable to codify "percepts" according to the single characteristics subjects verbalize as most salient in their responses. Such assumptions do not provide a good basis for understanding how perceptual tasks are handled, but they accord well with how meaning is assigned in representational or symbolic tasks (Goodman, 1976).

This point can be demonstrated by imagining a grossly simplified Rorschach card consisting of nothing more than a single curved line (Figure 4). If we ask subjects to tell us what the card "looks like" and refuse to accept the perceptual response ("it is a curved line"), a common reply might be "a hill." From a purely perceptual standpoint, our card does not look much like an actual hill. The only information it provides is its shape, and one could photograph a thousand hills without finding one that has the smooth, regular form of our figure. Yet most people would accept that because of its roundness the line could

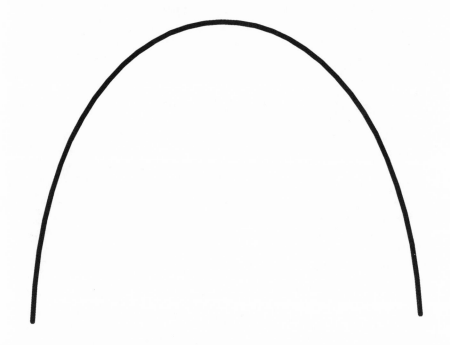

Figure 4. Card XI.

"stand for" a hill. As an immediately recognizable representation of a hill, we might well score it as a popular response with perfectly adequate form.

In ordinary perception, we expect that information will converge to allow us to determine what we are truly perceiving. In contrast, we would not only accept that our curved line "looks like" a hill, but would see nothing amiss if we were also told that it "looks like" the Gateway Arch in St. Louis, a noteworthy attribute of a reclining Playboy bunny, or the changing values of a bogus gold mine stock over a six-month period. With representations, it is perfectly reasonable that the same stimulus may have a variety of utterly different meanings.

Conversely, imagine we commission three artists to produce a work called *Fire*. Conceivably one might simply draw a few jagged lines resembling the outline of the top detail of Card VI when looked at from the side; a second artist, using charcoal, might produce an amorphous shaded area similar to Card IV; and a third might paint a vivid red blotch like the top detail on Card II. Each artist could insist, and a Rorschach examiner would accept, that their work "looks like" fire. On the Rorschach, as in tasks of representation, not only can the same stimuli have a variety of different meanings, but utterly different stimuli can have the same meaning.

We need not rely on hypothetical situations, however. The manner in which test instructions are interpreted by normal subjects reveals the representational nature of the Rorschach task.

As has been noted, when subjects take questions such as "What do you see?" literally and reply that Rorschach cards look like inkblots, examiners are inclined to suspect that there is something wrong with them, that they have limited cognitive capacities or, perhaps, some form of organic damage. This reaction only makes sense if we assume that Rorschach instructions are meant to be taken differently. And they are. With very few exceptions, subjects know that what is being requested is not an identification of the inkblots, a matter so obvious it hardly warrants comment. Instead they assume correctly that what is being requested is that Rorschach cards be "seen as" something. In Piaget's terms, they realize the task is a semiotic or symbolic one in which one thing, an inkblot, is to stand for or signify an object, event, or concept (Piaget and Inhelder, 1969, p. 51).

As has been seen, this recognition that the task is representational probably underlies Rorschach's observation that a near universal belief among subjects that they are dealing with a test of imagination is almost a precondition for offering percepts (Rorschach, 1964, p. 16). Clearly subjects do not believe that they are free to ignore the inkblot and make up any response they wish. Rather, their characterization of the task reflects a conviction that it is a creative exercise, that the blots or part of the blots are to be treated as visual metaphors and made to depict some object or concept.

Examiners, too, act on an implicit assumption that the Rorschach is a representational task. For example, consider the interpretations made about intelligent, able individuals who note that Rorschach cards do not really look like much of anything other than inkblots, give relatively few responses, all of adequate form or better, and comment often that even these percepts are imperfect replicas of objects because one detail or another is far from right. Their steadfast commitment to a perceptual interpretation of the task is unlikely to be met with praise for the accuracy of their perception and their heroic, if stubborn, defense of the reality principle. To the contrary, Rorschach (1964) characterizes such individuals as dull, rigid, emotionally inhibited pedants and probably no group is less liked by most of his followers. If honest, many examiners would confess to a greater respect for the florid responses of psychotic patients than productions so solidly grounded in "reality."

This negative attitude does not stem from hidden bias. A cursory survey of the Rorschach literature should be sufficient to demonstrate that compulsive personalities are far more prevalent among those who write about the test than are schizophrenics or schizotypal characters. Nor do such attitudes arise because Rorschach examiners fail to appreciate clear perception, good reality testing, or a conscientious commitment to a task, even if that commitment is carried to extremes. In fact, as the attention lavished on scoring of form attests, they value these qualities highly. Were the Rorschach a test of perception, the productions of these compulsive subjects would be viewed in a more positive light.

Examiners' attitudes toward such subjects reflect an intuitive appreciation that the Rorschach is a creative exercise, one of artistic expression. Their greater respect for the approach of psychotic subjects to the test arises because the Rorschach task is accepted and thoughts and feelings are expressed in open and striking, if also uncontrolled and disturbing, ways. In contrast, examiners sense that the self-critical, restricted approach of many compulsive personalities is not based chiefly on a devotion to reality, but rather on an aversion to engaging in a creative process. They recognize that this manner of handling the test reflects a fear of and resistance to the Rorschach task, not an exaggerated compliance with it.

The representational concept of the Rorschach also offers an escape from an awkward problem. As long as the task is viewed as perceptual, it is hard not to imply that there is something deficient in the responses produced. For example, in spite of his devotion to the Rorschach, Exner (1986) speaks of the importance of "misperception" in his theoretical discussions of the response process. Yet we cannot have much respect for an enterprise based on mistakes or self-deception. In fact, we admire good Rorschach responses because they do not involve misperception to the slightest degree. Subjects never doubt that they are dealing with inkblots. Rather, they treat blots as a medium to be shaped into visual representations, a creative act similar to those of artists who form other material into paintings and statues. It is precisely this quality of the task that undoubtedly attracted Rorschach, with his deep interest in the graphic arts, to the test in the first place (Ellenberger, 1954).

SCORES

In contrast to other alternate interpretations of the Rorschach, a representational one accords as well as or better than perceptual theories with the assumptions upon which Rorschach scoring is based. For example, form, color, shading, and the expressive aspects of forms that give the impression of movement are not only qualities of the world as we perceive it; they are also used as means of artistic representation. Such scores, and those for location, may be understood as ways of codifying the manner in which individuals make use of the symbolic medium. Others, those of content and special scores involving confabulation, fabulized combinations, and perseveration, bear on the choice of referents. Still others, such as those of form level and contaminations, reflect the effectiveness with which individuals are able to coordinate symbol and referent. A conception of the Rorschach as a representational task thus requires no alteration in standard scoring categories, because each is related to one or another aspect of the representational act.

In fact, this conception of the test provides a stronger foundation for scoring practices than do perception theories. For example, as has been seen, the idea implicit in most Rorschach scores that a "percept" is typically based on a single determinant is not one that academic students of perception take seriously. Yet such an assumption poses no problem for a representational theory. Whereas visual representations may be determined by a variety of factors such as color, shape, or shading, it is by no means unreasonable to believe that their meanings are based on only one. As examples from our simplified Rorschach card demonstrate, a curved line provides a readily recognizable representation of a hill. Similarly a shape, a color, or a shaded area alone is sufficient for an artist to represent fire.

More important, a representational conception of the Rorschach is not subject to the problems around reliance on "untrained introspectionists" that bedevil perceptual theories. Because perception is a private, internal process, serious questions can be raised about how faithfully subjects' verbal descriptions of their "percepts" convey what they actually perceive and about whether they are truly aware of the processes underlying their perception of inkblots. When treated as a representation, however, a Rorschach response is not a description of an internal process at all but, rather, an explicit, shared symbol. It is formed through a process that involves not only a subject telling the examiner, "It looks like a bat," but also an inquiry that is not complete until the examiner "sees" what the subject is trying to represent and discovers the more or less explicit rationale for the representation. Since the general rules governing denotation in such cases can be made manifest with relative ease (e.g., "It looks like a hill because it has a rounded shape like a hill"), it is possible to give credence to subjects' accounts of the bases on which they have established their visual metaphors in ways that cannot be done with perception.

The concept of representation also provides a solution to the problem of form level. As has been seen, traditional criteria based on perceptual similarities or statistical frequency are problematic. Insofar as blots are unlikely to be mistaken for pictures of bats or butterflies, good form cannot be based on concrete likeness. Nor are statistical criteria alone a satisfactory basis for judging responses. The whole form on Card I would not look like a J even if, by chance, two out of three people claimed that it did.

Assessments of form quality make sense when viewed as judgments about the adequacy of "percepts" as representations. The quality of representations does not depend on exact correspondence to the object. For example, a caricature provides an immediately recognizable depiction of an individual with only a line or two if the artist succeeds in capturing some representative feature of the subject. Far from being based on concrete similarity, a sketch of Jimmy Durante is likely to exaggerate a single anatomical feature outrageously, though, if successful, it will "resemble" its subject more than a photograph taken from the wrong angle or capturing an uncharacteristic expression.

Rorschach "percepts" are richer and more complex than caricatures, yet they are representations as well. Consequently, the standards intuitively applied to them, whether by Rorschach examiners or large numbers of subjects in normative samples, are aesthetic ones appropriate to works of art. Good form is based on such criteria as whether percepts capture essential features of the concept represented, whether only one feature is involved or a variety are integrated, whether the approximate relationship of those features in the concept is maintained, and whether features that do not belong are excluded or whether the representation is spoiled by their inclusion.

INTERPRETATION

Finally, a representational conception of the Rorschach is not only consistent with ways in which the test is scored, but also requires no substantial alteration in the manner in which interpretation of determinants is undertaken. With only modest revisions, the assumptions underlying interpretive practices based on perceptual theories can be reformulated in representational terms that provide them with a more secure base.

Even aspects of interpretive theories that seem most closely tied to perception, those involving differential registration of various stimulus qualities of the blots, can be incorporated within a representational position. Take, for example, the presumed linkage between achromatic color and dysphoric tendencies. Though depressive subjects may be more sensitive to the dark, somber qualities of blots, it can still be argued that it is the decision to make use of these qualities in forming an image that is critical in Rorschach responses. In effect, the world may "look blacker" to these subjects, but what we score and interpret on the Rorschach is their effort to portray this aspect of their experience.

More important, perceptual explanations of determinants rest chiefly on theories about the manner in which a variety of central processes—cognitive, emotional, and motivational variables—"organize" percepts. Yet, if the Rorschach is treated as a form of artistic representation, the same factors would play equally prominent roles in the theories about such creations. Indeed, it is more reasonable to believe that these influences are accentuated in acts of creative expression than in perception, which is far more constrained by conditions of stimulation.

In most explanations that have been offered about the meaning of particular determinants, the word "representation" can, in fact, be substituted for "perception" with virtually no change in those formulations. The language used to describe the role of intellect in form responses, for example, applies equally to perceptual and representational theories. Other interpretations of determinants, notably those of movement responses which emphasize sublimation and symbolization, are already primarily representational rather than perceptual theories (Blatt, 1990). At the least, a representational conception of the Rorschach results in consistent explanations of such determinants instead of ones that can be called "perceptual" only by employing shifting definitions of the term along a hypothetical continuum.

A representational theory *does* introduce a change in the logic of the process by which inferences are made from Rorschach responses to personality characteristics. Traditional theories rest on the assumptions that inkblot "percepts" reflect modes of perception or perceptual styles that are, in turn, aspects of broader modes of cognizing, representing, and acting upon the world. The proposed alternative assumes that Rorschach performance already directly embodies ways in which subjects experience and represent the world. Generalizations from test responses are based on the premise that there are consistencies in how individuals represent their experience across different symbolic modalities and different situations. For example, it is assumed that individuals who make heavy use of dark colors to portray morbid, depressive themes when given free rein to depict their experience in visual modalities will emphasize themes of defeat, deprivation, loss, worthlessness, and hopelessness when giving autobiographical narratives or verbal descriptions of the day's events to a therapist (Beck, 1967). In effect, in place of the assumption that the same psychological factors influence perception and representation, the Rorschach inference process is now based on an assumption of commonalities across different modes of representation.

CONCLUSION

For many readers, the foregoing discussion may well seem tendentious and unfair. The form in which the perception theories of leading exponents of the Rorschach have been cast exaggerates differences between them and a representational position. A more generous reading of those theories, it could be argued, might well lead to a recognition that the theory that has been proposed is little more than another, perhaps more refined, restatement of views that have been implicit in the literature on Rorschach theory from the first.

In a sense, these readers are correct. I believe that a theory of the Rorschach as a form of representation embodies what Rorschach meant to convey about his test when he insisted that it dealt with "perception as interpretation." Similarly, embedded in a psychodynamic ego-psychological model of personality, Rapaport's cogwheel model always implied that more was involved in the Rorschach response process than perception and association. There are also links between a representational theory and Schachtel's emphasis upon the "form-giving" aspect of "perception" in the Rorschach situation, and Exner's efforts to advance a broadened definition of the task as a "perceptual-cognitive" one.

Yet a representational theory is not a restatement of earlier ones. To the contrary, the problems that have been highlighted with earlier theories arose because what Rorschach and his major followers intuitively sensed to be the essence of their test could never be encompassed satisfactorily by theories centering on perception and association. In formulating their positions, they struggled constantly to find ways of going beyond the constraints imposed by those theories, Exner's description of the

Rorschach as a task requiring "misperception" being the most dramatic example of efforts to escape those limits. The advantage of a representational theory of the Rorschach task is, above all, that it provides a way of capturing the insights implicit in earlier conceptions of the test, while articulating ideas that could not be expressed adequately in the language and concepts of perception theories.

21

Representation and
Children's Rorschachs

THE SYMBOL SITUATION AND THE ORTHOGENETIC PRINCIPLE

The model of symbol formation advanced by Werner and Kaplan (1963) readily lends itself to conceptualizing the stages through which the Rorschach is mastered. Organized around the orthogenetic principle, it portrays the development of the capacity for representation as a process in which the constituent parts of the symbol situation become progressively more differentiated and coordinated. From this standpoint, the earliest mode of handling the Rorschach, that represented by the inner ring of Figure 5, is one in which symbol and referent and addressor and addressee are experienced in global, undifferentiated ways and in which the resultant products are diffuse and unstable. In the transitional periods and stages that follow, designated by the middle and outer rings of the figure, each component is increasingly distinct from the others, more complex, and better integrated. While psychosocial aspects of the mastery of the Rorschach have been examined in the light of the addressor–addressee axis of this model (see Chapter 13), a full understanding of the salient features of young children's Rorschachs is possible only as changes in the handling of the symbolic vehicle and referent are considered as well.

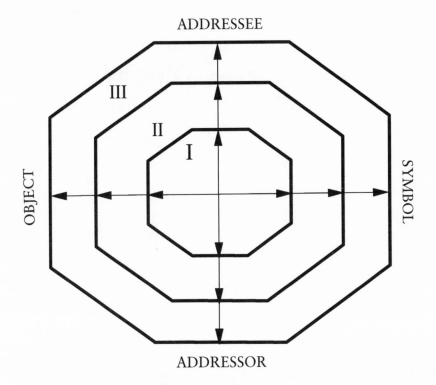

ADDRESSEE

OBJECT

SYMBOL

ADDRESSOR

Figure 5. Diagram of developmental changes in components in the Rorschach situation II. (This modification of the diagram of the symbol situation from H. Werner and B. Kaplan (1963), *Symbol Formation* [New York: John Wiley, p. 41] is included by permission of Bernard Kaplan and Lawrence Erlbaum Associates, Inc.)

STAGE I: PERSEVERATIVE RORSCHACHS

As has been seen, although isolated Rorschach responses may be given in the latter half of the second year of life, children typically begin to produce protocols in their third year. Their first responses are often perplexing and arbitrary ones that leave examiners puzzled about location and determinants and in doubt about whether they are truly responses at all. Inquiry into these responses is seldom undertaken because it confuses children or leads to new associations rather than clarifies ones they have given. Furthermore, responses to subsequent cards consist of repetitions of the original response. Hence, explanations of these earliest Rorschachs should address four sets of issues: the age at which children begin to produce responses, the nature of the initial response, the difficulties encountered in conducting inquiry, and the perseveration of the first response through the rest of the test.

Timing

If we had no experience with children's Rorschachs, it would be difficult to predict the age at which responses begin to appear by using perceptual theories of the test. For example, Rorschach's assumption that there is an unfolding of perceptual capacities until a threshold is passed at which children can manage "perception as interpretation" provides no guidance in estimating when that point is reached. We have no more reason to guess one year of age than five.

In contrast, when we assume that the Rorschach, while involving perception, is nonetheless based upon the emergence of capacities for symbolization, the timing of first responses presents no difficulties. We might well predict that some children will produce crude responses between the ages 18 and 24 months, the period in which symbolic representation becomes central to their thinking (Piaget, 1963; Piaget and Inhelder, 1969). And, if records typically begin to be produced a half year later, it would not come as a surprise. Given the complexity and unfamiliarity of the Rorschach medium and the fact that children have not used it as a primary means of communication, responses to the test might be expected to appear after more commonly used forms of representation such as language. In fact, it would be reasonable to predict that responses appear, as they do, in the third year of life at about the same time children start to use crayons and pencils to create their first artistic productions (Di Leo, 1970; Gardner, 1980).

The Nature of the First Response

The ambiguity and uncertainty surrounding the production of young children's initial Rorschach responses is in part a consequence of how difficult the task is for them. Presented with a strange object, they are asked what it looks like when it does not look like anything with which they are familiar. Moreover, appreciating the connotations examiners wish attributed to the phrase "looks like" requires a command of the nuances of language that is often beyond these subjects, and accomplishing the task set for them requires representational skills they are only beginning to develop.

Three ways of handling this situation can be inferred from different types of responses that can be distinguished by examiners' reactions to them. The most primitive of these responses are those whose determinants are obvious because the task is treated as purely perceptual. For example, in the first of a longitudinal series of protocols obtained by Allen (1955), a girl of two and a half reacts to Card I by noting: "Looks like a book; this is chalk on it." The cards that follow, she asserts, are chalk marks of different colors. Though no inquiry can be undertaken, it is unnecessary. The first card literally looks like the cardboard material from which young children's books are made and the markings on it resemble chalk. Paradoxically, the assurance with which the examiner can understand the response is possible only because it is still far from being a "true" Rorschach response. The child treats the task as one of perceptual recognition and has not, in Rorschach's terms, crossed that boundary beyond which it becomes one of "interpretation."

Children move closer to that border when they produce a second type of response, one that elicits the opposite reaction in examiners. In these cases, adults have little idea of the basis for the response and strongly suspect that, at best, children's associations bear only a tenuous relation to qualities of the inkblot. For example, a boy notorious for his preoccupation with vehicles says that Card I is a truck although he hardly looks at it, or a girl says that it is a "kitten" although the examiner strongly suspects that she is responding less to the inkblot than to a stuffed animal nearby. Behavior of this kind leads Klopfer and Margulies (1941) to suggest that a response in this stage "may or may not" be related to properties of the card, and Ford (1946, p. 36) to observe that it "may be determined by some rather vague impression received from the first card or it may have no relation to the first card." Fox (1956) argues that these are responses less to features of the inkblot than to the total test situation, which includes ideas and feelings subjects bring to the testing and their reactions to the examiner. In Wernerian terms, such associations grow out of the matrix of the symbol situation in a period when contributions of the addressor, addressee, and symbolic medium are not differentiated. In these cases, the Rorschach truly appears to be a test of association, but what the association is to remains a mystery.

The borders of the Rorschach as a representational task are reached only as children give a third type of response, one that examiners believe is a reaction to some aspect of the blot—a color, a form, or, perhaps, some physiognomic quality—even if children's inability to clarify the matter leaves the examiners in doubt. The case of Colin, which was used to illustrate Stage I phenomena in earlier chapters, provides a good example of such responses (A. Schachtel, 1942). Colin reports that the first card looks like a mountain and the examiner, drawing on her sense of how the child treats the card, believes, but cannot be sure, that the response is based on the slope of the lines of the card or an angular portion of it. Responses of this kind are, in many respects, a more differentiated version of the second type. The child's response still appears to arise from a "vague impression," but now an impression of some properties of the card rather than of the test situation as a whole. Colin's stance toward the perceptual medium and toward forming an idea of what it "might be" also still appears to be largely passive. The capacity to use the blot for representational purposes, to act as if it "is" or "stands for" a mountain because the medium and referent share a property (in this case, angularity), is at best only beginning to be operative and is present in transitory ways. More often, the response seems to be merely an association to some perceptual properties of the blot.

In this first stage, then, children approach and wander along an indistinctly marked boundary at which the Rorschach task becomes one of symbolization. As Werner (1961) suggests, mental functions and phenomena in the period are syncretistic; it is unclear whether responses derive from associations to the blot, unrelated ideas children bring to the test situation, or reactions to examiners. Even if children seem to be reacting to the card, examiners feel responses are based on a vague sense of the blot or perhaps a mood it engenders. Consequently, such responses tend to be diffuse and unstable, changing readily as children's impressions of the situation and moods shift. Above all, there is little hierarchic organization or central regulation of the functions responsible for these early responses. Perception and association are not subordinate to, and thereby transformed by, an overriding representational intention. No efforts are made to carve out and define aspects of the perceptual medium that will serve as the basis for a representation, and certainly ideas about the referent do not affect how that medium is treated. At most, a representational intention is present faintly and fleetingly, and thus the test is continually in danger of degenerating into merely a task of either perception or association.

The manner in which children deal with the Rorschach at this time is similar to their early approach to artistic representation (Rouma, 1913; Goodenough, 1926; Di Leo, 1970). Asked to draw a human figure, children of 24 months are likely to simply scribble in a manner that strongly suggests they are interested in using the crayon only for the sheer pleasure of making marks on paper. If pressed, they may give a name to the chaotic mass of lines. However, their production is not a true representation, but rather the record of an activity (Freeman, 1993). A few months later they announce beforehand that they are drawing a man, although adults question whether the scribbling that follows is truly an effort to represent a human being or merely an attempt to pretend to do so. Soon thereafter children may discern in what they have scribbled a part that by chance resembles some aspect of a person, and this feature becomes a basis for an early representation. As with the Rorschach, children create diffuse, ambiguous productions that approach and then cross the border at which representation can be said to be present.

Inquiry

Viewing the Rorschach as a symbolic enterprise permits a better appreciation of a number of factors that have already been introduced to account for difficulties in conducting an inquiry into responses in this stage. In considering the contributions of ego psychology, for example, note was taken of the fact that not only do young children lack the patience and self-control necessary to bear with a difficult task, but also the cognitive capacities required to reflect on their productions (see Chapter 10). Their rudimentary representational abilities are a major factor in limiting this capacity for reflection. Symbols help arrest the flux of experience by concretizing phenomena and allowing them to be represented. For example, adults can later recall parts of a complex lecture if they write a brief word or two about it; the clearer and more detailed their notes, the more they can remember. However, children's initial Rorschach responses are not well-articulated representations in which the response bears a recognized relation to the medium. Rather, they are often associations arising from a global experience of the blot, and, as such, are difficult to reflect upon or explain. Doing so is like trying to recall a lecture using notes that consist of cryptic references to passing thoughts written in rapidly fading ink.

Equally important, young children experience the task in an egocentric manner (Piaget, 1952, 1959). As has been noted in analyzing psychosocial aspects of the mastery of the Rorschach (see Chapter 13), because of their limited differentiation of addressor and addressee, they have little sense that others see the card differently and that any explanation is required.

Finally, whereas the original response arises out of a global experience of the test situation, the inquiry process changes that situation by adding a set of demands from the examiner. Rather than viewing questions as an opportunity to clarify or explain the original response, children experience a new situation altogether. They assume either that the first responses must be wrong or that the adult is seeking some other association to the blot. Hence, inquiry in this period produces confusion and resistance and may lead to different responses if pressed.

Perseveration

A number of explanations have already been offered of the most distinctive feature of children's earliest Rorschach protocols, the pattern of pervasive perseveration in which children repeat their initial response on all subsequent cards. In particular, emphasis has been placed upon the manner in which this strategy serves defensive and adaptive functions, providing a "magic key" that allows children to cope with a task they experience as too difficult to handle in other ways (Klopfer and Margulies, 1941; Fox, 1956).

In addition, however, a cognitive explanation can be advanced that allows perseveration to be understood as a perfectly reasonable way of dealing with the test. As has been seen, at a stage when primitive forms of representation are not well established and frequently give way to perceptual approaches to the task, children struggle to find an answer to the question of what Card I might be even though it does not look like much of anything. When presented with Card II and asked to perform the same difficult task, they can now draw on previous experience. They know that this inkblot resembles nothing in the world so much as Card I. If the original response is adequate for first card, it is no less appropriate for the second. Moreover, Card III looks remarkably like its two predecessors. Hence, as children proceed through the test, the response becomes automatic, although it may be given in an ambivalent and uncertain way if children sense examiners are not satisfied with their answers.

TRANSITIONAL PHENOMENA: MODIFIED PERSEVERATIVE
PROTOCOLS

Each of the three patterns of modified perseverations described by Klopfer and Margulies (1941) and Ford (1946) are steps away from the most primitive ways of handling the symbol situation. For example, the most modest of these steps, simply substituting the phrase "I don't know" for a repetition of the original response, is significant in that it suggests that the absolute hold of perseveration on the response process is giving way. Magic repetition is no longer an automatic means of dealing with the blot; rather, children give some consideration to the card's characteristics, if only to reject a response.

The pattern of partial perseveration, in which children produce a few additional responses in predominantly perseverative records, is a clearer indication that they are approaching the test in a more mature way. All cards are no longer treated in an undifferentiated manner. The fact that protocols contain a few new responses indicates that more note is being taken of characteristics of the blots and that the range of referents is starting to expand, if only modestly.

Ford's pattern of perseverated logic, in which children give the same response to each card but try to find features of the blot that justify their association, is the most sophisticated of these transitional strategies. To be sure, insofar as the referent remains constant, the task is still approached in a rigid and inflexible way. Yet in searching the card for perceptual qualities to support the response, children treat the blot as a symbolic medium. They no longer seek to determine what the card truly looks like, but strive to establish a relationship between symbol and referent, using the medium differently on each card in order to do so. Thus, the process underlying the responses is clearly representational as it is in Stage II even though in outer form these protocols are like the perseverative records of Stage I.

STAGE II: CONFABULATORY RORSCHACHS

The Range of Responses

The production of protocols that include a different response to most cards, the change that most clearly reveals that three- and four-year-olds have entered the next stage in their handling of the Rorschach, is an outgrowth of new ways of dealing with the test as a representational task.

In offering varied responses to the cards and answering questions about their responses by noting that one is a bird because of the wings and another a dog because of the head, preschoolers are obviously dealing with the perceptual medium in a more differentiated way. Rather than basing their initial association on vague impressions of the first Rorschach card and repeating it without regard to the qualities of subsequent designs, they now single out particular aspects of each inkblot for consideration.

The different responses to each card are evidence of increasing flexibility in the choice of referents. In pure perseverative protocols, there is, in fact, only one response to all ten cards; now there are ten or more.

Most important, in implying that a card is fire because it is red or a monkey because of its tail, children demonstrate that they are treating the perceptual stimulus as a symbolic medium and using it to represent a concept on the basis of a shared common feature (e.g., a color or the shape of a tail). When vehicle and referent are linked in this way, there is no longer any ambiguity about the Rorschach being approached as a representational task.

Inquiry

The ability of children, when they choose, to participate in a crude form of the inquiry process, the second distinctive characteristic of Stage II Rorschachs, is also based on changes in their handling of the symbol situation. As has been noted, although still highly egocentric, preschoolers begin to appreciate differences between addressor and addressee. Thus, for example, in conducting experiments in which he sought to elicit children's explanations of their thinking, Piaget found that they began to become testable around the age of four (Flavell, 1963). In the case of the Rorschach, preschoolers have only a limited ability, and often even less inclination, to explain their responses. Nonetheless, they do have a growing sense that some reponse to examiners' questions may be necessary because others do not see things exactly as they do (see Chapter 13).

In addition, answers to inquiry questions become possible because the representational nature of the task is now firmly established. Even if they wish, Stage I children can give examiners little idea of the bases of responses that are little more than associations arising from hazy impressions of the blots. In Stage II, at least part of the blot is articulated in a way that bears a distinct relationship to the concept it is meant to represent. With this delineation of the symbolic medium and its relationship to the referent, children's responses are more stable and questions about them can be answered in ways that give examiners some idea of their location and determinants.

Confabulatory Whole Responses

The location and determinants of responses are, in turn, characteristics that distinguish Stage II Rorschachs from protocols of later developmental periods. The typical preschool response is one to the entire blot that is of poor, and frequently extraordinarily poor, form. Because of limitations in the inquiry process and scoring conventions, these responses usually do not receive a formal DW designation. Nonetheless, as Klopfer, Spiegelman, and Fox (1956) observe, the process underlying them is often that of confabulatory whole responses. Responses are advanced on the basis of a single detail or aspect of the card without concern for whether other aspects of the design fit the concept or not. If by chance the rest of the blot roughly corresponds with accepted images of the response a child has offered, it receives a respectable form level score. If, as is more likely, there is little or no correspondence, the response receives a poor form level score and may well be described as "crude," "arbitrary," and even "pseudopsychotic" (Kay and Vorhaus, 1943).

Traditional theories of the Rorschach attribute these responses to deficient approaches to a complex perceptual task. Because of an incapacity to delay and difficulty integrating a variety of details into a percept, it is suggested, preschoolers react hastily with an association based on limited information, thereby short-circuiting the process necessary to form an appropriate percept. It is puzzling, however, that children would believe this is an acceptable strategy, for their response bears little resemblance to any recognizable image of what they claim to see. Were the Rorschach task chiefly perceptual, it would make better sense if early responses were confined to simple, vague, or ordinary ones that require relatively little organization and look more like the object or concept depicted.

From the standpoint of a representational theory, the preschoolers' DW response is not a sign of an intellectual deficit, but rather a remarkable cognitive achievement. It is the decisive step in moving beyond approaching the Rorschach as a task of perceptual recognition to treating the inkblots as a medium to be interpreted. In Stage I, children either try to identify the blot or offer responses that appear to be associations based on a diffuse impression of it or the test situation as a whole. In contrast, with the DW response, they use the inkblot as a symbolic medium, singling out a distinct aspect of the card to serve as a means for representing an idea. If questioned when they are in the right mood, they can give examiners a sense of the relation linking their use of the vehicle to the concept or object for which it stands. The prevalence of this strategy of dealing with the Rorschach reflects the fact that for these children a single shared attribute is sufficient for an adequate representation.

This use of a part of an object or concept to stand for the whole is a respectable, if unsophisticated, mode of representation that continues to operate later in life. For example, the country's most successful fast-food franchise spends millions of dollars each year on the assumption that the public recognizes that golden arches are symbols of hamburgers, chicken nuggets, and wholesome family life. Moreover, the entire populations of such cosmopolitan centers as Boston and Chicago choose to represent their baseball teams by their socks, while citizens of Cincinnati, perhaps more prone to C responses, designate theirs by the color of players' socks alone.

As a predominant method of handling the Rorschach, DW responses are analogous to the simple one- and two-word sentences children use as they begin to master language. Judged by adult standards, the latter constructions are remarkably limited grammatical structures. Yet, as every parent knows, what is most significant is not those limitations, but rather the fact that these sentences are a major milestone in language development. They indicate that children are embarked on a course that will rapidly lead to the acquisition of increasingly complex linguistic forms. So, too, the preschooler's confabulatory whole response, however primitive it seems, is a giant step along a similar developmental line leading to the mastery of a form of visual representation.

Rorschach responses of this kind, of course, appear later than early forms of language, but at the same time as analogous types of visual representation in artistic productions. For example, typically, between the ages of three and four, children produce their first recognizable pictures of human beings, which consist of a circular form with perhaps a crude effort to include some facial features, notably the eyes (Rouma, 1913; Di Leo, 1970; Gardner, 1980). Shortly thereafter, during the "tadpole stage," legs and arms may be added as appendages to the figure. Whether this rounded form is meant to designate simply a head or a global combination of head and torso is still subject to debate (Gardner, 1980). Like Rorschach responses in the period, the whole human being is depicted by a crude representation that at best captures only a small part of the concept and certainly bears little concrete resemblance to it. Yet in both cases, children's productions are, for them, perfectly adequate representations.

Some of the problems in scoring and interpreting Rorschach responses in this stage arise because of differences between the manner in which children approach the test and the forms of thought and modes of analysis examiners bring to their work. Questioned about a response that does not resemble the card as a whole, preschoolers reply by noting one aspect of the inkblot. For example, they may state that Card IV is an elephant because it has a trunk. For them, that detail is all that is necessary for the card to represent an elephant. Thus, when examiners, firmly believing that responses should be determined by the shape of the blot as a whole, seek to discover "What else makes it look like a elephant?", communication breaks down. Because there is no "what else," children, depending on their predispositions, respond in confused, willful, impish, or anxious ways. Examiners, in their turn, describe the response as vague, arbitrary, or peculiar and call attention to limitations in children's cognitive development.

Confabulatory Responses

Perhaps the most distinctive feature of Stage II Rorschachs is the prominence of confabulation in its more general sense. Silly language and nonsensical associations abound as three-year-olds describe seeing, for example, boonjis, sissers, and piadigats (Allen, 1954). Rorschach images are not merely enlivened by elements of fantasy, but made into the subjects of stories as if the inkblot were a CAT card (Halpern, 1953). So vivid are these fantasies that, confronted with children who claim a bear on Card VIII has bitten them, Ames et al. (1952) suggest that there may be some impairment in reality testing.

Perceptual theories of the Rorschach view such phenomena as a result of the disruption of the response process by extraneous, reality-distorting influences. Whereas some allowance is made for kinesthetic sensations and physiognomic properties of blots contributing to a modest degree of fabulatization in normal percepts (E. Schachtel, 1966), blatant confabulations are seen as the consequence of fantasies and loose associations derailing children as they seek to formulate genuine percepts. In Rapaport's model, for example, these responses are interpreted as the association phase of the response process run amok.

From a representational perspective, confabulations do not arise because children are deflected from the true Rorschach task, but rather because they are beginning to grasp it. As has been stressed, the crucial step in mastering the test is the decision to approach it as a creative exercise rather than a problem of perceptual recognition. Only as children appreciate that the task is one of artistic expression are they able to treat the inkblot as material to be molded into an image of their choosing. No longer utilizing a strategy of "perseverated logic" in which they devise ways of making card after card into the same response, they now recognize that the choice of referents is, at least in principle, infinite. In short, confabulations demonstrate that children understand that they may give free rein to their imagination in selecting referents.

The problems examiners experience with this stage arise because preschoolers throw themselves into this task with such relish that freedom becomes license. Whereas those administering the test wish it taken in ways that conform to a particular set of rules, preschoolers do so only sporadically and strive to convert the task into a more interesting form of play (see Chapter 11). Hence, the funny language and behavior, the absurd associations, and the readiness to transform the Rorschach into a CAT.

Even when these children do conform to the general requirements of the test, they are far less concerned than older subjects with a broader set of social rules governing responses that should and should not be given. Three-year-olds are egocentric beings who have only a limited sense of how they are seen by others. Readily assimilating the Rorschach situation to their own needs and interests, they see nothing amiss in producing absurd, fantastic, and idiosyncratic responses as long as the process is fun. In this respect, piadigats, sissers, and boonjis may be particularly satisfying associations and offering fantasies about Rorschach images can perk up a process that might otherwise quickly become tedious. In contrast, because older subjects are sensitive to how they are viewed by others, their creation of Rorschach images and decisions about which to share are influenced by considerations of rationality and social propriety. From a developmental standpoint, what requires explanation is not the existence of confabulation in Rorschach responses in Stage II, but rather the manner in which inhibitory factors later enter into the response process to restrict what subjects represent and share with examiners.

When the Rorschach is viewed in this way, the timing of Stage II becomes clear. Confabulatory Rorschachs appear at precisely the point at which there is a quantum leap in children's interest in forms of artistic expression and dramatic play (see Chapter 11). Preschoolers begin to handle inkblots flexibly in the same period that crayons, paint, and clay become standard equipment in their playrooms, and they produce varied referents, often heavily invested with fantasy, in the same period that there is a flowering of their capacity for and investment in pretense play. Far from being aberrant phenomena, preschoolers' flamboyant confabulations are simply exaggerated manifestations of the processes that make taking the Rorschach possible. As such, they are reminders that the ability to take the Rorschach has its roots in the human capacity for imaginative play (E. Schachtel, 1966).

TRANSITIONAL PHENOMENA: CONFABULATORY
COMBINATIONS

The changes in children's Rorschach protocols at the end of the preschool years that mark the next transitional phase are the result of further development in their handling of key aspects of the symbol situation.

The confabulatory combinations, which Klopfer, Spiegelman, and Fox (1956) consider the characteristic response in this period, reflect an increasingly differentiated treatment of the symbolic vehicle. Formerly one detail was sufficient to serve as the basis for representation; now children make use of two. However, the integration of details in the overall form is still not the overriding consideration in creating representations as it will be in the third stage. In a manner that accords with Piaget's description of the latter part of the preoperational stage, these children juxtapose a variety a details but have difficulty synthesing them in an integrated structure (Piaget, 1952).

Equally important, there are apparently paradoxical shifts in the manner in which children choose referents. On the one hand, the wild confabulations of the preceding year diminish and associations to the blot tend to be more realistic. On the other, four and a half is the age at which what Ames et al. (1952, p. 168) describe as "extremely confused and unrelated concepts" are at their peak. Thus, for example, children in this period offer significant numbers of responses such as "a fireplace with feet," "a dog with two heads," or "a person with a chicken head."

These incongruous combinations are typically interpreted as signs of confused thinking, ideational instability, and difficulties with reality testing—and with good reason. They consist of odd mixtures of ideas that result in strange and fantastic images. Nonetheless, in children of this age such responses are, in fact, products of a growing sophistication in dealing with the perceptual medium and an effort to treat the Rorschach in a more realistic manner.

The origins of incongruous combinations can be appreciated by considering an illustration of a pushmi-pullyu, a creature from the Dr. Doolittle stories (Lofting, 1967). Asked to identify the picture (Figure 6), most adults would describe it as an animal with two heads. In a like manner, we could obtain responses of three-headed dogs, creatures that are half human and half animal, and other incongruous combinations if we asked adults to describe sketches of Cerberus, the guard to the entrance to Hades; mermaids; satyrs; and similar mythological figures. In each case, subjects' perceptions are accurate, although what they perceive are "unrealistic," imaginary beings.

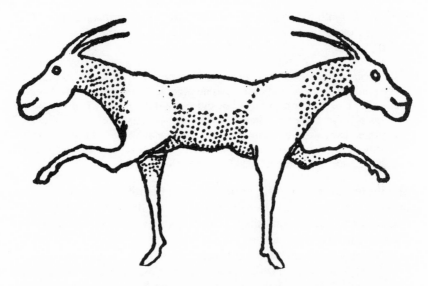

Figure 6. A pushmi-pullyu. (From H. Lofting's *Doctor Doolittle's Circus,* copyright Christopher Lofting.)

The situation confronting children as they begin to take account of several features of inkblots is similar. Seeing a blot that looks like a chimney and legs, they define it as fireplace with feet. Finding that both sides of a symmetrical blot have details that look like dogs' heads, they describe it as a dog with two heads. Such images do not represent flights of imagination, but rather attempts to deal realistically with stimuli that are now treated in a complex manner. The problem is that realism can be defined in two ways, one related to the medium and one to the referent, and children opt for the former.

STAGE III: "THE RORSCHACH"

Attitudes Toward the Test

In the early years of elementary school, children exhibit new forms of cognition and social relatedness that contribute to marked qualitative changes in the manner in which they take the Rorschach. As they move into Piaget's stage of concrete operations, they display an increasing ability to recognize that others' perspectives and viewpoints differ from their own and to understand rules governing social interactions (Piaget,

1951, 1952, 1959). Moreover, they not only now appreciate such rules; they also experience a strong need to conform to them. As Gardner (1982) observes,

> they gain a heightened awareness of, and concern with, the standards of their culture. Indeed, children become occupied, and preoccupied, with the rules and standards honored by those about them—how to dress, how to speak, how to play games, how to behave in a morally approved manner. They even become obsessed—they want to get these practices exactly right—and it becomes important for their psychological well-being that they not violate them [p. 100].

Manifested in further differentiation and integration of addressor–addressee components of the symbol situation, these new cognitive capacities and motivational dispositions have a profound effect on how the Rorschach is approached.

In Stage II, children have a general sense of how examiners are trying to define the Rorschach task. Yet, their grasp of "the rules of the game" is not especially refined and, more important, they have few compunctions about modifying those rules or making up their own if doing so makes the test a more interesting play situation. In Stage III, children understand the definition of the task clearly—for example, that it is one of producing visual representations, not an occasion for telling stories or engaging in pretend play. Furthermore, they are invested in playing the game right. To tell stories or claim an animal on a card is attacking them is to act childishly, behavior they are now trying hard to outgrow.

The clearest indication of this new attitude toward the test is in the handling of the inquiry process. Instead of struggling to get often resistant subjects to give them some idea of the bases of responses, examiners now find children ready and able to provide clear accounts of the location and determinants of responses. In part, this change results from children's awareness that their perspectives and those of others differ. If the examiner is to understand their responses, an explanation is necessary. In part, it reflects the fact that in the stage of concrete operations children are better able to reflect on their mental processes and hence provide such an explanation. In part, it is a product of school age children's ability to grasp the rules governing interactions and their readiness to play games by the rules. Hence, for example, after responding to inquiries about a card or two, they often anticipate the examiner's questions and provide answers without being asked.

With Stage III, then, children have a differentiated sense of the test situation that includes a recognition of differences between their own perspectives and interests and those of the examiner. They also have the integrative capacity to engage in a social enterprise conducted according to a set of shared rules. As a consequence, the Rorschach is now taken in more or less "standard" ways that include a serious engagement in both the tasks of producing responses and responding to questions about them.

Handling of the Symbolic Medium

The cognitive and motivational factors responsible for shifts in attitudes toward the Rorschach situation have an equally significant influence on how children deal with the symbolic vehicle. Although preoperational children take account of a number of details of a situation, they often simply juxtapose them. As they enter the stage of concrete operations, however, the integration of these details in coherent, organized forms becomes the paramount consideration. Moreover, in creating visual representations, school age children use their new capacities chiefly to produce "realistic" depictions of objects and concepts.

These changes are apparent in children's aesthetic judgments and in their artistic productions in general. Rejecting impressionistic and abstract works of art that once were of some interest to them, elementary school students prefer realism and literalism (Gardner, 1982). Their sketches and paintings reveal increasing technical sophistication used in the service of these aesthetic standards. For example, Burt (1921) observes that, whereas the drawings of five- and six-year-olds are governed by a "descriptive symbolism" in which there is a crude scheme of the object, but limited attention to shape and proportion, those of seven- to ten-year-olds are characterized by a "realism" in which there is increasing attention to detail and organization. Recognizing this growing differentiation and integration in visual representation, psychologists use quantitative measures of the number of details included in human figure drawings and realistic standards pertaining to how details are integrated and figures proportioned to assess children's intelligence (Goodenough, 1926; Harris, 1963). Even Gardner (1980), who dislikes these tests because of their insensitivity to aesthetic issues, concedes that they have some validity because school-age children and the psychologists testing them share the same narrow standards.

The principles that govern children's artistic productions can be seen in their handling of the Rorschach medium. Their capacity to analyze inkblots, already apparent in the attention to several details of figures seen in the latter part of Stage II, accelerates. For example, they give more responses in general and more detailed responses in particular.

More important, whereas earlier simply including details in representations was acceptable, now the integration of details to achieve more or less "realistic" depictions of objects or concepts is the overriding goal. Consequently, in this stage, children and examiners use the same principle of form level as a critical criterion for judging responses, and examiners intuitively feel more comfortable analyzing protocols in standard ways.

Handling of Referents

Stage III Rorschachs are also distinguished by new principles regulating themes to be represented. There is continuing differentiation of thematic content in the sense that children give more responses chosen from a larger number of content categories. Yet these changes are relatively modest. What is most significant is the change in standards governing acceptable representations. Increasingly aware of and sensitive to the opinions of their audience, school age children are influenced heavily by concerns about realism and conformance to social conventions in the responses they create and share.

As Gardner (1980) observes, "the reach toward realism" affects artistic productions of all kinds in the elementary school years. For example, there is a decline in the playful and poetic metaphors in children's speech. "Figurative language is despised and spurned – a person should not be called *sour*, a tie dare not be termed *loud*" (p. 149). Similarly, visual representations, including Rorschach images, portray more or less realistic subjects. To be sure, unicorns, superheroes, and other imaginary beings are acceptable themes, but only because they are part of a shared cultural reality. Idiosyncratic, personal creations or elaborate stories about Rorschach images are no longer appropriate because they are unrealistic and immature.

The new criteria by which referents are judged and the coordination of constituents of the symbol situation in this stage are well illustrated by the decline in confabulatory combinations. In the preceding stage, children had few qualms about producing images such as a fireplace with feet or a dog with two heads because they conformed to the "perceptual reality" of the inkblot. Now images must conform to a conceptual sense of reality as well. A card may look like a dog with two heads, but dogs do not in fact have two heads and hence some alternative should be found. Making use of a new flexibility in thought and a growing capacity to coordinate mental operations (Flavell, 1963), school age children can devise a variety of strategies for dealing with the problem. Ignoring one side of the card, they can describe the other as a dog or treat an even smaller part of the card as a dog's head. If they are more ambitious and talented, using the whole card they can create responses such as two dogs or a dog looking in the mirror. Underlying all of these strategies is the assumption that "good" representations must integrate perceptual and conceptual senses of reality, those related to the vehicle and the referent. With the emergence of this norm, incongruous combinations and other confabulatory phenomena become signs of immaturity and often of pathology.

CONCLUSION: STAGE III AND BEYOND

Freedom and Constraint in the Rorschach

With Stage III, the Rorschach becomes in some respects a less expressive instrument. In the elementary school years, much of the spontaneity that earlier characterized normal children's play with the test disappears. Gone are the boonjis and boo-carriers, the pink sissers and krozokuses, the two-headed dogs and fireplaces with feet. Gone, too, are the flights of fantasy about responses, which, however problematic from the standpoint of obtaining a respectable Rorschach protocol, were nonetheless a rich source of clinical data (Halpern, 1953). In their place we encounter the more staid, serious responses of children who try to stick strictly to the rules and who are conscious of how others will judge their productions. The result is test records that are more conventional, but also often less interesting.

These developments parallel those in children's art as well. Latency age children display a marked improvement in technical skills that enables them to turn out recognizable drawings of objects, yet most have less interest in art, produce less, and, many observers believe, are less creative. "Following closely upon entrance into school," Gardner (1982, p. 94) observes, "the charm, originality, and attractiveness of works by children are no longer as apparent."

Though commonly attributed to the stultifying effect of our educational system or the process of socialization in general, as Gardner points out, these changes can be understood as aspects of a natural developmental progression and have their own contributions to make to the mastery of art. Works of five-year-olds may bear a resemblance to those of Klee, Miró, or Pollock, but not because they are produced by budding masters of abstract expressionism or, for that matter, of primitivism. Mature artists draw and paint as they do by choice, young children because they know no other way. The work of latency age children is no longer spontaneous in part because of self-imposed restraints on form and content as children seek to use new cognitive skills to depict objects realistically. The practice and mastery of these skills enables talented artists to represent their ideas later in myriad of styles *by choice.* In effect, the constraint evident in the art of school age children reflects a form of self-discipline that is essential to learning a craft and one that opens the possibility of a higher degree of freedom of expression within a medium.

An analogous process can be seen in the manner in which children treat the Rorschach in Stage III. Their approach to the inkblots is governed by rules that limit their freedom of action. The task is now strictly one of visual representation; they will not allow themselves to treat it as an open-ended expressive exercise that can eventuate in a CAT-like story. More important, integrating details of figures and producing adequate forms become major considerations in determining acceptable responses. In some respects, such standards make the task harder, narrow the range of responses, and lead to more ordinary and banal responses. At the same time, insofar as the Rorschach task is one of visual representation, operating within such rules is necessary to its mastery. As subjects are able to work within the confines of the medium, ultimately a richer range of expression opens up to them. This new balance of constraint and freedom in how the Rorschach is approached provides the rationale for its interpretation. On one hand, with Stage III, children exhibit a more differentiated capacity to use the symbolic medium. In forming images, they can draw upon the whole blot, a part of it, or even a small detail. They can base responses on form, color, shading, physiognomic qualities of the blot, or some combination of characteristics of the medium. Form is a major factor in determining the responses they produce, but how rigorously this standard is applied is left to individuals' discretion. In effect, the handling of the Rorschach is now subject to self-imposed constraints, but the nature of these constraints and the choices made within them become the bases for interpreting formal characteristics of responses.

With Stage III, children also place restrictions on the content of their responses. In contrast to preschoolers, who can display their thoughts and feelings all too freely as they work on the test, older children are better able to control themselves and far more sensitive to how they are viewed by examiners and how they wish to be viewed. As a consequence, they are careful, even guarded, in their choice of referents. Able to express more in the tests, they impose their own limits on the range of images they allow themselves to create and censor some of these images rather than share them with examiners.

These changes, however, do not render the Rorschach any less useful in personality assessment. To be sure, children no longer reveal their thoughts, desires, and fears as directly in the Rorschach situation, although the unfamiliarity and expressive potential of the medium and the open-ended nature of the task may allow examiners to catch glimpses of these matters when their subjects' guard is down. Yet, as has often been stressed, the test is not an x-ray of the unconscious. Producing responses involves not only expression of thoughts, wishes, and feelings, but also efforts to shape and control what is expressed. The changes encountered in Stage III Rorschachs are a product of children's increasing capacities to organize and regulate their thoughts and actions and as such enable the test to be used to explore critical aspects of their personalities. Responses grow out of a process in which their creators struggle to maintain a balance of spontaneity and control, impulse and defense, and self-expression and inhibition that are present in all aspects of their lives. Accordingly, much of the formal scoring of the test as well as analyses of individual responses and their sequence are concerned with how these antithetical tendencies are played out. The value of the Rorschach as an instrument for personality assessment lies precisely in the unique opportunity it affords to witness this process in a novel situation.

Stage III and Later Development

There is no reason to believe that developmental changes in the manner in which the Rorschach is handled cease with the elementary school years. For example, Hemmendinger (1953) suggests that as children mature they handle the symbolic medium in more differentiated and integrated ways. In his study, by the age of ten, the trend of diminishing percentages of whole responses characteristic of the early elementary school years begins to be reversed and children give more whole responses. However, in contrast to the global whole responses of preschool children, he notes, these percepts "are composed of separate details integrated together into a larger whole" (p. 164).

Nonetheless, the early school years is an appropriate point to end this narrative. Prior to this time, children are still in the process of mastering the Rorschach, and their often curious performance on the test reflects stages in that process. Now they understand and accept the rules that define the standard form of the Rorschach at all subsequent ages. They produce responses in a manner similar to those of subjects at later ages and participate in the inquiry process in ways that allow examiners to have a clear idea of the determinants of responses. As a consequence, examiners have confidence that they are obtaining valid test records and that those records can be interpreted according to the same principles used with older subjects. Hence, although further developmental changes occur after Stage III is reached, they are changes that can be measured and understood by typical modes of administering and analyzing the test.

V

Clinical
Applications

Problems in the Clinical
Assessment of Young
Children

INTRODUCTION

The preceding sections have explored the manner in which children master the Rorschach and the implications of this developmental process for our understanding of the nature of the test. Yet to be worthy of consideration theories about a diagnostic instrument should have some contributions to make to its clinical applications. In the case of a study of how normal children between the ages of two and seven handle the Rorschach, the obvious area in which such contributions might be expected is the use of the test with troubled children of these ages.

The clinical evaluation of young children has received little attention in the Rorschach literature. As has been seen (Chapter 1), works on preschoolers compose a small portion of those on children, which, in turn, are a modest fraction of those on the test as a whole. Of the publications on young children's Rorschachs, most are concerned with normative trends rather than clinical problems. Moreover, much of what has been written about this age group in general raises serious questions about whether the test can or should be used for evaluation of psychopathology.

This chapter will examine problems that have become apparent as psychologists have tried to employ traditional Rorschach techniques in testing young children. Those that follow will explore what a developmental framework can add to an assessment of these children and of profoundly disturbed youngsters in the early elementary school years.

PROBLEMS RELATED TO TEST ADMINISTRATION

Rorschach evaluations of children have typically involved simply an extension of the modes of administration and interpretation used with adults. Yet as children are tested at younger and younger ages, these efforts become more strained. Thus, as all who have worked with preschoolers recognize, their level of cognitive, social, and emotional development makes it hard to elicit responses and even harder to conduct a satisfactory inquiry into those responses.

The nature of these difficulties and attempts to cope with them are discussed at length at the outset of this book. For the present purposes, we need only recall the pronounced, unresolved disagreements among Rorschach authorities regarding appropriate ways of testing young children.

Those most inclined to use the Rorschach in evaluating preschoolers seek to counter problems in administration and scoring by introducing modifications in procedures that may go beyond the letter of Rorschach law but, they believe, remain faithful to its spirit (see Chapter 2). For example, they suggest such alterations in test procedures as trial inkblots (Ford, 1946), restricting the rotation of cards (Ford, 1946), extensive intervention on the part of examiners to support and encourage children (Halpern, 1953), inquiry after each card and even after each response (Ames et al., 1952), and so forth. Even more important, because of young children's difficulties with and resistance to the inquiry process, some propose looser and more intuitive approaches to scoring (Ames et al., 1952; Halpern, 1952, 1960).

Others who use the Rorschach with young children object to any significant departure from standard administrative procedures. For example, Klopfer, Fox, and Troup (1956) stress the importance of maintaining the integrity of the administrative technique even if it means that records obtained in this way will be less rich and that there will be greater doubt about scores of particular responses.

Carrying this line of reasoning a step further, still others, probably most of the Rorschach community, believe that because of the magnitude of problems in test administration and the meagerness of the data obtained, the Rorschach simply is not a valid and reliable instrument with young children. Thus, major books on children's Rorschachs, such as that of Exner and Weiner (1982), often consider work only with school age youngsters.

In short, there are widely shared reservations about using the Rorschach with preschoolers at all; among those who do, there is no consensus about the administrative techniques that should be used; and even those most committed to work with young children concede that they experience more uncertainty in scoring and interpreting responses than they do with older subjects.

PROBLEMS IN INTERPRETATION

Most authorities on children's Rorschachs agree that the principles that should be employed in interpreting the protocols of children, even young children, are the same as those governing evaluations of older subjects. For example, Klopfer, Spiegelman, and Fox (1956, p. 25) assert that "the phenomenological analysis of a child's Rorschach record, for the purposes of obtaining clues to structural aspects of the child's personality," and "the hypotheses used in combining these clues and connecting them to structural aspects of personality organization" are the same with children and adults. Similarly, Exner and Weiner (1982, p. 14) contend, "Rorschach behavior means what it means regardless of the age of the subject."

To be sure, these and indeed almost all discussions of interpretation of children's records also stress the importance of considering results within a "developmental framework." Yet in practice the latter recommendation consists chiefly of comparing a child's scores with norms for other subjects of the same age and making inferences about the pathognomonic significance of particular test signs that try to take into consideration whether the presumed personality characteristics associated with those signs are typically found in children at that age or not. Insofar as the Rorschach is used with children, however, it is assumed to be the same basic test at each age.

A number of problems arise with regard to this approach to interpretation of young children's Rorschachs. One is a direct consequence of the problems of administration. Analyses based on a comparison of test data with norms can hardly be secure when there is little agreement about the methods of generating data to establish those norms. For example, the most extensive normative data on young children, that of Ames et al. (1952), is gathered by means others (e.g., Klopfer, Fox, and Troup, 1956) find suspect.

Another problem is that of the "meagerness of data" (Ames et al., 1952). Even after preschoolers advance beyond the stage of perseverative protocols, they give relatively few responses. Their average number of distinct responses is well below the figure most Rorschach practitioners consider sufficient for a satisfactory analysis of test protocols. Perhaps for this reason, most research studies of young children have focused on normative trends and comparisons of groups of subjects across ages rather than on differences among subjects of the same age.

The most significant problems for applications of traditional modes of Rorschach interpretation to preschoolers center on the assumption that determinant scores have the same meaning with this population as with others. As has been seen, Klopfer, Spiegelman, and Fox (1956) argue that the Rorschach protocols of young children may be based on modes of thinking fundamentally different from those of older children. If this is the case, as this book suggests it is, such differences may take precedence over any other findings related to determinant scores. Indeed, scores at times may be artifacts of those thought processes and the difficulties examiners have in grappling with them.

UNCERTAINTY ABOUT PATHOGNOMONIC SIGNS

Another set of difficulties in using the Rorschach for clinical assessment of young children lies in uncertainty about what constitutes a sign of pathology in this population. As Ames et al. (1952, pp. 282–283) observe, "many responses commonly considered to be danger signals in the adult" occur "relatively benignly" in the records of children. To state the problem more crudely, if pervasive perseveration, poor form level, and extensive confabulation are normal in young children, what isn't?

There is remarkably little in the literature on this issue and works that do address it create as many problems as they solve. The efforts of Klopfer and Ames in this regard are instructive.

Contending that "concept formation" is the only area where "age patterns have emerged sufficiently to be ready for conceptualization," Klopfer, Spiegelman, and Fox (1956, p. 25) suggest two indicators of pathology. First, the presence of perseveration, confabulation, and confabulatory combinations beyond the age range in which they are typically encountered, especially after the age of seven, may be indicative of "mental retardation, emotional infantilism, or a temporary emotional disturbance" (p. 28). Second, contaminations, a form of "deviant concept formation," may reflect schizoid tendencies in subjects of any age (pp. 29–30). However, though these observations may be apt, what is most significant about Klopfer's discussion of pathognomonic signs is what it does not include—almost every Rorschach score and index used in assessing pathology in adults!

The most comprehensive attempt to delineate "danger signals" in the Rorschach protocols of young children is that of Ames et al. (1952). In the first edition of *Child Rorschach Responses*, they list 13 kinds of responses they consider "immature, dangerous, atypical or indicative of disturbance in the child." These include: (1) a preponderance of leaf or tree responses in children over the age of four or five; 2) greater than 75% pure form responses in children over the age of five; (3) pure color responses, although they are more common in young children than older subjects; (4) color naming in children over the age of five; (5) more than one achromatic color response; (6) more than one inanimate movement response; (7) contaminations in children over the age of five and a half; (8) less than 40% to 50% whole responses; (9) Do responses; (10) a lack of human responses; 11) refusals of cards after the age of three and a half; 12) position responses after the age of four; and 13) bizarre responses or actions. Clinicians seeking guidance in evaluating preschoolers are likely to find this list less useful than it appears. A third of the signs apply only to school age youngsters and others are described as merely "suggestive" of pathology because they are more prevalent in young children than older subjects. Even more important, efforts to test these "danger signals" empirically have not been encouraging.

Comparing Rorschach protocols of 40 children between the ages of eight and ten in treatment in a child guidance clinic with those of a matched control group of normal subjects, Elkins (1958) found effects for a group of nine of Ames's signs, *but in the wrong direction*. Normal subjects exhibited a greater number of them than the clinical population. However, Elkins's study can hardly be considered a reasonable test of the efficacy of the Rorschach in this regard since she eliminated four of the most potent indicators of disturbance (e.g., contaminations, confabulations, color naming, and bizarre responses and actions) because she believed that they called for "subjective judgments."

Ames et al. (1974) sought to test the power of an expanded list of 16 "danger signals" to discriminate 50 boys between the ages of six and 12 receiving psychiatric treatment from a normal control group. Of their original group of 13 items, four, most of which had been excluded from Elkins's study, yielded statistically significant differences in the groups. These items included an absence of human responses, bizarre or troubled content, contamination and confabulation, and positional responses. In addition, Ames and her associates found several new signs, notably excessive card manipulation, F% exceeding

F + %, elimination and sex responses, and static perseveration, which also discriminated the two groups. Nonetheless, their findings offer little encouragement to those who would use these signs with preschoolers, in that their youngest subjects are already of school age.

PROBLEMS IN CLINICAL APPROACHES TO PRESCHOOL ASSESSMENT

Not surprisingly, those who are most inclined to use the Rorschach in the evaluation of psychopathology in young children have been clinicians who favor an idiographic approach to interpretation and rely heavily on their own experience and judgment. Yet the Rorschach literature contains few cases describing how clinicians actually work, and those that have been published underline the problems inherent in such assessments.

Clinical approaches to the Rorschach evaluation of preschoolers are perhaps best exemplified by the work of Halpern (1953), their most enthusiastic advocate. As has been seen, in order to elicit as much material as possible, she is prepared to take substantial liberties with the administration of the test. She notes, for example:

> The preschool child is often unable to point out with any clarity or definiteness the area of the blot that he used in giving a response. Here once again the examiner must be flexible because too much insistence will only disturb the child and prevent him from responding to subsequent blots. Far more important than formal factors at this age are the associations that the child brings to his responses. It is therefore quite useful to use the responses almost as one might use a CAT picture [p. 15].

Of necessity the interpretation of material gathered in this way is based heavily on the examiner's clinical skills and impressions of the child.

As might be expected, the chief criticism of such an approach is the one Klopfer, Spiegelman, and Fox (1956) raise about Halpern's work: It is largely speculative.

The nature of this problem can be seen in Anna Schachtel's (1944) interpretation of the protocol we have used to illustrate perseverative approaches to the Rorschach. On the basis of observations of her subject Colin's behavior during the testing and her intuitive sense of the processes she believes responsible for his repeated response of a mountain, she offers an analysis of his personality that includes suggestions that he exhibits a striving for power and superiority, that he reacts with defiance and opposition as his sense of efficacy is challenged, and that "he is not quite satisfied with himself, but does not make it easy for himself to be satisfied" (p. 5). Commenting on her analysis, Beck (1944a) observes:

> The interpretations which Miss Hartoch [Schachtel] makes of the Rorschach findings appear to me impressionistic. They may be accurate, but all we have is the examiner's qualitative judgment. Another examiner may have a different qualitative reaction. Working in this way the door is left wide open to what becomes the examiner's free association [p. 18].

His critique, in effect, is roughly the same as Klopfer's critique of Halpern.

There are more rigorous interpretations of cases reported in the literature. For example, Klopfer, Spiegelman, and Fox (1956) offer an example of a phenomenological approach to the interpretation of the protocol of a five-year-old boy. However, although their formulation is based on more data and a more extensive analysis of that data than in Schachtel's case, one would be hard pressed to explain how it would escape the same charges of being speculative and impressionistic that they level at Halpern's work.

CONCLUSION

The problems faced in the Rorschach assessment of preschoolers are hardly surprising. As any clinical technique is extended further and further beyond the domain for which it was originally developed, a point will be reached at which serious doubts arise about whether the assumptions governing the use of the instrument hold and, beyond that, another point will be reached at which doubts give way to a conviction that those assumptions cannot be made. In moving from work with adults to the testing of young children, almost all who use the Rorschach recognize that they at least have entered the band of uncertainty by the preschool years and many, if not most, have reached the point at which they believe the test, at least in its standard form, cannot be used in a valid and reliable way. Thus, at the peak of Rorschach's popularity, less than a tenth of child guidance clinics used it in assessing children under the age of seven (Anderson and Higham, 1956) and leading authorities who have tested preschoolers extensively are extremely cautious in recommending clinical applications (Klopfer, Spiegelman, and Fox, 1956; Ames et al., 1974).

A Clinical-Developmental
Approach to Preschool
Rorschachs

PRESCHOOL ASSESSMENT AS A PROBLEM

At first glance, the developmental perspective that has been advanced in this book affords little reason for optimism about clinical applications of the Rorschach with young children. It highlights the erratic, changing ways in which preschoolers approach the test, the marked qualitative differences in how the Rorschach is taken at each stage of its mastery, and the diverse strategies examiners have adopted to cope with such behavior. It also calls attention to the perseverative and confabulatory responses characteristic of early Rorschach performance and the extent to which these protocols are less rich and quite different from those produced in the last stage. Given these facts, it is to be expected that (1) there will not be a consensus among authorities about appropriate techniques for testing young children; (2) many will be skeptical about whether conditions presupposed by standard interpretations of the Rorschach are met when it is used; (3) individual examiners will often be unsure about whether particular children have taken the test in ways that meet their own criteria for valid testing; (4) even advocates of preschool Rorschachs will acknowledge that protocols of these subjects are "less revealing" than those of older ones (Ames et al., 1974, p. 27); and (5) doubts will be present about whether the same processes underlie the Rorschach responses of young children and adults and about whether scores can be interpreted in the same way with each group (Bohm, 1958). In short, our model provides a theoretical basis for accounting for why controversy and uncertainty surround the use of the Rorschach with this age group.

Nonetheless, this perspective need not lead to pessimistic conclusions about clinical uses of the test with young children. Modes of interpreting Rorschach data that presuppose standard administration inevitably appear questionable when subjects take the test in immature ways. Yet, as has been seen, children who are only beginning to acquire the skills necessary to handle the Rorschach produce striking behaviors and responses that may well be valuable diagnostic material. The questions that have been raised about preschool Rorschachs thus center on techniques of analysis, not on the utility of the instrument itself. The possibility remains that the Rorschach can be of assistance in assessing young children if a suitable approach to interpretation of their test performance can be advanced.

The conception described in the preceding sections of how young children deal with the Rorschach should provide a foundation for such an approach. If theories introduced to explain how normal children treat the Rorschach at different stages are truly of value, they ought also to provide concepts through which individual differences and deviations in development may be understood as well. At the least, exploring how these theories can be applied to clinical problems affords a means of showing their heuristic potential even if the result falls short of demonstrating that the Rorschach should be accepted as a major instrument for evaluating preschoolers.

MODES OF INTERPRETATION

Debates about clinical use of the Rorschach with preschoolers arise because interpretation of the test with this population is similar to that with older subjects in some respects and different in others. The similarities are enough for a few authorities to advocate the instrument; the differences sufficient for many others to discount it. To go beyond simply reiterating opposing positions, it is necessary to have a clear recognition of these similarities and differences *and*, where differences exist, to consider alternative ways of analyzing preschool Rorschachs that are, at least in some crude way, functionally equivalent to those employed with older subjects.

The concept of the Rorschach as a task of visual representation provides a way of looking at the interpretive process that can clarify these issues. When viewed from this perspective, the different types of analyses used in Rorschach interpretation may each be seen to address different components of the symbol situation in which representations are formed. The scoring and analyses of location and determinants of responses are chiefly efforts to understand how subjects use the visual medium or symbolic vehicle; analyses of content of responses center on the choice of referents; and examinations of interpersonal aspects of the Rorschach situation or "the patient–examiner relationship" focus on the other basic dimension of the symbol situation, the experience of self and other. There are, of course, wide variations in how these types of analyses are conducted and the weight attributed to each in final interpretations of protocols. Yet Rorschach assessments typically involve a combination of these basic approaches.

In principle the Rorschach task is the same for preschoolers as it is for older subjects. It is one of visual representation that should be analyzed in terms of each of the components of the symbol situation. In practice, however, there are differences, some quite profound, in how these analyses are undertaken.

With regard to interpretations of the self–other dimension or the patient–examiner relationship, differences are minimal. Examiners rely largely on clinical sensitivity in trying to conceptualize the dynamics of the testing relationship with both children and adults. If anything, because children are less guarded and less influenced by social convention, such data are more easily acquired and can be used with greater confidence.

There is also relatively little difference in the manner in which the content of responses is interpreted with both populations. To be sure, with perseverative Rorschachs, there is not much content to interpret. However, three-and-a-half- and four-year-olds give more responses, including dramatic confabulations, that provide examiners with suitable material with which to work.

It is with regard to the handling of the symbolic medium that interpretations of preschool Rorschachs differ markedly from those with older subjects. Rorschach's seminal contribution to projective technique lay in his emphasis on this aspect of his instrument, and major systematizers of the test have been concerned chiefly with applying and elaborating these ideas. As a consequence, Rorschach interpretation has traditionally depended heavily on scoring of determinants and comparisons of a subject's scores and combinations of scores with established norms. Controversies about preschool Rorschachs have centered on the applicability of these interpretive procedures. It is, after all, ridiculous to spend time making inferences from psychograms of perseverative protocols and, as has been seen in the preceding chapter, the analysis of the confabulatory protocols of three- and four-year-olds is fraught with the methodological problems.

From the standpoint of the developmental model we have advanced, approaches to interpretation of preschool Rorschachs based on comparisons of scored protocols with norms for children of a particular age may be seen to founder as a result of three sets of methodological problems. First, the application of such techniques presupposes that subjects engage seriously in the task of producing responses and provide the information necessary for accurate scoring, assumptions that cannot be made with confidence when young children respond to the inkblots in such mercurial ways and to inquiries so capriciously. Second, the extent to which examiners are involved in the test process — the extra help they must provide to enable preschoolers to manage the test and produce responses and the leeway that must be granted in making judgments about scoring — may be a confounding variable. Third, even if examiners believe they have a good sense of the determinants of an individual youngster's responses, how are interpretations of scores on the basis of norms to be trusted, when data produced by different examiners and by preschoolers at different stages appear to be incommensurate? Insofar as there is no consensus about how testing should be conducted with these subjects, there can be no agreement about what constitutes normative data. As a consequence, traditional interpretations of preschool Rorschachs seem at best only a poor approximation and at worst a caricature of how the test should be used.

Even so, the problem of interpretation of preschool Rorschachs is circumscribed. Analyses of content and the interpersonal aspects of testing can be conducted in forms that are not fundamentally different from those used with older subjects. It is only with regard to analyses of the use of the medium that difficulties arise. Thus, the critical issue in interpretation of preschool Rorschachs is whether other ways of analyzing this aspect of the representational process can be found.

One path to solving this problem lies in considering the two rationales advanced for the analysis of determinants. First, Rorschach practitioners emphasize the importance of scoring responses because they believe the procedure provides a quantitative method of inferring individuals' preferred modes of experiencing, perceiving, or representing their worlds in certain delimited circumstances. Second, modes of representation on this particular task are assumed to reflect broader aspects of personality. For example, the passivity and reactivity thought to underlie the production of pure color responses are associated with personality traits such as impulsivity and a proneness to express emotions in raw, unmodulated ways.

To question the reliability and validity of quantitative analysis of preschool protocols is not to suggest that there are no ways of addressing how young subjects handle the representational task or making inferences about their personality characteristics in general. Indeed, as is the case with assessment of profoundly disturbed children who cannot take tests in standardized ways, the very problems that raise doubts about traditional analyses of Rorschach responses may be themselves sources of data bearing directly on these issues (Leichtman and Shapiro, 1980; Leichtman and Nathan, 1983).

Consider, for example, problems in test administration. Most older subjects are relatively easy to test because they clearly appreciate the task and use overlearned, automatized skills in dealing with it. These skills operate so smoothly we have little sense of the processes underlying them and rely on scoring systems to understand them. In contrast, it is difficult to trust scores with young children because the Rorschach is new, unfamiliar, and often only partially grasped and, as a consequence, they approach it in erratic, unpredictable ways. Yet this situation affords valuable opportunities for understanding the processes underlying their management of the task. Because the problem posed by the Rorschach is new for young children, because their solutions to it are not yet guided by habit or social convention, and because preschoolers are relatively open and uninhibited, their behavior often involves striking displays of the manner in which they are grappling with the representational task. In a sense, the situation is analogous to how we might try to learn about motor skills. We can discover more about the nature of walking from a few moments' observation of infants taking their first steps than from hours of watching adults engage in an action they now accomplish smoothly and effortlessly.

Moreover, because the Rorschach task can be difficult and frustrating for young children, we can also observe directly personality characteristics that facilitate and interfere with its negotiation. Thus, for example, we do not need an analysis of color responses to make inferences about impulsivity and emotional lability with subjects who are so impulsive and emotionally labile that it is difficult for them to produce color responses.

Similarly, the extent to which examiners are deeply involved with young children as they establish rapport and help them cope with the test is not simply a factor that contaminates test results. It also affords examiners access to another domain of data bearing upon questions of how children manage the representational task and the demands of the Rorschach situation in general. Insofar as examiners act as "auxiliary egos," they are responding to problems children have with the task. By reading back from the assistance they provide intuitively, they can gain an appreciation of the problems of their subjects for which they are compensating.

In effect, then, observations of the test process—of children's behavior and of examiners' efforts to help them cope with that test situation—provide ways of dealing with many of the issues addressed through analyses of the formal determinants with older subjects.

DEVELOPMENTAL STAGES AND LEVELS OF FUNCTIONING

The use of determinant scores serves other important functions in Rorschach interpretation with older subjects. In contrast to analyses of content and of the testing relationship, which often appear impressionistic, this aspect of Rorschach interpretation is based on a body of established norms and can be done with a reasonable degree of reliability. Hence, the psychogram is a good starting point for the interpretive process because readings of it provide a normative framework within which other types of inferences can be grounded.

The concept of developmental stages in the mastery of the test can play an analogous role in the interpretation of preschool Rorschachs. For example, although there is no consensus in the Rorschach literature about norms related to particular determinants or, indeed, about whether and how scoring should be undertaken, authorities agree about the two broad trends upon which the concept of stages is based. First, regardless of the administrative techniques used, they offer similar descriptions of the ways in which children take the Rorschach and the problems they present for testing at each stage. Second, there is agreement about broad patterns of test performance across the stages. Children progress from perseverative and modified perseverative to confabulatory protocols that are in turn superseded in the early elementary school years by the more sophisticated and familiar protocols children produce as they are able to take the test in a standard way.

An immediate advantage of using these stages as a framework for clinical interpretation of young children's Rorschachs is that it enables us to put to practical use the controversies that bedevil efforts to apply traditional modes of analysis. We need no longer be troubled by questions of whether the Rorschach is or isn't the same test with preschoolers, but instead we can accept the obvious. Because these children are learning the instrument, it is the same in some respects and different in others. The particular pattern of similarities and differences becomes a basis for categorizing protocols.

Moreover, judgments of this kind are not subject to the criticisms about reliability that plague efforts to score individual responses. Pervasive and modified perseverative protocols are unmistakable and confabulatory ones are easily recognized. The very problems of test administration that make the scoring of responses difficult are defining characteristics of different stages. It is also easy to discern Stage III Rorschachs in which examiners obtain full records, are able to score them with relative ease, and have few qualms about subjecting them to standard modes of analysis.

In practice, difficulties in assigning Rorschach records to particular stages arise at two points. When youngsters appear to be at transitions between stages and substages, decisions may be harder to make. This is especially true as children move toward Stage III protocols. However, these records are rich enough and their scoring sufficiently dependable that when such concerns arise, Rorschachs can begin to be analyzed in traditional ways.

There are also cases in which there is a discrepancy between assignments of stages based on test protocols and on the handling of the test process. For example, a child may give modified perseverative responses but respond to inquiry in a relatively sophisticated manner or give confabulatory responses but be unable to handle the inquiry process. In these cases, categorization should rest on judgments about the quality of the protocol rather than the mode of taking the test. However, the discrepancy between the two can be a valuable source of clinical information. Problems in conducting inquiry with a child who is able to give a range of confabulatory responses might lead us to suspect that the youngster is action oriented and unreflective even by the modest standards used in making such judgments about four-year-olds.

Because stages reflect levels of functioning in cognitive and psychosocial spheres that are roughly correlated with age, they provide a natural starting point for analyzing preschool test performance. Imagine, for example, that we are asked to evaluate a boy who produces a florid confabulatory protocol and responds to efforts to obtain determinants in ways that lead the examiner to consider devoting the rest of his career as a diagnostician to administering MMPIs to adults. Knowing no other information except the child's age, we could begin making inferences of potential clinical significance. If the child is two and a half, we might entertain hypotheses that he is a bright, socially precocious little fellow; if he is three and a half, his test performance appears age appropriate; and, if he is six or seven, we might scrutinize the protocol carefully to decide whether cognitive limitations or psychological factors account for such a developmental delay.

Assignment of a level of functioning is, of course, only the beginning of the interpretative process with preschool Rorschachs. A three-year-old may produce a perseverative protocol because of intellectual limitations or because of a number of other reasons. At this point, qualitative analysis of test behavior and responses is needed to formulate and test hypotheses about the sources of the problem. Furthermore, even if children manage the test in age-appropriate ways, it is still important to examine the qualities that distinguish their particular ways of dealing with issues characteristic of their stage of development from those of their peers. Thus, in addition to offering a crude measure of development, categorizing how children handle the Rorschach according to stages or levels of functioning provides a springboard for more refined analyses of styles of dealing with the challenges inherent in the task as well as of factors responsible for delays and distortions in the developmental process.

EGO PSYCHOLOGY AND PRESCHOOL RORSCHACHS

Each of the perspectives that have been introduced to understand how children master the Rorschach can make a variety of contributions to such "refined analyses." For example, ego psychological theories have implications for many aspects of the ways in which young children handle the Rorschach.

As has been seen, from this perspective the Rorschach is an adaptive task whose negotiation requires a number of skills children acquire in the course of their early years. The most obvious of these skills are the cognitive ones required to grasp a reasonably complex task and devise strategies for accomplishing it. However, they also include abilities to tolerate anxiety around meeting with a stranger; accept tasks that involve subordinating one's own wishes to the expectations of another; sustain attention; inhibit impulses that interfere with working in a goal-directed manner; manage affects such as fear, anxiety, boredom, and frustration that can disrupt work; and cope with concerns about the adequacy of one's performance and others' judgments of it.

To illustrate how such a perspective can be applied, let us take the liberty of assuming that Colin (A. Schachtel, 1944), whose protocols (see Appendix) have been used to illustrate Stages I and II, is not simply a child selected from a nursery school class as a research subject, but rather one who has been referred for testing by teachers who would wish to know what we can tell them about his personality and about the kinds of problems they should anticipate in working with him. We can then consider the process by which we make inferences that enable us to answer such questions.

Although Colin's first protocol at the age of three consists of the repetition of a single response whose determinants are unclear and though no inquiry is possible (Chapter 6), we can nonetheless draw a number of conclusions about the boy that may be of use to his teachers. For example, reflecting on his handling of the examiner and test situation, we could offer some thoughts about his character and modes of relating to others. Clearly Colin does not appear shy or bashful. Rather he presents himself as an outgoing youngster who handles uncertainty in circumstances not too different from the ones he will no doubt face in preschool by trying to take charge and impose his will on those around him.

What is most striking about Colin's protocol, of course, is that it is perseverative. Since he produces this type of protocol somewhat late, we could consider the possibility that he is of below-average intelligence. However, there is reason to doubt this explanation. He displays a good deal of practical intelligence in getting the examiner to let him direct the testing as he wishes.

There are more plausible explanations of why Colin does not deal with the test more effectively. One is that he is distractible. Certainly he jumps hastily from one card to another and from one activity to another. Yet the chief problem with which the examiner must cope in testing him is not so much one of attention as impulsivity. From the beginning of the test to the end, Colin insists on doing what he wants at the moment he wants it. After rapidly producing a response on each of the first cards, he immediately orders the examiner on to the next; seeing a more interesting activity across the room after the fifth card, he dashes off to join it; when he later returns to the Rorschach, he begins dropping cards through a crack in table before the examiner can act to protect her equipment; and, as soon as the test is over, Colin runs off again. No doubt in the interest of completing the test the examiner seeks to channel his energy rather than confront or contain him. One suspects she senses he has little tolerance for being frustrated.

In her interpretation of this protocol, A. Schachtel (1944) suggests that he exhibits a striving for power and superiority and will respond defiantly when thwarted. Others might hesitate to make such inferences on the basis of his repetition of the mountain response on ten cards or his use of space and color. But we might accept them more readily if they were made on the basis of what the examiner experienced as she tried to test the boy. Lacking access to this information, we may be more cautious in our interpretation. Nonetheless, even on the basis of interactions around a brief perseverative protocol, we might well be comfortable suggesting to his teachers that Colin will be an engaging but also willful and action-prone addition to their preschool who is likely to require considerable help in learning to settle down.

Tested a year later at the age of four, Colin produced a confabulatory protocol, filled with images such as men and birds with "pinchers" (Chapter 7). The fact that he is now handling the test in an age-appropriate way indicates that his delay in moving beyond perseverative responses the preceding year was not due to significant intellectual limitations. Although his responses have changed, however, Colin's handling of the test only reinforces earlier impressions of his distractibility and impulsivity. At a time when other youngsters begin to participate in an inquiry process that requires some capacity for delay and reflection, Colin is having none of it. Instead, he simply races from one card to another. His difficulty modulating impulses is even more apparent in his treatment of the cards. For example, on Card VIII he responds, "That's a bang, bang, bang," and hits each color spot on the card.

In addition to noting these qualities again, our report might well comment on a number of others as well. For example, the content of some of Colin's responses (e.g., his preoccupation with things that pinch) and his haste to get away from disturbing responses suggest that we are now seeing a highly anxious little fellow. His behavior, his remarks in the course of testing, and the images he produces (e.g., on Card IX, "That's a pound, pound, pound, that pounds people's heads. A hammer.") point to particular problems managing aggressive thoughts and feelings. And, given such behavior as well as other raw expressions of emotion (e.g., he begins his responses to Cards IX and X by blurting out that he hates them), it requires little clinical sophistication to recognize that he is having difficulty modulating and controlling affect in general.

SOCIALIZATION AND PLAY

Consideration of the manner in which subjects and examiners negotiate the definition of the Rorschach task (the perspectives of socialization and play discussed in Chapter 11) can also make a variety of contributions to clinical assessment. For example, when the Rorschach was a more popular instrument with young children, some authorities sought to find measures of school readiness in it. Assuming that the task is an unfamiliar, anxiety-arousing one, Halpern (1960) argued that an ability to handle the first card might be such a predictor. Overcoming distress rapidly and responding effectively to the initial inkblot, she reasoned, is a mark of the kind of ego strength required to handle the demands of other new and unfamiliar situations like school. Halpern's position has received little support in the Rorschach literature, but there may be a simpler and more plausible way of using the Rorschach to predict the ability to negotiate the demands of a classroom—the capacity to take the Rorschach in its standard form. As has been seen, that capacity, like the skills required to handle the demands of the first grade, is the culmination of a socialization process through which children come to be able to appreciate the rules of a task prescribed by others and to accept and carry through with that task regardless of their own wishes and predilections.

The concept of socialization can make only modest contributions to the assessment of preschoolers, however, since their grasp of the rules of the examiner's game is limited and their interest in following those rules even more limited. The younger the children, the less their inclination to work and the greater their determination to use the Rorschach for play. Yet, insofar as children make the Rorschach into a form of play, its value as a clinical technique increases.

Three aspects of the manner in which preschoolers play with the Rorschach are of particular relevance. First, play has a social dimension. In Stage I, children engage in largely parallel play whereas in later stages they include others more and treat them in increasingly reciprocal ways. By considering whether and how they seek to engage examiners in their activities, we thus have a measure of social maturity. In addition, regardless of the level of that interaction, its quality—whether playmates are treated benignly or roughly, catered to or controlled, entertained or ignored—is obviously of clinical significance.

Second, the formal quality of the play is no less important. In Stage I, children are inclined to use the Rorschach card chiefly as a toy and are concerned with its manipulative rather than imaginative possibilities. The confabulation characteristic of the next stage may be seen as a measure of their capacity for dramatic play. Far from being a sign of problems, such behavior is encountered earliest in bright children from intact families (Rubin, Fein, and Vandenberg, 1983) and indicates they now have open to them the opportunities for creativity, problem solving, emotional expression, and sublimation afforded by fantasy play (Singer, 1973, 1991; Fein, 1987). In Stage III, the Rorschach is treated more as a rule-bound game, although, as children come to appreciate rules pertaining to the Rorschach card as a medium, their capacity to use the test as a form of creative expression increases, as does the examiner's ability to assess the capacity for self-discipline that enters into that expression.

Finally, the content of children's play is clearly of particular significance in the diagnostic enterprise. Most child psychiatrists and psychologists encourage young children to play in order to use the themes that emerge to learn how youngsters experience their worlds, their anxieties and conflicts, and their defenses and coping strategies. These opportunities are present when children treat the Rorschach card as a toy and even more when they use it as a launching pad for flights of fantasy.

When we consider Colin's testing at the age of three in these terms, a number of inferences can be made. For example, although his perseveration gives us little thematic content with which to work, his Rorschach "play" is immature. Like children a half year younger, he engages chiefly in parallel play with the examiner (see Chapter 11) and treats the card as a toy. In addition, Colin is a bossy playmate who insists on having things his own way. All the same, because the examiner is not acutely uncomfortable with him we probably would not suspect the presence of severe psychopathology. As Colin drops the last three cards through a crack in the table, she finds it amusing. At the least, he seems capable of having fun and sharing it.

The presence of extensive confabulation in his protocol a year later is reassuring since he is now engaging in imaginative play characteristic of his age. Yet there are a number of signs of strain. First, although some of Colin's responses are loose and silly, for the most part the content and quality of the play are more anxious and driven than that of the last testing. Second, much of his anxiety seems to center on themes of threats to bodily integrity and, if we are inclined toward psychoanalytic formulations, castration fears. For example, his responses to the first two cards are "a man with pinchers" and "a bird with pinchers"; his next response involves peacocks "pulling some out of it and they are smack"; and by the time he has completed his ten-response Rorschach, he gives one more pinching response and another of a "chopped off" and "broken down tree." Third, as has been noted, his responses (e.g., "That's a pound, pound, pound that pounds people's heads") and what the examiner describes as his "forceful, play fights" with the last three cards leave few doubts that aggression and its management are a significant issue in Colin's life. We might also advance hypotheses about whether Colin's anxiety about external threats stimulates his aggressive behavior or vice versa, although without direct experience of what he is like in the test process, it is hard to have much conviction about such speculations.

INTERPERSONAL ASPECTS OF THE RORSCHACH

In exploring interpersonal aspects of the process of administering tests such as the Rorschach (Chapter 12), note was taken of two aspects of the "patient–examiner relationship" that can be used in clinical assessments of young children.

First, even while playing the formal role of tester, examiners must work hard to establish and maintain a relationship with their subjects that allows them to administer and score the test. In Stage I, children seem to have little idea of what the Rorschach task is or how to accomplish it and little sense that the examiner does not perceive the cards as they do. Consequently, examiners must provide extensive help in negotiating the task and must be closely attuned to what children are experiencing to have any idea of where responses are or on what they are based. In contrast, in Stage III, children are able to handle the Rorschach without help and have a clear sense that examiners may not see what they are seeing and need some explanation of their responses. Thus, the formal relationship of child and examiner at each stage reflects different degrees of social maturity and may be used to make inferences about such issues as the subject's degree of egocentricity (Flavell, 1963), of differentiation of self and other (Werner and Kaplan, 1963), or simply of the need for adult assistance in negotiating adaptive tasks that bear some similarity to the Rorschach situation.

Second, the subjective definitions of relationships that emerge in the course of testing young children can make even greater contributions to clinical assessment. In the course of trying to establish rapport with particular children, examiners sense that they are being experienced by children in particular ways and feel a pull to enact reciprocal roles (Chapter 12). Working with an immature first grader, they find themselves acting like the parent of a three-year-old; testing a frightened, withdrawn youngster, they behave like a soothing, protective figure; or trying to deal with a provocative, oppositional youngster, regardless of their intentions, they find it hard not to feel like an exasperated authority figure or to keep themselves from entering into conflicts around compliance and defiance. With young children no less than with adults (Schafer 1954; E. Schachtel, 1966), such relationships provide valuable information about how subjects experience themselves and others and the nature of the transference–countertransference paradigms that are likely to emerge in their treatment.

We have little information about these aspects of Colin's testing. When A. Schachtel (1944) suggests that the content and repetition of responses in Colin's first protocol indicate that he is preoccupied with issues of power and superiority, Beck (1944a) questions whether this interpretation is anything more than speculation, pointing out that the data could easily be read in different ways. He is undoubtedly correct, yet we might lend greater credence to Anna Schachtel's views if they are based not simply on a reading of the content of Colin's responses, but even more on first hand impressions about what it is like to interact with him during the test. As has been seen, often it is only as psychologists reflect on the rationale for their actions and their feelings during the test process that they can find metaphors capturing the roles they and their subjects seemed to enact.

Although we are at a disadvantage in trying to interpret this aspect of Colin's Rorschach performance because of a lack of this kind of firsthand experience, we can make some educated guesses about those roles on the basis of his behavior and that of the examiner. For example, if we reflect on the description of Colin's testing when he was three, it is safe to conclude that he does not present himself as a shy, anxious waif seeking to elicit protective parenting. Nor is he unduly intimidated when confronted with the formidable presence of a Rorschach examiner. To the contrary, from the start of the testing to the end, he acts like an assertive little male trying to take charge of a relationship with a female examiner and impose his will in a vigorous way. He dictates where and when the test will take place, imperiously orders the examiner to go from one card to the next, and abandons her and the test in the middle when he feels like joining other children in more interesting play. When she is able to lure him back, he continues to do as he pleases, creating a game by dropping cards on the floor after the eighth card. At the same time, though headstrong, he does not seem unduly oppositional. Although we do not know what the examiner is experiencing, she does not appear inclined to enter into a battle of wills with him, but rather seems amused by his actions and shares in the fun. In a report, we probably would not go far wrong describing him as a willful, assertive little fellow who, while feisty, is not without charm with indulgent older women. In preschool, we might suggest, his teachers will probably find him likeable, but a handful, and discover the major task in working with him to be that of reining him in without quashing his initiative and self-confidence.

When seen at age four, Colin appears to play a role similar in many respects to that of a year earlier. Certainly he is eager to take charge and impose his will on the examiner. Now, however, we may suspect that he has more concerns around exhibiting and maintaining a masculine identity. As has been noted, he seems anxious about percepts of figures with "pinchers" and themes related to threats to bodily integrity. Both his fighting with the cards through the last part of the test and his imagery may be read as a four-year-old's display of macho aggression intended perhaps as much to impress a female audience as anything else. Certainly, again we might well advise his teachers that their work with him is likely to center on efforts to domesticate a little roughneck.

CONCLUSION

In effect, then, by beginning analyses of young children's Rorschachs with a consideration of their developmental stage or level of functioning and examining both responses and test behavior in terms of the theoretical perspectives used to account for the manner in which normal children master the test, we can address each of the issues covered by traditional approaches to Rorschach interpretation with older subjects. Though by no means focusing on only one aspect of the symbol situation, the ego-psychological perspective provides a way of analyzing how young subjects deal with the symbolic medium; consideration of preschool Rorschachs as a form of play affords, among other things, a way of examining the referents subjects chose in a manner similar to traditional Rorschach analyses of content; and analyses of interpersonal aspects of the response process are essentially identical to those undertaken with adults.

Nonetheless, in reflecting on this clinical-developmental approach to the interpretation of the preschool Rorschachs, most psychologists who employ the test with older subjects will be far more sensitive to differences in how the test is used than to similarities. Although they do not ignore test behavior with adults, many may feel that this interpretive strategy almost subordinates analyses of responses to behavioral observations. Whereas the quantitative analyses of scores around which traditional interpretations of the Rorschach are organized accentuate psychometric properties of the test, this way of assessing young children resembles a clinical interview in which interactions revolve around play with a specific toy. Moreover, even if they accept that the Rorschach can be used in this manner with children, few psychologists will believe that the test in this form is comparable in the data its generates and the role it plays in clinical assessment with the instrument used with older subjects.

Each of these points has merit, but all should be understood in the context of the nature of clinical assessment of young children in general. For example, most clinicians who evaluate children and adolescents utilizing batteries that include projective instruments would contend that their reports are based on an integration of behavioral observations, results of intelligence tests, and projective data. With few exceptions, they would also acknowledge relying far more heavily on observational data with young children than on projective material and giving increasing weight to information from projective tests as children get older. They do so, in part, because material gathered from projective tests of all kinds is relatively scant with young children and grows in richness and volume with age. Yet they also do so because young children are less inhibited and display problems more openly than older subjects whose more effective defenses allow them to cover their true thoughts and feelings beneath a veneer of social convention. Thus, in relying heavily on behavioral observations with preschool Rorschachs, examiners are not simply compensating for limitations in the instrument. Like miners, they are most inclined to dig where they find a vein of ore.

The similarities between the way the Rorschach is used with preschoolers and clinical interviews is also a result of what young children are like. As a Wernerian conception of the experience of the Rorschach task makes clear (see Chapter 13), the ability to recognize that "the Rorschach" is a distinct activity governed by its own set of rules is the culmination of an extended developmental process. In the first stage of that process, children do not differentiate the test from their own wishes or their interactions with the examiner. Only gradually are they able to treat it differently from a play therapy session with a particular toy. Hence, to interpret their handling of the test in ways that are similar to those used in clinical interviews is not a violation of the spirit of the test but a recognition of a fact of life and a readiness to act accordingly.

Similarly, although it may be conceded that what can be learned from preschool Rorschachs rarely comes close to matching the often unique and distinctive insights that can be obtained from adult Rorschachs, this comparison is not a critical one for clinicians. A better measure is how this use of the Rorschach compares with other projective tests for children. Judged by these standards, preschool Rorschachs do not fare badly.

It is not easy to obtain projective data from children, and the material derived from all such tests is relatively crude and limited when compared with that obtained from older subjects. For example, the human figure drawings of three-year-olds, which often consist of little more than a poorly executed circle and a few marks to denote facial features, are hardly as revealing as drawings of seven- or ten-year-olds. The information that can be garnered from tasks involving projective stories such as the CAT is also limited by young children's levels of cognitive development. For example, a subtest at the three-and-a-half-year level on the Stanford–Binet Intelligence Scale Form LM asks subjects to "tell about" a picture of a boy and girl approaching a house with a birthday cake in the window. Representative examples of passing answers include: "Look—girl—clean," "Those are candles—that's a window—that's a little boy," and "Boy and girl taking a walk" (Terman and Merrill, 1960, p. 134). Needless to say, this level of complexity of characterization and narrative does not provide clinicians with the amount or kind of information they will obtain from projective stories of children several years older. Hence, though the Rorschach is a far more limited instrument with preschoolers than with older subjects, it is not more so than any other projective test. Given the paucity of projective data typically available on young children, some clinicians may find it a worthwhile addition to their batteries.

Even if the Rorschach yields some clinical information with preschoolers and a suitable mode of interpretation can be advanced, however, a critical question remains. Does the test produce enough data of a kind unavailable from other sources that a strong case can be made for making it a regular part of test batteries with young children?

All but the most partisan advocates of the test are likely to conclude: "Probably not." With Colin, for example, we were able to use the test to generate inferences about a variety of aspects of his personality, yet most would have come from other sources had the Rorschach not been administered. Little that was gleaned about his impulsivity, assertiveness, concerns about aggression, or ways of relating to others would have been missed in a good clinical interview or other opportunities to observe his behavior. Issues such as those regarding his cognitive development could be addressed better by other tests. Hence, although the Rorschach can be used with preschoolers, it is hardly an indispensable diagnostic tool.

The best arguments that can be mustered on its behalf are modest ones. It takes only a few minutes to administer; many children find it diverting; it can satisfy the curiosity of examiners and give them a better perspective on an instrument they use with older children; and, perhaps in some cases, it may produce diagnostic information that may not come from other sources. These reasons cannot be said to be compelling. All the same, there are a good many worse ways for examiners and children to spend a few minutes of their time together.

The Rorschach and
Severely Disturbed
Children

Although the Rorschach can begin to be used in its standard form with most children in the early elementary school years, severely disturbed youngsters present many of the same problems in administering the test encountered with preschoolers (Leichtman and Nathan, 1983; Leichtman, 1988). Their protocols bear some resemblance to those of young children as well. This chapter will explore what can be learned about the Rorschach and its clinical applications from developmental interpretations of the records of four deeply troubled children between the ages of five and eight.

BILL

As the very label suggests, children who manifest pervasive developmental disorders display the most profound form of early psychopathology. Bill was one such child. A thin, pale boy whose deep-set eyes and vacant expression gave him a peculiar and unsettling appearance, he exhibited such severe delays in cognitive, social, and emotional development that, when referred for evaluations in preschool and kindergarten, he had taken little notice of the examiners or their tests.

When seen again at the age of six, Bill began in a similar fashion. He wandered around the office more cognizant of the furnishings than of the man he was with, and he responded to the first tests like an automaton. Encouraged to do a drawing, he moved the pencil back and forth mechanically over the same area without looking at what he was doing. He did some items on intelligence tests, but acted as though in a fog. The examiner's questions went into the mist and Bill's answers floated out, but how much the boy understood of the tasks at any given time was unclear. Over a number of brief sessions, periods in which Bill was in and out of contact became more differentiated as the examiner provided him with candy and had a stuffed animal the boy liked ask some test questions. Yet even when Bill was most engaged, social interaction was limited. For the most part, he acted as if his companion were a distant, impersonal, vaguely sensed inquisitor.

To the examiner's surprise, on the third day of the evaluation, Bill was more intrigued by the Rorschach than he had been by other tests. Consequently, by remaining sensitive to fluctuations in Bill's attention and involvement with the task, presenting cards only when the boy seemed ready to look at them, and plying him with M & Ms when he was not, the examiner was able to elicit responses to all ten cards. Inquiry was conducted after each of the first several cards, although the examiner asked questions only when he felt he might get an answer and would not threaten Bill's tenuous engagement with the task. Occasionally, Bill outlined or pointed to his percepts, but typically in so confused or confusing a manner that the location or even whether Bill knew the location was unclear. At times, the examiner felt he had a sense of the determinants of Bill's percepts because of the way the boy looked at or pointed to the card, but such intuitions hardly seemed a proper basis for scoring the protocol.

Protocol 1: Bill (Age 6 : 2)		
Card	Free Association	Inquiry
I	Bird	[When handed the first card, Bill gives this one-word response quickly and then loses interest. Asked where the bird is, he points in a way that seems to indicate the whole blot, but the examiner cannot be sure. When asked about the determinants, Bill looks away distractedly. He nods when asked if it was a bird.]

	Protocol 1: Bill (Age 6 : 2) *(continued)*	
Card	Free Association	Inquiry
II	A cat, duck	[The examiner cannot clarify whether this is two responses or whether Bill sees one animal which he decides is a duck. Again Bill points vaguely when asked about the location, but this time the examiner has little idea where the percept is. Bill does point to the top red detail when asked about the duck's head. He acts as if questions about the wings have no meaning. He again looks away distractedly when asked about the cat.]
III	Chicken	[Bill indicates that the card is a chicken and seems to point to the detail that resembles a chicken's head. He is unresponsive to further questions about location and determinants, and retreats into himself until the next card is brought out.]
IV	A boy	[Bill points in a way that probably designates the whole figure, but is unresponsive to questions about his percept. The examiner decides to discontinue regular questions about responses, because they tax Bill's limited commitment to the test.]
V	A butterfly	[Probably the whole figure.]
VI	A butterfly coaster	[The examiner is not sure he hears this response correctly. Asked to repeat it, Bill says, ''a fly.'' When asked about a ''butterfly coaster,'' he looks away.]
VII	A rabbit	[Probably a side detail, but Bill is unresponsive to questions about location.]
VIII	Dog	[Probably the popular side detail. Bill is now far more interested in breaking M&Ms into small pieces and playing with them than in anything the examiner is doing.]

Protocol 1: Bill (Age 6 : 2) *(continued)*		
Card	Free Association	Inquiry
IX	[Claps hands excitedly] Tree	[Bill is again vague about the location. The examiner believes that he is probably using the green area.]
X	Clouds, sky clouds	[Bill points haphazardly at the blot. The examiner thinks he may be designating the blue area, but is not sure.]

As is true with most children with pervasive developmental disorders, the Rorschach is hardly needed to diagnose Bill's condition. In responding to the test at all, Bill does better than many of these children, whose pathology is clear from the very problems that make testing so difficult. Nonetheless, we can still ask what can be made of Bill's Rorschach from a developmental standpoint.

Bill's use of the Rorschach medium is more advanced than we might anticipate. Having moved beyond the perseverative treatment of the blots characteristic of Stage I, he produces distinct responses to each card. Yet his handling of the symbolic medium is not more sophisticated than that of an early Stage II child. When the examiner believes he has a sense of the manner in which Bill forms representations, the approach is a DW one. For example, Card III appears to be a chicken because of one feature, the head. Questions about other details seem meaningless.

In other respects, Bill approaches the task in a more primitive manner. Like a two-year-old, for example, he is unable to participate in the inquiry process in any meaningful way. Often the examiner has no idea of the determinants of his responses or even if there are any. At some times, he feels Bill is simply naming pictures; at others, it is not clear that the response is determined by any features of the blot. Thus, Bill's mode of handling the task is, at best, that of the typical three- or three-and-a-half-year-old.

Although the content of all except perhaps one of Bill's responses is unexceptional, two aspects of his choice of referents are significant. First, as noted, he advances ten distinct responses indicating that he has the cognitive capacity to produce Stage II protocols. Second, in contrast to most such protocols, there is a striking absence of imaginative elaboration in his responses. The only response that even hints at a fantasy life is the "butterfly coaster" on Card VI, but the examiner is uncertain whether the fantasy is Bill's or his own. The play in which Bill does indulge in the testing is the sensorimotor manipulation characteristic of Stage I.

Though he does not make the card into a toy, he spends his time breaking up his candy and playing with the pieces. There is little indication that Bill has much capacity for the kind of symbolic play and imaginative activity so important to preschoolers' adaptation to their worlds.

From a diagnostic standpoint, the critical features of Bill's Rorschach are interpersonal. His performance along this dimension is far more primitive than the cognitive abilities he displays in handling the symbolic vehicle and referent. For Bill, self and other are relatively undifferentiated in his testing. He pays little attention to the examiner. At most, the man is not a distinct figure, but rather a periodic intrusion to be accommodated or warded off when too noxious. In contrast to his responses themselves, which are handled in a Stage II manner, Bill's treatment of the inquiry is more like that of a Stage I child. He feels little need to explain his responses to another and, as a consequence, the examiner can only make educated guesses about the location and basis for Bill's responses.

On the examiner's part, there is also a relative lack of differentiation in the relationship. He spends much of the test trying to read Bill's mood and he paces the evaluation in a manner intended to catch Bill at the right time to get a response. The examiner believes he probably knows the location and determinants of some of Bill's percepts because of an intuitive sense of how the boy treats the cards. Yet even advocates of a loose approach to Rorschach administration might well suggest that such scores reveal more about what the examiner is reading into Bill's responses than how the boy arrived at them. Regardless of whether scores of this kind are taken as indications of the examiner's sensitivity to the child or a mistaken attribution of the examiner's own ideas, they point to a relationship in which self and other are not distinct.

Qualitative aspects of the test relationship are noteworthy as well. Even at his best, Bill is unable to sustain anything remotely resembling an ordinary human interaction with a concerned adult who goes to extraordinary lengths to make contact with him. Like a parent of an infant, the examiner constantly tries to sense Bill's mood, seeks ways of engaging him without pressing the interaction too far lest the boy withdraw, and attributes meaning to the youngster's behavior in an effort to relate to him. Doing so, he finds it possible to interact with Bill around the test task for periods of time, but always with a sense of the child's fundamental "otherness." Searching for metaphors to capture their relationship, the examiner initially suggests that Bill behaves like an automaton, or he compares interacting with him to trying to make contact with a shadowy figure in a fog. Even when more comfortable, Bill at best tolerates only superficial exchanges around mechanical aspects of the Rorschach, and whenever these are pressed too far, he experiences them as an intrusion and withdraws. This lack of true, reciprocal social interaction in the course of the test strongly suggests that for Bill something has gone terribly wrong with the most fundamental aspects of human attachment.

In summary, were the Rorschach the only test given, we might note that Bill's protocol has many of the characteristics of the Stage II Rorschachs of children half his age, suggesting marked developmental delay; that the delay in cognitive development is less pronounced than that in the social sphere; and that the fundamental problems Bill exhibits are profound deficits around the formation of attachments and the capacity to enter into reciprocal social relationships of any but the most primitive kind. In making recommendations, we might stress that it is possible to interact with Bill in more extensive and predictable ways than suggested by earlier reports describing him as untestable, but that doing so requires remaining attuned to moods and interests as if he were an infant, striking a balance between engaging him, on one hand, and avoiding intrusiveness and allowing him to withdraw as needed, on the other. Obviously, the treatment process with Bill is likely to be a long one in which progress will be slow and parents and treaters will be well advised to set modest expectations for themselves and Bill.

PAUL

When referred for testing at the age of five and a half, Paul exhibited not only marked delays in all areas of development, but also oddities of thought and behavior that led to questions of whether he manifested childhood schizophrenia. Many of these problems were apparent to the examiner the moment she met the child. In contrast to Bill, who wished to be left alone, Paul craved attention. A wild-eyed, desperately anxious child, he glaumed onto her when introduced in the waiting room as if he was being reunited with a lost parent. Whereas Bill would wander around the office quietly and occupy himself with solitary activity, unless restrained Paul whirled about like a tornado, leaving toys and papers strewn in his wake. As she worked with Paul, the examiner learned to provide a mixture of firmness, support, and gentleness that enabled him to stay with the tests if sessions were kept relatively brief. Although the examiner administered the Rorschach in the same manner that had been effective with other instruments, she found that the test was particularly difficult for Paul and her. In reflecting on the process, she was struck by how much she had used her tone of voice, posture, expression, and pacing of the test to help Paul focus on the task and, even more, contain anxiety that threatened to escalate into panic.

Protocol 2: Paul (Age 5 : 6)		
Card	Free Association	Inquiry
I	Two fingerprints. I'm fingerprinting the walls. . . . My dad's office, the street buckled and he had to park his car.	[Asked the location of the first response, Paul points around the blot. He seems to settle on an upper detail, but the location is unclear. He is unable to respond to questions about why the card looks like fingerprints or whether his remarks about his father's office are a response to the blot or extraneous information he wishes to share with the examiner for some reason.]
II	Paint prints from these paints. There's an overcast place in the north. . . .	[Paul again has difficulty specifying the location of his image and the examiner ceases pressing the matter after trying twice. She believes it is a whole response. When asked why the card looks like ''paint prints,'' Paul replies only, ''Paint.'']
III	Paint prints, too . . . overcoat. . . . Do you want to chop into the stone walls and fall into the . . . on the grass. [Asked about what he is thinking, Paul briefly settles down, but then goes on.] Fingerprints, daddy tire prints, trucks full of pollution, old war tanks, old-fashioned trucks.	[The examiner helps Paul settle down again. Convinced that questioning him about responses yields little and makes him anxious and loose, she decides to discontinue inquiry on subsequent cards.]
IV	Paint prints, blue, black paint prints.	

Protocol 2: Paul (Age 5 : 6)*(continued)*		
Card	Free Association	Inquiry
V	Some finger paints, categories would work.	[Trying to help Paul move beyond perseveration and model an alternative way of responding to the cards, the examiner asks, "Could it be a bird?" Paul replies, "Bird, too."]
VI	Bird, too.	
VII	Birds, too. . . . That's a sad story. . . . Daddy put the blue paint up in the trash.	
VIII	A tree. Two of them. I'm going to think . . . as trees get dead ax,a chain saw, and crowbar people.	[Points to the upper, center detail.]
IX	Two monkeys. There's one lost in the tree branch. That's a mad one.	
X	Finger paints, finger paints I put on the ceiling.	

Paul produces the kind of modified perseverative record encountered in normal children half his age. His response to the first inkblot is repeated on the next four. When the examiner introduces a new theme, he perseverates it for several cards, though the pull of his initial response can be seen on Cards VII and X. However, he is able to introduce a few new responses on the last cards. His Rorschach is thus that of a child beginning to move beyond Stage I.

Two other aspects of his handling of the test are characteristic of this period. First, although we can only speculate on the origins of his initial response, it is hard not to suspect that it is based less on effort to use the medium to represent an idea than on crude perceptual similarity. The card does in fact look like a mess, like fingerprints or finger paints on a wall. Second, as with children in Stage I, there is little to be gained from inquiring into responses because Paul is unable to reflect on them or offer coherent answers to the examiner's questions. When she tries to move him away from perseverative responses on Card V, he is so suggestible he merely repeats her response for a while.

Paul's use of the medium is significant in another respect as well. As those who interpret the test in traditional ways would observe, he seems hypersensitive to color and shading. Hypotheses about impulsivity and affective lability based on these characteristics would no doubt gain immediate assent from the examiner, who is preoccupied with trying to help Paul contain his anxiety, volatile emotions, and poorly modulated behavior throughout the evaluation.

The contents of Paul's responses are noteworthy in a number of respects. As is characteristic of children in this stage, the range of his responses is limited. However, in contrast to most young children, Paul's perseveration is around disturbing, idiosyncratic themes, suggesting that the overvalent nature of these ideas may be more responsible for the primitive structure of his Rorschach than cognitive limitations. In fact, the confabulatory activity characteristic of Stage II protocols is apparent throughout his protocol. His fervid imagination shapes almost every response from the first ones of fingerprinting walls to the last one of mad monkeys lost in trees or finger paints on ceilings. The problem for Paul is that such fantasies are so anxiety-laden they can rarely be integrated into representations. Instead they lead to a train of personal, frightening associations that pull him away from the test task altogether. For example, it is hard to determine whether Paul's second response to Card I, the street buckling near his father's office, is a genuine representation (perhaps the card resembles broken asphalt) or whether it is an extraneous idea occurring to a child who is no longer attending to the card at all. The latter appears to be the case on Card III when Paul jumps from thoughts of fingerprints to daddy tire prints, trucks full of pollution, old war tanks, and old-fashioned trucks. On many responses he is simply too anxious to integrate "perceptual" and "associative" processes in a representational act.

Although there are formal similarities between the manner in which Paul handles the Rorschach and that of late Stage I and early Stage II preschoolers, he exhibits disturbances in thinking not encountered in normal children. His first response is probably a contamination, a condensation of two ideas that are superimposed upon one another because he cannot keep them distinct. He talks about fingerprints, an idea one suspects that arouses upsetting memories of having been responsible for messing up walls at home. Simultaneously, he seems to be thinking about finger paints, an idea linked to fingerprints by the sound, by the nature of the activity (making a mess), and by fears that an urge to make messes will get out of control. Quite possibly it is the arousal of such wishes that triggers the anxiety and subsequent loose associations that interfere with his ability to stay with the representational task through his early responses. In addition, these loose associations, his disorganized thinking, his odd uses of language (e.g., "dead ax" "crow bar people"), the intrusion of disturbing memories (e.g., streets buckling), and his peculiar aggressive fantasies all point to the presence of a thought disorder.

Paul's relationship with the examiner in the course of the testing also exhibits an undifferentiated quality characteristic of the earliest stage in handling the test. When he first meets her, Paul acts as if she is a familiar caretaker, and the examiner falls naturally into this role. As with younger children, she functions as an "auxiliary ego," making extraordinary efforts to help him focus on test tasks, control his impulsivity, and manage his anxiety and disorganization.

On her part, the examiner experiences an unusual sense of closeness to Paul, a capacity to share his thoughts, that would be difficult to convey to a skeptic. When Paul speaks of fingerprints, fingerprinting walls, and the street buckling by his father's office on the first card, she has an intuitive sense of what he is conveying. Although the thoughts come so rapidly they are difficult to put into words, she believes he begins by saying that the card looks like fingerprints because it is messy, that this reminds him of dirtying walls at home, and that this thought, in turn, leads to others about something messy and, perhaps, destructive associated with him. Later, similar thoughts of messing lead to dysphoric, foreboding associations (an overcast place in the north) and destructive ones (chopping into stone walls, pollution, old war tanks, etc.). Resonating with such experiences, the examiner feels the intensity of Paul's anxiety, the fluidity of his thinking, his fears about being unable to control his actions, and not only his preoccupation with aggression getting out of hand, but also his uncertainty about whether he is its source or victim. She has a direct sense of what it is like to live in a world in which thoughts about messing and losing control meld with actions (e.g., unless she exerts firm control of Paul, the office can become a disaster area). While interactions of this kind have some formal characteristics in common with those encountered with young preschoolers, they also leave the examiner with a conviction that she has been working with a profoundly disturbed little boy who experiences himself as a destructive, yet vulnerable little being in a dangerous, gloomy, chaotic world.

In sum, Paul's Rorschach reveals serious pathology. It is similar in formal respects to children half his age. Equally important, in contrast to those of preschoolers, the disturbances in formal thought processes apparent in his handling of responses, the presence of primary-process thinking and peculiar fantasies in the content of his responses, and the nature of his interaction with the examiner all point to early manifestations of a schizophrenic process. It is also clear that parents, caretakers, and treaters will need to work with Paul in a very different manner than with Bill. Because Bill cannot tolerate closeness with others, the central issues in treatment are those of finding ways of making contact with him without being experienced as a noxious, intrusive force. Paul craves an almost symbiotic relationship. Treatment recommendations might well stress the intimate engagement he requires, his lack of boundaries, and his need for containment and soothing to help him cope with the flood of disorganizing thoughts and uncontrolled urges that threaten to sweep him away.

SARAH

Sarah was referred for testing at the age of seven and a half because of questions about whether she exhibited a psychotic process. A tall, awkward youngster, she had many odd mannerisms such as flapping her arms as she walked. In spite of her size and age, the examiner responded to her as if she were a needy, dependent four-year-old. Like Paul, for example, she formed an immediate intense relationship and required constant reassurance to contain her anxiety. Trying hard to be polite, Sarah exhibited better control over her behavior than Paul, yet that control was tenuous. She felt compelled to remind the examiner repeatedly how well she was behaving and that she was not like other children who probably tore his office up.

On the first day of the evaluation, she tried to maintain her concentration on intelligence tests, but often lost track of her thoughts and forgot the problem on which she was working. She also occasionally advanced odd ideas, but did not give unambiguous evidence of a thought disorder.

When given the Rorschach the next day, Sarah was not only anxious, but excited. She seemed to be overstimulated by the test and raced through each response. The examiner tried to slow her down and calm her, but with little success. Sarah had particular difficulty with the inquiry process, perhaps because it required her to stop and think about her ideas. When asked the location of percepts, she hastily pointed around the card as if each response was a whole. The examiner often believed that she was responding to only a part of the blot, but did not pursue the matter because of her anxiety and low tolerance of

Protocol 3: Sarah (Age 7 : 4)*

Card	Free Association	Inquiry	Scoring
I	Dog	The whole thing. Cause it's standing up. It's not a dog when it stands down. (What about it looks like a dog?) . . . turns over a turtle cause it just does. Ears. (Ears?) Legs. Got one leg. Doesn't have legs. Those are squares. I'm done. [Because even this level of questioning produces anxiety and loose thinking, the examiner decides to be more cautious in pursuing questions on subsequent responses.]	Wo F– A 1.0 ALOG, DR$_2$ (CONFAB–Rapaport)
II	Birds, birds with legs. [Points all over the card]	(Looks like?) Cause it just does. That's a round circle in it. I'm not done yet. A butterfly. (Looks like?) Butterflies don't sting you. Butterflies just fly. (?) Yep, it's flying.	Wo F– A 4.5 Wo FM^{a}o A 4.5 DR$_1$
III	Square [referring to the card]. An owl.	(Looks like?) It's got eyes and a tail, but the tail's tore off. Its got a ribbon and the eyes and arms and a monster. [Getting loose and anxious.]	Wo F– A 5.5 INCOM, MOR, CONTAM(?)

*Although Rapaport's procedures were used in testing Sarah and the other children discussed in this chapter, the protocols are scored according to Exner's Comprehensive System, which is most familiar to readers. Rapaport's confabulation scores for responses in which there are extensive fantasy elaborations are also included because they have no suitable counterpart in the Comprehensive System, as are his scores for the arbitrary use of color that Exner codes as incongruous combinations. The meaning of both sets of scores will be examined in the chapter that follows. Needless to say, Sarah's agitation and difficulty dealing with questions about her responses make many scoring decisions, especially those related to thought disorder issues, little more than educated guesses.

Card	Response	Inquiry	Scoring
V	What does owls do? I'll show you in . . . a monster bird? Ooowee Ooowee, Ooowee. . . . That's a monster bird. I'm done. I think it's an owl and owls do this. [Flaps her arms about.]	(Looks like?) Because it's going . . . it's got ears, feet, and a scary body. (Scary?) Cause he's got scary eyes. Square. [Counts the cards.] He's just scary. I'm done now.	Wo Fo (H) P 2.0 (CONFAB—Rapaport)
IV	A monster.		Wo Fo A P 1.0
V	Let me take this one. Here he is! He's a bat! There he is. There.	(Looks like?) Cause it's got bat wings and stuff. Bats fly. Bats got legs, too. It's a butterfly. But don't do nothing but fly. Butterflies. Flies go zzzz. Bumble bees go zzzz. What happens if you get stung? What does sting start with? An S. (What about it looks like a butterfly?) Cause it flies. I don't got nothing else to say.	Wo Fo A P 1.0 DR$_2$
VI	I can't tell what it is. . . . Square. [Turns card] It's a sheriff. He's got arms, legs, feet. A waggy [dog] sheriff and this and this. [Points around the card as if locating the percept]	(Looks like?) Cause it just is. Gots arms. I'm not done yet. It looks like . . . I'm done, I'm done.	Wo F— (A) 2.5 DV$_2$ CONTAM(?)

Protocol 3: Sarah (Age 7 : 4) (continued)

Card	Free Association	Inquiry	Scoring
VII	It's bunnies and a butterfly. It's got an ear and a tail. And that's a tail and that's a bunny and that's a butterfly. Square. [Squeals]		Do Fo (2) A
			Do Fo A
VIII	Where's that at? Square. [Turns card] A top. Got toys on it. Got toys on it. [Appears to mean that the top has toys on it]	(Looks like?) How could it be a top? Cause I think it is!! Dinosaurs, pigs, blue, wings on it. Pigs. [Loose, starting to get upset]	Wo FC− Hh 4.5 CONTAM, DR$_2$
IX	It's an elephant.	(Looks like?) The elephant got green arms and pink ears, pink eyes. It's got orange for . . . there. There, there, those orange things are there. I'm done with it.	Wo FCu A 5.5 INCOM$_1$ (FCarb−Rapaport)
X	How many more will there be? It's a pineapple. Wings. It's got green eyes and green wings.	[Appears to indicate that there is a single image, a pineapple with eyes and wings, but Sarah is so anxious and stirred up, and the examiner does not pursue further inquiry.]	D+ FC− Fd, Ad 4.0 INCOM$_2$

frustration. Instead he concentrated on trying to obtain determinants. At times, Sarah responded to these questions by noting a detail of the figure that justified her percept. More often she blurted out a string of loose associations. After the test, she confided that her mind does not work well and that a voice tells her to do "bad things" or not to listen to other people because "they are bad."

Although the looseness of Sarah's thinking is reminiscent of Paul's, she is almost two years older and responds to the test in a more advanced, though still far from age appropriate, manner. Her Rorschach most resembles the later confabulatory protocols of four- to four-and-a-half-year-olds.

This similarity can be seen in her handling of the medium. At times she seems to use a DW approach to forming percepts, in which one detail is sufficient to create a representation, and at other times she appears to rely on form (e.g., the bat on Card V and the elephant on Card IX). For the most part, however, her responses are based on a juxtaposition of a couple of details with little regard for how they fit together. Card I is a dog because of the ears and legs even if the design as a whole bears little resemblance to a dog. The difficulty she has in outlining her percepts for the examiner may well stem from the fact that form is not important to her. Several parts are sufficient to justify a representation irrespective of the manner in which they are combined.

She deals with the inquiry in a manner characteristic of children in Stage II. Questions elicit information about percepts, but not in a consistent way. At times, the examiner is able to learn about the determinants of her representations; at others, he simply gets a string of loose associations. Rarely does one have a sense that Sarah is trying to explain the basis for her images.

What is perhaps most striking in her protocol is the prominence of confabulatory activity. Sarah's thinking is pervaded by fantasies that seem to run wild. To begin to consider the dog on Card I is to get caught up with ideas of dogs overturning turtles. The owl on Card III becomes a monster bird with a ribbon. Even in describing the bat on Card V, she quickly becomes lost in word play and disturbing ideas. As is characteristic of this stage of confabulation and confabulatory combinations, concerns about reality play little role in regulating the choice of percepts. If a card looks like a pineapple and one sees wings, it is a pineapple with wings.

There is also little coordination of how the medium is used and the ideas represented. At times the medium dominates, as with her incongruous combinations. At other times associations are primary, as when she gets caught up with a string of loose associations. Seldom are the two aspects of representation integrated effectively.

Although the confabulatory activity that is so prominent in Sarah's Rorschach is similar to that of normal preschoolers in some respects, it is very different in others. Examiners usually experience the confabulations of young children as what they are, a form of play that, however inconvenient from the standpoint of obtaining a sensible test record, suggests that the children are trying to have fun. Little in Sarah's protocol seems playful. From the beginning of the test until the end, her responses are driven by intense anxiety and the fantasies that pervade those responses (e.g., those of overturned turtles on Card I, butterflies that might sting on Card II, monster birds and torn-off tails on Card III, scary monsters on Card IV, and so forth) are almost invariably frightening and strange. Equally important, even when throwing themselves into uninhibited play with words and ideas, normal preschoolers can reassert control over their thoughts and actions. Their thoughts race as if they are excitedly riding a bike down a hill, but they can still steer. Sarah is overwhelmed. She is almost helpless as her thoughts careen down a steep slope into dangerous terrain. Sarah's protocol contains a number of clear signs of thought disorder that can be understood as manifestations of an anxiety-driven confabulatory process running amok.

The most obvious of these signs are her loose associations. For example, in the inquiry on Card V as she tries to explain why the blot looks like a bat, she shifts gears abruptly and adds: "It's a butterfly. But don't got nothing but fly. Butterflies. Flies go zzzz. Bumblebees go zzzz. What happens if you get stung? What does sting start with. An S." There are perseverations of content (e.g., the recurrent idea of shapes) that do not reflect the cognitive limitations underlying preschoolers' repetitions of themes, but rather intrusive, often irrelevant ideas that interfere with her capacity to respond flexibly to each new blot. There is, of course, her readiness to read frightening and, at times, peculiar fantasies into each card. And there is evidence of contaminatory thinking in which ideas fuse and contradictory images are simultaneously ascribed to the same areas of the blot (e.g., monster birds and waggy [dog] sheriffs).

One other feature of Sarah's protocol that would be labeled a sign of thought disorder in standard scoring systems is also worth noting. On the inquiry to her first card, Sarah appears to explain her response by noting that it is a dog " 'cause it's standing up. It's not a dog when it stands down." Rapaport et al. (1946) and Exner (1986) would describe this answer as an example of autistic logic. It is certainly illogical when viewed from an adult standpoint that assumes Sarah is making an effort to justify her percept. From a developmental standpoint, however, her response probably does not reflect a disturbance in logic. Little in the inquiry process throughout the testing suggests that Sarah is, in fact, trying to explain her images. Rather, she seems to find answering questions anxiety arousing and reacts with loose associations and desperate play to avoid the task. In this respect her answer resembles the silly language and confabulatory behavior characteristic of Stage II Rorschachs. What is pathological is her problem in undertaking the explanatory process in a manner characteristic of seven-year-olds.

As with Bill and Paul, Sarah's relationship with the examiner and what can be inferred about her experience of self and other during the test can make significant contributions to diagnosis as well. Like Paul, Sarah cannot handle the test situation in an autonomous way. For her to manage the Rorschach even in the erratic manner she does, the examiner must remain sensitive to her psychological states and work constantly to help her focus on the task, manage her vulnerability to overstimulation, control her anxiety, and regulate her activity level. Sarah does exhibit somewhat more differentiation from the examiner than Paul in that she is beginning to be able to participate in the inquiry process, yet the examiner must still be closely attuned to her moods and ideas to understand how she forms representations. She is also prone to sharp regressions, as with her reaction to the inquiry on Card V when she ceases engaging in a social interaction and retreats into a chaotic world of her own.

With Sarah, too, there is a relative lack of differentiation on the examiner's part. As the child reels off strings of loose, idiosyncratic associations, he often feels he understands some of what she is trying to convey (e.g., the struggle between being drawn to frightening ideas and desperately trying to escape them that she plays out on the inquiry on Card V). If correct, this understanding is based on a capacity to share Sarah's experience of herself and her world much as one would with a young child; if the examiner is mistaken in the belief that he senses what Sarah is experiencing, if he is simply attributing his own feelings and ideas to her, the situation is still a relatively undifferentiated one, albeit of a different kind.

From a clinical standpoint, the nature of the examiner's relationship with Sarah may well make the greatest contributions to planning treatment. Never during the testing does he have a sense that he is working with a seven-year-old. In order to do the Rorschach and, indeed, any tests with Sarah, the examiner acts as if he is working with a needy, easily overstimulated, intensely anxious child who struggles with fears of dangers in her environment and concerns about her mind going out of control. What she needs from him is no doubt what she requires from caretakers and treaters generally. In carrying out specific behavioral, psychopharmacological, and psychological programs addressing aspects of her pathology, those working with her must be able to respond to her as though she were a preschooler who needs constant attention, calming, and help from sensitive parents in regulating her affects and actions.

JAY

Jay was referred for testing at the age of six and a half because of hyperactivity, uncontrollable tantrums at home, and aggressive outbursts and unmanageable behavior at school. According to his parents, he was always on the go and always getting into trouble. He also seemed driven to violate any rules set for him. When they placed limits on his activities, he would throw or break objects, punch, kick, or spit. His teachers, too, were at a loss about how to handle him. Reasoning, persuasion, limit-setting, time-outs, and behavioral programs had little effect on him in class. On the playground, with less supervision, he was worse. Within a few months of the start of the semester, Jay's school file bulged with reports of his running into other children, pushing them over, and trying to choke them. Not surprisingly, he was universally disliked by peers. Although Jay had been diagnosed as manifesting an Attention Deficit–Hyperactivity Disorder and treated with Ritalin, his parents now sought further evaluation because they were convinced that he had more serious problems.

When Jay came for testing, there was little about him that suggested a hellion. A child of average height and build, he looked like a rather ordinary first grader. He began the first session cautiously, trying to control his behavior and be ingratiating. However, there was soon abundant evidence of his hyperactivity and distractibility. Finding it hard to remain in one place, he answered questions on verbal intelligence scales while pacing the room. If the examiner did not intervene, he would roam around the room, crawl on the floor, and open drawers or closets. Keeping him seated posed problems of its own. At one point, he got his neck stuck between the supports of a chair with which he was playing.

The most striking aspect of Jay's test behavior was not his activity level or impulsivity, but rather his relationship with the examiner. As Jay became comfortable, he began acting like a stubborn, controlling, obnoxious child. Frequently, he would refuse to do test tasks, asserting imperiously, "I'm not answering *any* questions!" He sought to dictate the amount and kind of work he would do, offering, for example, to exchange five minutes on the tests for a considerably longer period of play. The examiner never felt that this resistance arose because the tests were too difficult. Jay's intelligence was in the Superior range and he had little trouble with any of the subtests once he tried them. Moreover, the examiner kept sessions brief, allowed time for play, and, where possible, made tasks like games. Yet no matter how much the examiner tried to engage Jay in a supportive way, the boy seemed driven to alienate him. The harder the psychologist tried to be patient, the more Jay seemed determined to defeat his efforts and get under his skin.

Administering the Rorschach to Jay required greater effort than is typical though far less than with Paul or Sarah. The examiner had to make sure Jay was attending to the cards and keep him at the task when he wished to slough it off, but Jay was able to give responses to each card and answer questions about them in ways that afforded a sense of the location of images and, when he was willing, their determinants. What is less apparent from the protocol, but of particular importance, is that throughout the test the examiner was trying hard to maintain a benign, tolerant facade, while feeling like an angry, exasperated, demanding parent locked in battle with a stubborn, obnoxious child.

Although Jay's Rorschach contains evidence of loose and idiosyncratic thinking, it is considerably more advanced than Sarah's. His is the protocol of a youngster who is completing the transition to Stage III, but for whom the hold of confabulatory approaches on the test is still strong. It is thus now possible to analyze his record in standard ways. However, to gain an appreciation of its differences from the protocols of more disturbed children and of the manner in which earlier trends can still be discerned in more advanced protocols, let us consider it from a developmental perspective.

The greater sophistication of Jay's handling of the Rorschach can be seen in his use of the medium. His first response, that of a doily, raises questions of whether he is going to say literally what the cards look like, but his second makes it clear that he has the capacity to use the inkblot as a representational medium in a mature way. The blot is an angel because of the wings and body, a percept in which details are not merely juxtaposed, but well integrated. His protocol contains many other images, some of them popular ones, that demonstrate a similar capacity to shape the medium in ways in which parts are combined in coherent forms. The level of Jay's capacity for representation is also apparent in the inquiry. With Paul and Sarah, examiners were often unsure of the location of images and had to guess about determinants. With Jay there are no such doubts. If he wished, Jay could give the

Protocol 4: Jay (Age 6 : 7)

Card	Free Association	Inquiry	Scoring
I	10″	We've done these! (?) I don't know. A doily.	(?) It's half a doily (Looks like?) I don't know because I didn't make these. It just looks like a doily.	Wo Fu Hh 1.0
		An angel. I've had enough, but I've got a gun. [Starts playing with a toy gun.] (Anything else?) No, but it's icky because it doesn't have any color!	(?) 'Cuz it had wings and a *body* and everything. I'm not doing any work. I'm going to sleep.	Wo Fo (H) 1.0
II	6″	A little bit of color, a volcano.	(?) See, that's lava. [Sprawls across the table.] Why does that clock make so much noise? (Looks like?) It's red! It's erupting, Mount St. Helens. Do you know what a volcano is? Tell me . . . There are diamonds. There are always diamonds in the middle of a volcano. I've been in a volcano before.	W$_v$ m^a. CF$_u$ Ls, Ex DR$_1$ (CONFAB—Rapport)
		An inkblob. Hey, did you guys make them inkblobs?		

III	5"	Everyone is red! This looks like a crab. The whole thing. It's a blood-crab . . . and I'm getting one some of these days. One of these days I mean.	(?) There's the teeth and there are the feet and this is all the body (Blood-crab?) Blood crabs, when they go pee, they pee out blood. I was just imagining that. (Looks like blood-crab?) Because it's blood. I just know it is. (Are there really blood-crabs?) Nope, there's no such thing.	Wo FC– A, B1 5.5 DR$_2$, CONTAM (?) (CONFAB—Rapaport)
IV	6"	It doesn't have color! It looks like *nothing* to me! [Tosses card away.] [Given card back.] I won't be doing anything. I get tired on days when my parents come. A monster with giant feet.	(?) Every part of it. They made an inkblot that looks like a monster, a big, fat monster. There's the butt and there's the feet. There's the butt and there's the head. He had a long butt. You know what I'd like you to do. I'd like you to butt out. [Playing in chair.] Do you like your chair or do you hate it.	Wo Fo (H) P 2.0 DR$_1$
V	7"	A bat. That's all it could be. . . .	(?) Bats are very mean. It's got antlers. These are the feet. It's got antlers. [Angry] Those are the wings.	Wo Fo A P 1.0 DV$_1$

Protocol 4: Jay (Age 6 : 7) *(continued)*

Card	Free Association	Inquiry	Scoring
	and a man or a flying man	(?) It's *not* a flying man. It's a bat. It's a bat, a bat, a bat, bat, bat. It's not a man. It's a flying fox. They both look like bats and everything.	Wo Mu H 1.0 $INCOM_1$
V	Now it looks like a butterfly		Wo Fo A P 1.0
VI 7″	Looks like another volcano erupting. A flying volcano. A volcano that flies.	(?) That is where it's erupting. Lava. It's exploding. (Flying?) See, these sort of look like wings and so it's a flying volcano.	Wo m^a- Ls, Ex, Ad 2.5 $INCOM_2$
VII 8″	A dood brain. A dood about to erupt. It's rain.	(?) It's stupid. It's just a dood-brain. It looks like dood coming out. (Brain made from dood?) Yup, so it's a dood-brain, dude. It's a dood-brain.	Wo m^a- An , Ex DV_2 $CONTAM$ (?) (CONFAB—Rapaport)
VIII 6″	I saw it. (?) Two animals trying to get up a hill. It just looks like it. Gray! Gray! Gray! Gray's on it! White! White! White! You said it would be all colors.	(Tigers?) They're the red part. They're red tigers. (Hill?) It's all those colors in the middle—blue, green, the everything. It just looks like a hill. (?) It's just colors.	Wo FM^a. FC. CFo (2) $INCOM_1$ (FCarb—Rapaport)

		Response	Inquiry	Scoring
IX	8"	An elephant	(?) I just know by the eyes and the trunk and the ears and the feet. All he's doing is sitting. It's a two-feeted elephant.	Wo FM^p_u A 5.5
		Grass. It doesn't look like anything else.	(?) That's in the background. Grass. (Look like?) Because it's green. Grass is green.	Dv C B$_t$
X	15"	Okay, one more. I saw it! It's too hard! (?) It is. . . . It's all different colors.	(?) That's the bunny. That's his eyes. That's his body, man!	D+ F. m^a – CA, Hh, Na 4.5 DV$_1$
		I don't know what it is. No. I can't and I don't want to do any more of this talk, mushy stuff. (?) There's a bunny blue in there. There's his house and it's raining outside.	(House?) Just his house. That is the dirt pile rabbits make. And it's raining outside and this blue is rain. [Playing with the gun.] I wish this was a real gun and I'd pull the trigger.	(CONFAB—Rapaport)

examiner a clear idea of where his percepts are and of the rationale for them. It is these advances in forming and explaining representations that make it possible to score his protocol with a reasonable degree of confidence.

To be sure, not all of Jay's percepts are well organized. He is hypersensitive to color and shading. The "icky" dysphoric qualities of the achromatic cards which he notes at the outset of the test stir feelings of anger and irritability that can contribute to resistance and disrupt his performance. For example, on Card IV, he begins, "It doesn't have color?! It looks like *nothing* to me." After tossing the card away, he continues, "I said I won't be doing anything and I get tired on days when my parents come." In contrast, he is eager for color and seems to crave the excitement he associates with it, which can lead to more poorly organized images. In addition, the quality of his representations can be affected by his impatience, his dislike of the task, and his conflicts with the examiner.

For the most part, however, these reactions affect the nature and quality of images Jay produces rather than interfere with the representational act itself. For example, as he takes Card II, Jay has just made comments indicating that he is angry and resistant ("I'm not doing any work"); that he dislikes dark, shaded cards; and that he wants cards with color. Given a blot with dark shading and bright red, he produces an image of a volcano erupting. The response is one in which there is little distance between Jay's feeling state and the idea being represented. Yet he uses the color to produce a raw, powerful representation that effectively expresses his feelings. Because he can do so, traditional methods of scoring and analyzing protocols now provide a means of using modes of representation to make inferences about personality functioning.

Jay's handling of referents or themes to be represented is also more advanced than Paul's or Sarah's. Rather than repeatedly superimposing overvalent ideas on the blots, Jay is able to allow himself to start fresh with many of the cards and let his thoughts be guided by possibilities suggested by the medium. As a consequence, he gives a greater number of popular responses and ones with which examiners are familiar. Nonetheless, his success in this regard is relative to the extent of the others' problems. There are still hints of perseverations of content as overvalent ideas lead to repetitions of themes across a number of cards. For example, the idea of flying that begins with the bat on Card V carries over into the next responses, a flying man and a butterfly, and intrudes utterly inappropriately into Card VI (a volcano that flies). In addition, as noted, there is only a limited degree of differentiation between his feeling states and relationship with the examiner and what he chooses to represent. His responses of butts and brains with dood (fecal matter) erupting are probably more influenced by his effort to use the test to express his feeling about the test and provoke the examiner than by any considerations about shaping the medium into ideas that can be well represented.

The confabulatory tendencies of Stage II are still much in evidence in Jay's protocol. He would much rather play than work on the tests and, in fact, he pretends to be shooting a toy gun through much of the test. Like younger children, he engages in language play during the Rorschach, though more often with the intention of being obnoxious rather than cute (e.g., his reference to "inkblobs" on Card II and his shift from talking about the monster's butt to telling the examiner to "butt out" on Card IV). While he reluctantly allows the examiner to keep him at the task, like Stage II children he gives free rein to his imagination throughout the test. For example, on the second card, the idea of a volcano leads to the beginning of a fantasy about diamonds in their middle that, one suspects, he would have elaborated had the examiner given him any encouragement.

Jay exhibits some of the pathological forms of combinatory thinking seen with Sarah and Paul. His representations can move from incongruous combinations of ideas toward contaminations in which boundaries between concepts blur (e.g., dood brains, blood-crabs). Yet there is a different quality to Jay's thinking. Sarah and Paul are swept along by loose associations and idiosyncratic ideas. Whether representations are realistic or not and how they will be received do not seem to occur to them. Jay throws himself into primary process ideation with some sense of what he is doing. When he launches into a series of odd associations about blood-crabs that pee blood on Card III, he knows the ideas are "unrealistic" ("I was just imagining that"). When he produces peculiar or inappropriate ideas (e.g., butts and dood brains), he has a pretty good idea of how others will experience them. Indeed, that reception is why the ideas have appeal for him. In a manner characteristic of borderline children, Jay often plunges willfully into primitive and arbitrary modes of thought and is not so much unaware of social convention or out of contact with reality as indifferent to such considerations (Leichtman and Shapiro, 1980a, b).

Interpersonal aspects of the test process with Jay also differ significantly from those with Sarah and Paul. Jay is capable of functioning at a Stage III level. He grasps the formal roles of tester and testee. He also recognizes that the examiner does not see his responses as he does and needs to have the location and determinants explained. He quickly anticipates that the inquiry will always include questions about where his responses are and why they represent what they do.

To be sure, testing Jay does require extensive, often nonverbal intervention on the part of the examiner. Like Sarah and Paul, he is impulsive, easily frustrated, and difficult to test. Yet without the examiner's help, the other two children could not manage the Rorschach task itself. Jay can. With him, the examiner does not function so much as an auxiliary ego – certainly Jay experiences little the psychologist does as helpful. Rather, the examiner is an external agent who keeps him at a task he would like to avoid.

In certain respects, the struggle between them resembles the conflicts around work and play characteristic of preschool Rorschachs in Stage II. The examiner expects Jay to do tasks in conformance with particular rules and expectations. Jay has no wish to. The tone of the testing is set on the first card. Jay begins by noting he has done the task before and doesn't want to again, reluctantly gives two quick responses, and asserts, "I've had enough." When inquiry is conducted after the card, he again complies briefly, before asserting "I'm not doing any work. I'm going to sleep." Jay is much more interested in playing and does so with a toy gun as the examiner continues the test. Through the rest of the test, Jay reluctantly accedes to the examiner's insistence on work, while engaging in extensive confabulatory activity.

Yet this process differs in important respects from that with normal preschoolers. Young children oscillate between work and play with only a limited recognition that the two are distinct. Jay has the cognitive capacity to function at a higher level. He appreciates the formal social roles involved in the test situation and knows the rules of the Rorschach game, but they do not matter to him. For reasons having to do with his own needs, defenses, and character organization, his own definition of the interaction, one centering on the enactment of roles he has set before the test began, takes precedence over the task.

What we encounter with Jay is the pathological variant of Stage II functioning characteristic of borderline personality organization. In contrast to the relationship with Paul and Sarah in which boundaries between self and other blur and in which examiners are closely attuned to the children's states, with Jay roles are usually quite distinct. Yet the manner in which these roles are manifested is quite different from that found with normal children in Stage III. With the latter, formal social roles that define the testing situation are so prominent that examiners must reflect carefully to discern subjective definitions of the situation that are subtly enacted in the test process. With Jay, the playing out of roles defined by intense, peremptory personal conflicts is primary.

Moreover, it is not Jay alone who enacts these dramatic roles. The examiner wishes to be a benign, helpful professional or, at the least, a responsible, objective one, but the intensity of the reaction Jay elicits and Jay's capacity to get the examiner to experience himself in a role reciprocal to his own is remarkable. The Rorschach is not so much a distinct test as yet one more battleground on which the struggles of an angry, noxious problem child are played out with a frustrated and enraged parent. Reactions of this kind may be seen as manifestations in the testing of the projective identifications that Kernberg (1975) describes as hallmarks of borderline pathology (Leichtman and Shapiro, 1980a, b; Leichtman and Nathan 1983).

From the standpoint of diagnosis, the particular qualities of Jay's relationship with the examiner are also critical. Paul and Sarah in their own ways resembled very young children desperately seeking a close relationship with parents who will minister to their needs, soothe them, protect them, and help modulate and control their affective states and behavior. When not simply seeming malevolent, Jay resembles an older preschooler locked in battle with parents he is driven to alienate. To some extent, these problems can be attributed to difficulties he and his caretakers experience in coping with the hyperactivity, impulsivity, emotional lability, and distractibility characteristic of ADHD. To some extent, too, Jay manifests the stubbornness, anger, and resentfulness characteristic of what currently is labeled an Oppositional-Defiant Disorder. Yet Jay's problems go beyond these diagnoses. Not only the looseness in his thinking but also the intensity of the hatred he feels toward others and elicits from them is extraordinary. Like an erupting "dood brain," Jay has an uncanny ability to attack and repel others and to make them wish to respond in kind. Although many are reluctant to diagnose severe character pathology in six-year-olds, the testing strongly suggests that, without intensive treatment, Jay will consolidate a malignant borderline personality disorder with antisocial features.

The quality of Jay's testing relationship is no less important for treatment planning. For example, when the examiner shared his reactions to Jay with the boy's parents, teachers, and treaters, they admitted similar experiences that they had long been reluctant to acknowledge. Hence, although what is clearly in order is a treatment program that includes medication to help manage impulsivity, irritability, and distractibility and behavioral programs to provide structure and containment at home and school, a crucial component of all aspects of treatment lies in understanding Jay's hate and hatefulness and both controlling and using countertransference reactions in his treatment.

CONCLUSION

Cases such as those of Bill, Paul, Sarah, and Jay provide means of addressing a number of critical questions bearing on whether and how the Rorschach should be employed in clinical practice with severely disturbed children in the early elementary school years. The most obvious of these questions is whether the Rorschach in any form is a useful instrument with these youngsters.

With our examples, the answer depends upon the case. The test is hardly necessary with Bill. His diagnosis is clear from behavior he exhibits in a wide variety of situations and the Rorschach generates little information that could not be obtained elsewhere. At most, his handling of the inkblots suggests that he may have more symbolic capacity than would be anticipated from observations of his behavior alone. The Rorschach has more to offer with Paul and Sarah. Their diagnoses, too, can be established easily on the basis of behavioral observations and information from other tests, yet the Rorschach does provide graphic demonstrations of the presence of thought disorder. With Jay, the instrument is even more valuable in assessing not only his formal thought processes but also his impulsivity, emotional lability, and experience of himself and others. Thus, it seems reasonable to conclude that the Rorschach can be a helpful, though hardly indispensable, instrument in working with many severely disturbed young children and that its utility increases as they move toward more mature, Stage III approaches to the test.

If we accept this answer, a question that follows naturally is how much a developmental-clinical approach to interpretation contributes to clinical applications of the test with this population. Again, even if we assume that the particular interpretations that have been offered are convincing, judgments will vary with each case. With Bill, we are better off with a developmental-clinical approach to interpretation than a traditional one by default. The former permits us to extract at least some reliable information from the protocol, whereas attempts to score and analyze a psychogram when neither the locations nor determinants of responses are clear would be ridiculous. With Paul and Sarah, we are also probably better off with a developmental-clinical approach to interpretation because of their erratic handling of the test and problems in scoring location and determinants. Special scores related to thought disorder can be used with some confidence, but even here a developmental perspective can help distinguish normal and pathological manifestations of primitive forms of thinking. With Jay, standard forms of interpretation can be used effectively, although a developmental perspective may offer additional insights into his handling of the test. Hence, the strongest case for the utility of a developmental-clinical approach to the Rorschach can be made for those profoundly disturbed early grade school youngsters who approach the test in a manner similar to preschoolers.

A third set of questions raised by these cases concerns the nature and meaning of differences in this type of interpretative process with pre-schoolers and with older children who exhibit significant pathology. As has been seen, a level of functioning can be assigned to more or less normal three- and four-year-olds like Colin with relative ease. In contrast, it is only possible to identify central tendencies in the Rorschachs of seriously disturbed children before focusing attention on variations in the manner in which they handle different aspects of the symbol situation and on shifts in their functioning across the test as a whole. For example, Bill's is a Stage II protocol in that he gives a distinct response to each card, yet his interaction with the examiner is more primitive. In Paul's record, the modified perseverations characteristic of the end of the first stage predominate, but he also exhibits confabulatory tendencies characteristic of Stage II. Although Sarah gives some DW responses found in the early confabulatory stage and some form-dominated responses found in Stage III, her typical approach to the test is that encountered in the period of confabulatory combinations. Jay is capable of handling the test in its mature form, but exhibits frequent dips into Stage II functioning. The neatness of the classification scheme used with Colin is clearly lacking as it is extended to seriously disturbed school age youngsters.

This observation, however, says less about the applicability of a developmental approach to interpretation than about the nature of the two populations. The manner in which normal preschoolers handle the Rorschach is determined chiefly by their level of cognitive development and their characteristic ways of dealing with their social environment. These factors do not result in a uniform approach to each card or consistency across every aspect of the symbol situation, but they do impose significant constraints on the amount of variation possible. Severely disturbed older children have more advanced cognitive capacities and are capable of a wider range of social interactions, albeit a range that now includes quite aberrant behavior. Though they exhibit responses and approaches to the test that are similar in certain formal respects to those of younger children, these result from a variety of disturbances that interfere with age-appropriate functioning. Because of their more extensive repertoire of behavior and the sporadic operation of pathological influences, these children should be expected to display greater unevenness in levels of functioning across the test protocols. Moreover, this variation becomes more pronounced as subjects get older. Thus, borderline and psychotic adults produce many of the types of confabulatory responses encountered with preschoolers, yet these responses usually occur intermittently in records in which higher level responses predominate.

Differences in levels of functioning encountered in the Rorschach performance of disturbed children increase rather than diminish the clinical usefulness of a developmental perspective. The discrepancy in Bill's handling of cognitive and interpersonal aspects of the Rorschach task highlight the nature of his pathology. The inconsistency in Sarah's protocol points to her proneness to a sharp deterioration in her thinking under stress. In such cases, detecting and generating hypotheses about the reasons for variations in performance across the test lie at the heart of the clinical inference-making process.

Finally, although case studies are hardly sufficient to provide definitive answers to questions about what constitute pathognomonic signs in children of this age, they can suggest ways of thinking about the problem that can be subject to both formal empirical tests and the informal pragmatic tests clinicians apply as they consider the utility of such ideas in their practice. For example, these cases support the contention of Klopfer, Spiegelman, and Fox (1956) that the best predictor of pathology is the presence of developmentally primitive patterns of test performance beyond ages at which they are expected. As has been seen, Bill and Paul approach the Rorschach in a manner that most closely resembles that of children half their ages and seven-and-a-half-year-old Sarah generally treats the test like a four- to four-and-half-year-old. Furthermore, the degree to which children depart from normative modes of dealing with the test is roughly correlated with severity of their pathology. For example, Jay comes far closer to age-appropriate ways of taking the test than the other three children. To the extent that there are differences between the approach taken here and Klopfer's, they lie in adoption of a more global view of test performance. Whereas Klopfer and his associates focus chiefly on concept formation, our scheme also includes modes of handling the test process itself, especially ways of dealing with inquiry.

As Klopfer, Spiegelman, and Fox (1956) and Ames et al. (1974) note, primitive modes of concept formation do, in themselves, point to significant pathology. The three psychotic children exhibit extensive perseveration, confabulation, and incongruous combinations long after these responses diminish in normal children. In addition, the two schizophrenic children exhibit one pattern of thought disturbance, contamination, not typically found in preschoolers' Rorschachs. Jay, too, displays some responses that have contaminatory qualities (e.g., blood-crabs and dood brains), although examples from his protocols are less blatant and subject to other interpretations that suggest he is either playing with language or that boundaries between concepts do not entirely dissolve.

What helps distinguish those forms of primitive concept formation that simply reflect developmental delay (e.g., retardation) from those indicative of more malignant psychopathology is, as Ames and her colleagues observe, the presence of either peculiar or bizarre content or primitive, primary-process themes (e.g., reference to sex and elimination). For example, Paul does not merely perseverate; he does so around highly idiosyncratic, anxiety-arousing themes. The same is true of Sarah's confabulations. In Jay's case, we are less struck by the oddness of the ideas he portrays than by their raw impulsive quality. He not only seems preoccupied with blood, pee, butts, dood, and aggressive eruptions, but uses such responses to assault the examiner.

The indicators of serious pathology underemphasized by Klopfer and Ames are those centering on the relationship with the examiner. The developmental-clinical perspective advanced here suggests two aspects of this relationship are of particular importance. First, there are the formal aspects of the relationship captured by assignments of levels of functioning. For example, the lack of differentiation of self and other in severe pathology is reflected in the extent to which examiners must assume the roles of auxiliary egos in order for children such as Bill, Paul, and Sarah to take the test at all. It can also be seen in their problems dealing with inquiry. Second, qualitative aspects of the relationship can be used to determine the specific nature of the pathology. For example, Bill and Paul both function at relatively primitive levels, yet the manner in which they interact with examiners and the roles examiners assume with them are billboards advertising radically different types of problems.

In addition, the testing relationship can be a guide in assessing the implications of particular responses. For example, it can assist in distinguishing borderline and psychotic patterns of thinking in children (Leichtman and Shapiro, 1980b). When Jay gives primitive, disturbing responses such as blood-crabs, the examiner does not feel the same kind of concern elicited by Sarah's looseness or Paul's. Their anxiety and their tenuous hold on reality evoke a protective, supportive reaction, whereas the examiner, sensing that Jay's responses reflect an indifference to reality and a provocation, reacts accordingly. Though hard to define and quantify in ways that lend themselves to empirical study, these aspects of the testing relationship are often a critical influence in the judgments of practicing clinicians.

25

The Rorschach and
Thought Disorder

THOUGHT DISORDER AND THE RORSCHACH TEST

From its inception the Rorschach test has been closely linked with the study of thought disorder.

Rorschach received his doctorate of medicine from the University of Zurich in 1912, doing his research on hallucinatory phenomena under Eugen Bleuler. At the time, Switzerland, with its state-supported asylum system, was the leading center in the world for the study of schizophrenia, and Bleuler, with the publication of *Dementia Praecox, or the Group of Schizophrenias* in 1911, was the preeminent authority on psychological aspects of the disorder (Kerr, 1993). In the years between 1915 and 1922, during which Rorschach developed his test, he was deeply concerned with the problem of schizophrenia in his capacity as associate director of the asylum at Herisau and as a member of the Swiss Psychiatric Society (Ellenberger, 1954; Oberholzer, 1955). Indeed, he conceived of his instrument as an empirical procedure for distinguishing types of psychopathology among which that disorder was primary. In this regard, he followed in the footsteps of other young Swiss psychiatrists of the time such as Jung and Riklin who, with

265

Bleuler's encouragement, sought to find ways of adapting psychological tests to the study of serious psychopathology.

Rorschach took note of a number of signs of disturbed thinking in *Psychodiagnostics* (1964). They include DW responses, poor form, and bizarre content. He also singled out two phenomena for particular attention: (1) "confabulatory-combined whole responses," combinations of confabulations and what would now be called fabulized combinations, which he believed are common in the psychoses, and (2) "contaminated whole responses," responses in which distinct concepts or percepts are superimposed upon one another and fused, which he contended are found only in schizophrenics (p. 38).

With the increasing popularity of the test in the years around the Second World War, interest in the manner in which it could be used to assess thought disorder grew. Rapaport (Rapaport et al., 1946) took the lead in extending this aspect of Rorschach's work. Stressing that "comprehensive and systematic work with the verbalization [on the Rorschach} . . . is a highway for investigating disorders of thinking" (p. 331), he elaborated a fifth scoring category to allow this dimension of responses to be recorded and analyzed. In addition to the fabulized combinations, confabulations, and contaminations noted by Rorschach, he included in this group such phenomena as autistic logic, peculiar and queer verbalizations, vagueness, confusion, incoherence, and absurd responses.

Rapaport's work provides the foundation for most subsequent efforts to use the Rorschach for the study of thought disorder. The Delta Index of Watkins and Stauffacher (1952) and the Thought Disorder Index of Johnston and Holzman (1979) are based largely on his ideas. The system for scoring primary and secondary process thinking advanced by Holt and Havel (1960) also draws heavily on his work, though adding a number of additional scores (e.g., composite figures and arbitrary linkages) and focusing heavily on primitive thought content. Similarly, all but two of the 12 "special scores" in Exner's Comprehensive System (1986) derive from Rapaport.

In spite of some relatively minor disagreements among authorities about the classification and meaning of particular thought disorder signs (Meloy and Singer, 1991; Kleiger and Peebles-Kleiger, 1993), there is a broad consensus about the value of such scores in the assessment of disturbed thinking and a substantial body of empirical research that supports this view (Watkins and Stauffacher, 1952; Friedman, 1953; Powers and Hamlin, 1955; Pope and Jensen, 1957; Zucker, 1958; Hertz and Paolino, 1960; Jortner, 1966; Dudek, 1969; Quinlan et al., 1972; Blatt and Ritzler, 1974; Wiener and Exner, 1978; Holzman, Solovay, and

Shenton, 1985; Exner, 1986). Consequently, many clinicians who are skeptical of inferences made from the Rorschach about other diagnostic issues are inclined to give credence to these test findings. In addition there is a growing literature offering empirical and theoretical justifications for the use of the test to distinguish distinct patterns of thought disturbance in different forms of severe psychopathology (Athey, 1974, 1986; Blatt and Ritzler, 1974; Leichtman and Shapiro, 1980b; Holzman et al., 1985; Lerner, Sugarman, and Barbour, 1985; Shenton, Solovay, and Holzman, 1987; Solovay, Shenton, and Holzman, 1987; Kleiger and Peebles-Kleiger, 1993).

Although the Rorschach is fulfilling its initial promise of providing a valuable tool for diagnosing disturbed thinking, theoretical problems bearing upon how it does so persist. Of these problems, the most fundamental is that of why Rorschach thought-disorder signs are signs of thought disorder.

To be sure, with many of Rapaport's "deviant verbalizations," the answer is clear. Peculiar uses of language, autistic logic, confusion, and incoherence are in themselves widely recognized manifestations of thought disorder. Thus, inferences about psychosis based upon their appearance in Rorschach protocols are likely to be convincing even to clinicians who are not initiated into the mysteries of the test. Rapaport, in fact, introduced many of his new scores because, with his sophisticated understanding of psychopathology and his view of psychological assessment as a standardized interview, he wished to assure that the opportunities testing afforded to observe such phenomena were not wasted. At the same time, apart from being an unfamiliar, anxiety-laden situation that is likely to elicit behavior of this kind, there is little that is unique about the Rorschach test in this regard. It is only one occasion among many to obtain a sample of strange thinking from people who think strangely.

The most distinctive Rorschach thought-disorder signs pose greater difficulties. Concepts of fabulized combinations, incongruous combinations, confabulations, and contaminations are not familiar to those outside the Rorschach community. More important, most explanations of these phenomena as well as those of the concept of form level are grounded in perceptual theories of the test that are problematic for reasons that have been discussed at length in earlier chapters.

Thus, we come to a third potential clinical application of a developmental theory of the Rorschach as a task of visual representation, explaining why particular Rorschach signs are indicators of disturbed thinking.

DEVELOPMENTAL THEORY AND RORSCHACH THOUGHT-DISORDER SIGNS

That a developmental theory of the Rorschach should have a bearing on this issue is hardly surprising. After all, many of the phenomena characteristic of young children's Rorschachs—perseverations, confabulatory responses, incongruous combinations, odd language, DW responses, and poor form level—would be taken as signs of disordered thinking if they occurred in the records of older subjects. Halpern (1953, p. 69) even goes so far as to suggest that preschool Rorschachs could be characterized as those of "healthy schizophrenics." At the least, as seen in the preceding chapter, the persistence of such responses beyond the preschool years often points to the presence of serious psychopathology.

The Rorschach productions of young children and severely disturbed adults, of course, are not the same. The pattern of specific test responses, the processes that give rise to those responses, and the functions the responses serve may differ significantly. Nonetheless, the broad formal similarities in the two types of thinking suggest that modes of analysis used with the former can illuminate the latter.

Certainly, the concept of the Rorschach task as a form of visual representation is as applicable with adults as with children. For subjects young and old, healthy and troubled, producing a Rorschach "percept" is an act in which an individual shapes a medium into a representation that stands for an object or concept and that is to be shared with an audience. Consequently, the Rorschach thought-disorder signs related to these representations—DW responses and poor form level, peculiar content, atypical uses of color, perseveration, and unusual confabulatory and combinatory responses—may be understood in terms of problems in various components of the symbol situation and their interplay. For example, while recognizing the influence of relationship of addressor and addressee on all aspects of Rorschach responses, DW responses and poor form level reflect, above all, distinct modes of handling of the symbolic vehicle; bizarre responses are outgrowths of factors bearing on the choice of referents; and the most important of the "special scores" such as fabulized combinations and contaminations codify ways of coordinating the symbolic vehicle and referent.

Equally important, the Wernerian concept of development provides a formal ordering principle for gauging the primitivity of these aspects of the representational process. Just as it is possible to think of early Rorschach performance in terms of increasingly differentiated and hierarchically integrated ways of handling components of visual representation and their relationships, so too can the unusual approaches to the task of troubled older subjects be understood as results of a process of de-differentiation and dis-integration in the representational act (Kaplan, 1959). Thus, the problem of thought disorder in adults can be conceptualized in terms of the same framework used for analyzing preschool Rorschachs (see Figure 7), although our concern will now be with regression rather than progression through developmental levels.

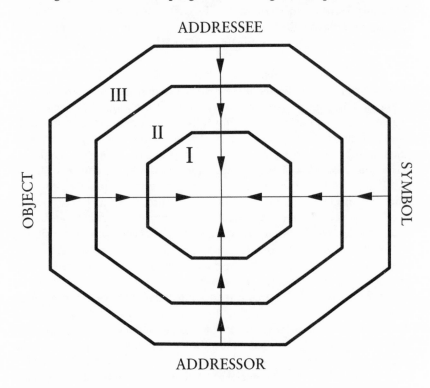

Figure 7. Diagram of developmental changes in components of the Rorschach situation in pathological regressions. (This modification of the diagram of the symbol situation from H. Werner and B. Kaplan (1963), *Symbol Formation* [New York: John Wiley, p. 41] is included by permission of Bernard Kaplan and Lawrence Erlbaum Associates, Inc.)

FORM LEVEL AND DW RESPONSES

From Rorschach's first publication to the present, perhaps the most widely shared tenet guiding interpretation of the test is that individual responses of blatantly poor form and low scores on aggregate measures of form level across protocols are indicators of problems cognizing the world and often of disturbances in "reality testing." While there is no reason to question such inferences, as has been seen (Chapter 16), one of the prime rationales offered for them—that good form reflects "accuracy of perception" or "correspondence of responses with reality" (Kimball, 1950)—is questionable. To cast the issue in the simplest terms, percepts that Rorschach authorities accept as embodying "good" form, such as a bat or butterfly on Card I, are awful facsimiles of those creatures.

Yet perceptual theories of the Rorschach are, in fact, peripheral in standard interpretations of poor form as a measure of reality testing. Rorschach examiners are not concerned with making inferences about problems in visual perception, but rather about disturbances in thinking. Adherents of almost every Rorschach system base their interpretations about reality testing on the assumption that complex cognitive activity is essential in the "perception" of form on the test (Levitt and Truuma, 1972). To produce a well-organized percept, subjects must scan and attend to blots carefully rather than react in hasty, impulsive ways; select critical features of the stimuli; organize and integrate them; match them with ideas or concepts that have similar features; and decide about the appropriateness of the fit. Thus, the production of good form responses is held to be based on reasoning, intelligence, and disciplined, "reality-oriented" thinking, whereas poor form responses are presumed to reflect deficiencies in these cognitive activities.

A representational conception of the Rorschach task requires no significant change in this understanding of the meaning of form level. To the contrary, insofar as inkblots are viewed not simply as objects to be perceived, but rather material to be shaped into symbolic forms, the assumption that form level is a measure of the effectiveness of cognitive operations through which individuals organize and structure their experience is more plausible than when the task is seen as primarily a perceptual one. Beyond simply supporting traditional interpretations of the processes presumed to underlie form responses, however, a representational theory of the Rorschach can deepen our understanding of the nature of "good" and "poor" form on the test and their relationship to the concept of "reality testing."

To appreciate these contributions, let us return to the principles upon which judgments of the quality of form are based. As has been seen (Chapter 20), in place of standards presumed to be based on perceptual accuracy, a representational theory would substitute four criteria related to how the medium is fashioned into a representation of an idea.

One such measure is the saliency of features chosen as basis for the representation. For example, assume that as part of a test in a class on French literature, we are asked to give a brief description of Hugo's Quasimodo that highlights only one impression of him. If our chief impression is that reading about him made us angry or sad, stirred fears that we might suffer a back injury in an accident, or reminded us of an old man down the block who scared us when we were children, we would not be pleased with our grade. We would do a bit better if we focused on a feature of the character in the book and would stand a reasonable chance of passing if the detail we chose is his hunchback rather than his age, height, or job as a bell-ringer at Notre Dame Cathedral. Similarly, a caricature can depict a familiar figure effectively by exaggerating a single distinctive feature. With the Rorschach, if a subject insists that Card V is a bat solely because of the wings, we assume that the form is adequate even if no other detail is taken into consideration. The wings are so prominent that they do make it look like a bat.

Typically, however, one characteristic is not sufficient to serve as a good basis for representation. In ordinary, commonsense judgments of such matters, the more features included, the better the form. For example, if children are asked to draw a face, we tend to judge pictures that include eyes and a mouth as superior to those that contain only the eyes. Faces that add a nose and ears are better still. For the same reason, a Rorschach "percept" of a dog that includes the head, body, and legs typically receives a higher score than one based on the head alone. Thus, for example, in a recent revision of the Mayman-Rapaport scoring system, Athey and Kleiger (1993) give the number of "supporting contour features" a prominent place among the "rules of thumb" to be used in making decisions about form level.

Most important, judgments of the adequacy of form are based heavily on the integration or relationship of parts of figures. In drawing a human figure, a young preschooler will sketch a circle for the head with arms and legs extending from it; a kindergartner may produce a large head and crudely drawn body; and a second grader will produce a figure with the head, body, and appendages in more or less the right places and the proportions of the head and trunk will begin at least to crudely approximate those of real people. Most observers would view these productions as getting progressively "better" or "more accurate" with age. Form level judgments on the Rorschach are based heavily on this criterion.

Finally, "good form" involves not only integration of parts in figures, but exclusion of parts that do not belong (Rapaport et al., 1946; Klopfer et al., 1954). For example, if, as a result of haphazard attention to Hugo's account of Quasimodo, we recall not only that he was deformed, rang church bells, and was deeply attached to Esmeralda, but also somehow confuse the description of his attire and hers, our portrayal of the Hunchback of Notre Dame would not only receive a poor grade but also make us an object of ridicule in the faculty lounge. Fs or spoil responses on the Rorschach are based on similar considerations.

Insofar as judgments of the form quality rest upon such criteria, they are, in fact, organized around the developmental principles of differentiation and hierarchic integration. The criteria of saliency and number of details are measures of differentiation in handling the medium; the more and better the choice of parts included in responses, the better the representation. Those of relationship and exclusion of details that do not fit are measures of the degree and adequacy of the integration of parts in figures.

These principles allow Rorschach responses to be ordered on a developmental scale. At one end are the most primitive responses such as the Stage I responses of young children. These responses seem to involve a DW process, but the basis for the "percept"—whether it is related to the referent or the child's mood at the time—is unclear and has so little saliency for observers that they have little notion of why the inkblot stands for the idea the child has associated with it. One step up the scale are the DW responses of Stage II Rorschachs. A single detail serves as the basis of the representation, but it is one that others can recognize and appreciate. The paradigmatic responses of the substage of confabulatory combinations are more sophisticated. Two or three details now form the basis for representation, but they may be juxtaposed rather than integrated. Spoil responses are also found in this transitional period, since they are related to the incongruous combinations characteristic of the period. These responses involve attempts to integrate details in a whole, but the integration is poor because of a failure to exclude those that do not fit. Finally, in Stage III, criteria of differentiation and integration apply simultaneously providing the basis for typical judgments of good form, although, of course, the scale may be extended further as the degree of differentiation and integration of components of representations are taken into consideration (Hemmendinger, 1953, 1960; Meili-Dworetzki, 1956). Rorschach systems seek to capture discrimations of this kind through distinctions between Fo and F + scores, Z scores, and Exner's scoring for Developmental Quality.

The same formal principles that apply to judgments of the degree of sophistication of children's representations can be used with adults as a measure of regression in cognitive operations. For example, we can now view DW responses as manifestations of the same processes involved in form responses rather than distinct, isolated phenomena and appreciate how far such responses depart from typical adult form responses. We should not assume responses of this kind are the same in children and disturbed older subjects. To the contrary, the former are typically found across protocols as a whole and reflect cognitive operations characteristic of the young; the latter occur sporadically in the protocols of individuals capable of a higher level of functioning who exhibit temporary regressions that may be caused by a variety of psychological factors. A developmental ordering of "form level" does not allow us to specify which factors are responsible, but it does enable us to appreciate the degree of regression in representational operations that is involved and provides a starting point for investigating why it has occurred.

A question remains, however, of why poor form on the Rorschach is associated with problems in "reality testing." One explanation is the traditional one. Production of higher level responses requires attention to stimuli, concentration, discipline, and advanced forms of thinking, whereas lower level responses result from disturbances in some or all of these functions. Certainly, with the regressions found in poor responses of adults, it is important to reflect closely on whether and how such factors affect the response process. Yet a developmental approach can add something more.

Representations are not only products of thinking, but means through which individuals codify their experience, retain it, and share it with others. Imagine, for example, that in trying to write an essay for a final exam on *The Hunchback of Notre Dame* we must rely heavily on notes taken on the book several months earlier. If our notes consist only of an idea or two and those ideas are about our feelings as we read the story, what we recall will be limited and whether our essay is even recognized as a description of Hugo's work may depend upon the reader appreciating and sharing our sentiments about it. If we remember only a salient detail of the book, our essay may be better but will be skewed in the direction of whatever detail we recorded. If we noted Quasimodo's back, what we write may sound like a discourse on prejudices against the handicapped through the ages, whereas if we recall his feelings for Esmeralda, we may convey the impression that the book is another story of unrequited love. If our notes included more details about Quasimodo and their relationship to his actions, we are likely to remember even more about the story and our description of it will be fuller, more recognizable to others, and more acceptable to the professor, who serves as the ultimate arbiter of reality in French literature classes. At the same time, the details we include and relationships we describe must be relevant lest our portrayal of plot and character be distorted. If our notes on Quasimodo are garbled and include information on Esmeralda's attire, our account of the book may make it sound like the tragic tale of a church employee struggling with a penchant for cross-dressing.

The Rorschach, of course, is a different situation and taps only one form of representation in a delimited, unfamiliar, often anxiety-arousing situation. Nonetheless, insofar as our idea of reality involves a representational act, we can assume that what we encounter in the Rorschach provides a basis for making inferences about such acts in other emotion-laden situations. Good form level may be viewed as a sign of a capacity to represent experience in comprehensive, coherent, integrated ways that are likely to remain stable over time, that provide a reasonable guide in dealing with the world, and that are shared with and recognized by others. In contrast, as Werner's model suggests, primitive modes of representation—those in which qualities of the referent and feelings about it are not distinct, those based on only a detail salient at the moment, or those in which details are not well integrated—result in ways of experiencing the world that are labile, diffuse, and inflexible. Individuals relying upon them are likely to have difficulty apprehending the flux of experience, maintaining a stable view of themselves and their world as their moods change, conveying their experience to others, and establishing a shared sense of reality with them.

DISTURBANCES IN THE CHOICE OF REFERENTS

Whereas some inferences about disturbances in thinking and reality testing such as those involving form level center on the use of the symbolic medium, others are based on the choice of referents. Even those who have little familiarity with the Rorschach suspect something is awry when subjects fashion inkblots into depictions of bizarre or idiosyncratic ideas. Typically such responses receive special scores such as incongruous combinations, fabulized combinations, contaminations, and confabulations because their strangeness derives in part from either unusual combinations of ideas or fantasy elaborations of blots. In addition, Rorschach scoring systems codify a number of types of subject matter that raise questions about thought disorder because of theoretical or empirical linkages with pathological conditions. These themes include raw expressions of Freudian drives such as those Holt and Havel (1960) seek to measure in their manual for assessing primary process thinking; sexual images or abstract symbols that may be given separate content scores; or morbid content and aggressive movement that are elevated to the status of "special scores" in Exner's Comprehensive System. Responses depicting or associated with disturbed "object relations" such as those receiving low scores on the Mutuality of Autonomy Scale (Urist, 1977), the Separation-Individuation Theme Scale (Coonerty, 1986), and the scale advanced by Kwawer (1980) for measuring borderline interpersonal relations on the Rorschach could also be included in this category (Lerner, 1991).

Offering a plausible account of why peculiar content on the Rorschach is a sign of disturbed thinking is not difficult regardless of whether a perceptual or representational theory of the test is advanced. Odd or socially inappropriate responses clearly indicate not only something about the kinds of thoughts individuals entertain, but also about their social judgment. Yet explaining why strange responses are signs of thought disorder is more complicated than the bare outline of such a theory suggests.

Consider the following hypothetical example. Looking at the large lower detail on Card IX, a man says, "That's two babies, the lively red color they would be if they had been dropped in boiling water." Obviously there is something wrong with the response. But what?

Many who hold a perceptual view of the Rorschach task might say that the subject has begun with a realistic percept, babies, but then distorted it as he became immersed in a peculiar fantasy about boiling them. If we hold a representational theory of the Rorschach, we do not have this luxury. Insofar as the inkblot is a medium that in principle may be formed into anything, we cannot say that it looks any more like a baby than like a boiled baby. In fact, from the standpoint of effective use of the medium, the latter response is superior. Both images integrate a number of details of the blot well enough to receive a good form-level score, but the second incorporates color as well. We would not have second thoughts if the response was, "It's babies, the rosy pink color they have after they come out of a warm bath." Our subject could argue his response is even more realistic in that the card is a darker shade of pink that would not have been present unless the baby had been in much hotter water.

The problem with the response is not the quality of the representation, but the thought being shared. We have reason to be concerned about the mental health of an individual to whom the idea of parboiling babies occurs, even if he claims to be merely offering an illustration of thought disorder signs on the Rorschach.

Yet the content of the response alone is not sufficient for it to be taken as a sign of disturbed thinking. We could induce responses of this kind in normal subjects if, for example, we administered the Rorschach to members of a creative writing course, telling them the test was being used to determine who will be offered a lucrative job devising plots for horror films. With minor variations in instructions and suitable rewards, we could also no doubt obtain protocols filled with wild sexual, aggressive, or morbid responses as well. To be sure, we would probably not get responses quite as bizarre as those of schizophrenics or as morbid as those produced by individuals suffering from a psychotic depression, but we might come close.

Judgments of disturbances in thinking thus depend not only upon the content of ideas, but the context in which they arise. The Rorschach is not given as part of a talent search for writers with macabre, aggressive, or lascivious imaginations. Typically it is administered as part of a clinical evaluation. When subjects give strange responses in these circumstances, an understanding of the nature of the disturbance in thinking and reality testing should be sought not simply in the ideas themselves but in an analysis of the self–other dimension of the symbol situation.

Most normal subjects approach the Rorschach with a set characteristic of children's Stage III Rorschachs. They recognize formal roles governing behavior in social situations, including clinical evaluations. Even when struggling with significant intrapsychic and interpersonal conflicts, they are concerned with how they present themselves and with others' reactions to them. Conventions governing what is real and appropriate affect how they approach the task, contributing to an inhibition of bizarre, primitive, or morbid ideation. If such ideas do occur, subjects seek to temper or suppress them. As Rapaport, Schachtel, and Exner recognize in their own ways in discussions of judgment and censorship in the response process, relatively healthy subjects impose restrictions on the content of their responses because standards bearing on the personal and social acceptability of ideas enter into the ways in which they form and decide to share Rorschach images. Paradoxically, a highly differentiated conception of ideas that may be represented includes criteria regarding unacceptable responses that actually narrow the range of themes they make public. "Reality testing," in this context, is not simply to be understood as a property of responses alone, but of judgments about the test situation itself.

Borderline patients produce Rorschachs containing more peculiar, personalized, and flamboyant sexual and aggressive themes. Though such responses may reflect a temporary breakdown of defensive operations and/or a greater propensity for primary-process ideation, often they are also a function of how subjects experience themselves and others. As seen in a nascent form with Jay (Chapter 24), individuals manifesting borderline disorders approach the Rorschach in a manner similar to children in Stage II. Though they have some sense of formal social roles that usually govern behavior in the evaluations, they are often indifferent to those conventions and take pleasure in flouting them. Like preschoolers, they may seek to redefine the test situation in their own ways, transforming it into a kind of play process, albeit a driven, idiosyncratic one. Depending on their character, they are ready to present themselves in eccentric, impulsive, histrionic, or aggressive ways and cast examiners in reciprocal roles. Their primitive, primary-process responses do not result so much from a "loss" of reality testing as from lack of interest in ordinary social definitions of "reality" and a readiness to redefine it in their own way. As a consequence, borderline subjects may produce more responses with peculiar content than psychotic individuals who try to suppress or hide their problems; examiners are often surprised in scoring borderline protocols by how much odd thinking they had taken for granted while immersed in testing these subjects; and, as with Jay, psychologists are more inclined to react with annoyance or frustration as such responses are produced than with anxiety for the patient or concerns about decompensation.

Psychotic responses on the Rorschach have a different quality. The affect of individuals who give them in the midst of acute episodes may convey to examiners the ego-dystonic nature of the ideas, the extent to which these productions reflect a breakdown in the ability to control and regulate thinking, and anxiety about a concomitant disorganization or disintegration in the sense of self. In contrast, chronic psychotic patients may offer disturbed responses blithely in ways that suggest that there is little differentiation in their sense of themselves and others. Not only do conventional notions of reality fail to regulate the production of such responses, but their creators seem to have little idea that others will see them as strange or fail to understand them as they do themselves. The loss of reality testing in such cases lies not only in difficulties regulating and inhibiting primary-process ideation, but also in the failure to appreciate how such thinking will be understood and interpreted by others.

PERSEVERATION

Of the Rorschach "special scores," perseveration appears most closely related to the referent dimension of the symbol situation since by its very nature it consists of a restriction of the range of content of responses. In its most extreme form, that which Rapaport (Rapaport, Gill, and Schafer, 1946, p. 299) describes as "thorough-going perseveration" and Exner (1986) labels "mechanical perseveration," the term may apply to protocols consisting of little more than the repetition of a single response. In other, seemingly milder forms, single responses may recur at a number of points in protocols. Rapaport gives perseveration scores to such "stereotyped responses" that reflect a preoccupation with "overvalent ideas." Using more stringent criteria, Exner confines his designation of "content perseveration" to cases in which responses are explicitly linked to earlier ones (e.g., "There is that bat again").

From a developmental standpoint, using the same score for the two sets of phenomena is questionable. They are similar superficially in that there is a repetition of responses, but the processes responsible for them are fundamentally different.

The "thorough-going" or "mechanical" perseveration of adults is like the pervasive perseveration of preschoolers who produce Stage I protocols. Because forming inkblots into visual representations is too complex and demanding a task for them, young children adopt a perseverative strategy for dealing with it that serves adaptive and defensive functions. Found chiefly in adults with severe neurological conditions and/or marked intellectual impairments (Exner, 1986), mechanical perseveration serves similar functions for individuals who lack the cognitive resources to deal with the Rorschach in a more sophisticated way.

In contrast, Exner's content perseveration and Rapaport's stereotyped responses are based on quite different processes. Responses of this kind bear some resemblance to perseverated-logic responses in which children begin with an idea or concept and try to make inkblots into them (Ford, 1946). Yet the modified forms of perseveration found as children are making the transition to Stage II protocols are still strategies for coping with the complexity of the Rorschach task. Adults who exhibit content perseveration have the ability to produce diverse responses. If they repeat a percept, they usually do so for reasons other than cognitive limitation. Moreover, the repetitive responses of normal preschoolers in this transitional stage are typically ordinary and benign (e.g., a bat or butterfly). The content perseverations of adults usually have disconcerting, conflictual, or emotion-laden qualities (Rapaport, Gill, and Schafer, 1946) that are indications of the intrusion of overvalent ideas and fantasies into the response process. As such, they reflect a distorted form of the kind of confabulatory processes characteristic of Stage II Rorschach, albeit one transforming what ideally would be a spontaneous creative process into a fixed, repetitive one.

DISTURBANCES IN THE COORDINATION OF VEHICLE AND REFERENT

The most distinctive Rorschach thought-disorder indicators are four types of responses that are usually grouped together: contaminations, confabulations in the broad sense of the term, fabulized combinations, and incongruous combinations. The first three have long been central to analyses of thought disorder within the Rapaport tradition and the last has gained increasing acceptance among its adherents as a scoring refinement consistent with their interpretation of this class of phenomena as manifestations of associative aspects of the response process running amok (Holt and Havel, 1960; Johnston and Holzman, 1979; Athey, Colson, and Kleiger, 1992).

The inclusion of confabulation scores within this group can result in some confusion since they are applied to two distinct sets of phenomena. On one hand, since Rorschach's original work, the term has designated DW responses or what historically have been viewed as "perceptually-based overgeneralizations" (Kleiger and Peebles-Kleiger, 1993). Holding to this narrow definition, Exner (1986) restricts his confabulation score to DW responses alone. On the other hand, Rapaport and his followers have also applied it to freewheeling associations to the blots, and in most of their discussions of confabulation the term is largely synonymous with the latter definition. A variety of alternative labels for this second process have been offered such as "autistic elaboration" (Holt and Havel, 1960), "extended fabulization" (Weiner, 1966), and "affect-laden fantasy embellishment" (Kleiger and Peebles-Kleiger, 1993). None, however, has gained currency. The following discussion of confabulation as a thought disorder indicator is concerned only with Rapaport's associative elaboration and not the DW responses, which, as has been seen, are best understood in terms of how the Rorschach medium is used.

The treatment of these four thought-disorder signs in the Rorschach literature is noteworthy in two respects. First, they are generally viewed as members of a class of phenomena linked by some underlying principle. Exner (1986), for example, considers incongruous combinations, fabulized combinations, and contaminations as "inappropriate combinations" that consist of "condensation(s) of impressions and/or ideas into responses that violate realistic considerations."(p. 163). Rapaport (Rapaport, Gill , and Schafer, 1946), as has been seen, contends that all are manifestations of associative aspects of the response process overriding perceptual ones. Second, although many authorities recognize different degrees of pathology within each category (Watkins and

Stauffacher, 1952; Johnston and Holzman, 1979; Athey et al., 1992), most agree that prototypical or modal representatives of these types of responses can be ordered along a continuum of pathology. Whether basing their judgments on empirical studies or clinical judgment, Rapaport's followers contend that contaminations are indicators of the most serious forms of disturbance followed by confabulations and then fabulized combinations (Watkins and Stauffacher, 1952; Athey, 1974; Blatt and Ritzler, 1974; Johnston and Holzman, 1979). While excluding confabulations from these scores, Exner (1986) holds that contaminations constitute a far more serious form of thought disorder than do fabulized combinations. With the exception of Blatt and Ritzler (1974), most who have included incongruous combinations in their schemes (e.g., Johnston and Holzman, 1979; Exner, 1986) see them as the least pathognomonic of these signs.

A comparative-developmental perspective provides support for this ranking in two ways. First, it supplies a theoretical rationale for the scheme, since each of the types of disorder may be seen to embody different degrees of difficulty in coordinating the use of the medium and the ideas to be represented in a symbolic act. Second, it also offers empirical support for the order in that, with the exception of contaminations, these phenomena occur in a regular sequence in children's Rorschachs. With children, however, the series is best understood by beginning at the lower end of the continuum and examining how, with increasing maturity, their productions reflect progressively more differentiated and integrated ways of approaching the task of visual representation. In contrast, with adults who have negotiated that developmental process, thought disorder signs are best appreciated if we move in the other direction and consider the manner in which increasingly severe pathology results in progressively more severe de-differentiation and dis-integration of the processes that constitute the representation act.

High-quality Rorschach responses in Stage III effectively combine processes encountered in more primitive forms in earlier stages. First, not only do such responses synthesize details of parts of the inkblot into a well-formed image, but some of the best bring together two or more images effectively. For example, separate responses describing the side figures on Card III as women and the lower central detail as a pot are considered quite decent. A single response describing the card as a scene with two women by a pot is better because it is more complex and sophisticated. Second, in addition to consisting of "good" percepts, high-quality responses often include ideational elaboration as well, particularly elaboration that includes affect, purpose, and action. For example, describing the two side figures as native women is better than simply describing them as women because the response is richer and more determinate. Characterizing them as native women cooking over a cauldron is better still, since it is not only consistent with the qualities of the blot but also speaks to a readiness to think of people in terms of purpose and intention. In addition, it suggests a capacity to think in narrative terms that move beyond the immediate present and see events related to antecedent conditions and leading to consequences in the future. In effect, Rorschach responses that are typically treated as signs of psychological strengths, for example, those involving high Z scores and/or human movement, are ones that effectively combine percepts and integrate affect and fantasy in ways that enliven and enrich images.

Incongruous combinations, such as a response in which the figures on Card III are described as women with birds' heads, arise from problems in coordinating these processes. Blatt and Ritzler (1974, p. 372) argue that these responses approach contaminations in the degree of pathology they reflect because of the extent to which they violate "the integrity of the object." However, Exner (1986) contends on empirical grounds that they are among the mildest of "inappropriate combinations." A developmental analysis of the phenomena supports Exner's view.

Such responses appear relatively late in young children's Rorschachs during the transition from Stage II to Stage III. As has been seen (Chapter 21), although they often contain strange themes, the process responsible for them is not so strange. Rather than resulting from an indifference to reality or an indulgence in wild fantasies, these responses are the product of children's difficulties dealing with two competing "realities." There is the "perceptual" reality of the blot, a form that partially resembles a woman, but also has an upper area that looks more like a bird's head. There is also a "conceptual reality" in which it is understood that women do not have bird's heads. Unable to resolve the conflict in a way that reconciles the two competing "realities," subjects who give incongruous combinations simply choose the former, a choice that leads Exner (1986, p. 375) to infer a propensity for concrete reasoning. To the extent to which such responses are the "healthiest" of their family of special scores, their relative strength lies in the fact that they arise from an effort to keep thinking bounded by the "reality" of the blot rather than from giving free rein to imagination.

Fabulized combinations, images that involve an implausible relationship between objects identified in the blot, are also forms of confabulatory combination that bear a resemblance to phenomena encountered in the later Stage II Rorschachs. On the surface, such responses appear better than incongruous combinations in that they consist of two "percepts" that may be well formed. However, the quality of the percepts, in fact, suggests why fabulized combinations are likely to be more pathological. Subjects begin with "realistic" images and must engage in an active, confabulatory process in order to attribute a peculiar or unrealistic relationship to them. Whereas incongruous combinations reflect an attempt to remain faithful to one of two conflicting senses of reality, fabulized combinations are based on an active fantasy-laden, reality-distorting thought process.

Confabulation scores are applied to a broad range of responses. Whereas some are an exaggerated form of the fabulization that enriches responses (e.g., "a blood thirsty vampire bat" or "a bat flying in search of prey"), others verge on unrestrained stories (e.g., "a vampire bat homing in on a victim and about to . . ."). Mild forms maintain a measure of grounding in the blot (e.g., Card I might be described as "smoke over a battlefield"), while others use the same card as little more than a launching pad for flights of imagination (e.g., "World War III, the line down the center divides it and the dark on each side is the conflagration consuming the opposing sides"). Scoring systems such as those of Johnston and Holzman (1960) and Athey, Colson, and Kleiger (1992) make use of quantitative measures to capture what clearly are differing degrees of pathology in such responses.

Confabulation in its more extreme forms of "uncontrolled fantasy elaboration" or attribution of idiosyncratic symbolic meanings to blots is formally similar to phenomena found in early Stage II Rorschachs. With young children, the inkblots are occasions for exercises in free play that quickly transcend the more mundane task of simply forming one image and going on to the next. The test becomes an opportunity to tell stories, free associate, or share personal experiences. With children, however, the ease with which the Rorschach task is transformed in this way results from an age-appropriate investment in play and a limited appreciation of anything else one could do with the inkblots. In contrast, adults have a capacity to shape the medium into complex forms and coordinate ideational content with them. With these subjects, blatant confabulations may be seen as more pathological than incongruous combinations or fabulized combinations because perceptual qualities of the blot no longer impose any constraints on fantasy and ideation.

Contaminations have been recognized as the most serious of this group of pathognomonic signs. Rorschach (1964) viewed such responses as indicators of schizophrenia, and since his time, clinical and empirical studies have offered support for their association with schizophrenic and schizotypal conditions (Zucker, 1958; Jortner, 1966; Wiener, 1966; Quinlan et al., 1972; Athey, 1974; Blatt and Ritzler, 1974).

From a developmental viewpoint, however, the justification for this belief is not immediately apparent. To begin with, no phenomena encountered with young children are analogous to contaminations except perhaps the curious words preschoolers produce when they engage in babbling-like language play as they work on the Rorschach. Equally important, it could be argued that confabulations, which involve little coordination of medium and referent, are less advanced than contaminations, which are based on some combination of images and ideas, even if a quite peculiar one.

The rarity of true contaminations in young children's protocols can be explained by the fact that they involve the disintegration of more sophisticated forms of thinking and retain traces of a complexity of which preschoolers have yet to attain. The second argument questioning the primitivity of such phenomena is not addressed as easily, since some contaminations consist of combinations of ideas that may strike observers as quite creative. These contaminations are like visual puns, as for example, when a subject takes part of a blot that looks like both a woman's head and a flower and describes it as "a Venus flytrap."

Nonetheless, typically contaminations are the more primitive of these types of responses. Most contaminations are not so much creative as bizarre. For example, seeing an area that might be a bug or ox, a subject describes it as "the face of a bug ox" (Exner, 1986, p. 162). Moreover, even when observers recognize responses like "the Venus flytap" as puns, the pun is usually neither intended nor even recognized by the subject. Whether crude or intriguing, such images do not derive from controlled, integrative activity. Rather, they have been likened to double exposures of film in which images and ideas simply run together (Exner, 1986). They seem to arise from a passive, primary-process operation similar to that encountered in dreams.

As Blatt and Ritzler (1974) observe, contaminations involve severe forms of "boundary disturbances" that are based on the syncretic forms of thought characteristic of Werner's earliest, global-undifferentiated phase of development. In such responses, the medium is not molded into determinate forms, but rather is diffuse. Images merge into one another and the same area is used in different ways simultaneously. Referents, too, are no longer stable and flow into one another. What might be a bug or an ox, each a concept with a fixed meaning, becomes "the face of a bug-ox," an idea that is literally nonsensical. These images are not so much puns as visual neologisms, and subjects must often coin verbal neologisms to put them into words (Exner, 1986). Distinctions between self and other are blurred as well, since ideas and the means of representing them are purely idiosyncratic. To the extent there is any recognition that another human being is present, it is not of an independent person to whom meanings must be communicated, but rather of someone whose sees and thinks exactly as the subject. Indeed, it is easy to doubt that an effort is being made to form a representation that will be communicated to another; rather, the subject is engaged in a strange kind of play in which there is little concern for the customary meanings of visual forms, words, or ideas.

In effect, there is not a true integration of medium and concept in contaminations. Instead, such responses arise from syncretistic modes of experience in which visual forms, language, and concepts are intermixed and in which distinctions between self and other collapse.

ATYPICAL COLOR RESPONSES

Although color responses are typically interpreted as measures of the handling of affect, three such scores—those for the arbitrary use of color in Rapaport's system, color projection in Exner's system, and color naming—have implications for thought organization as well.

From a developmental standpoint, arbitrary color responses in which the color does not match the concept (e.g., "a green bear" or "a pink lake") are the most benign of these phenomena. They are based on modes of thinking characteristic of the late Stage II confabulatory combinations of children. Faced with a conflict between the perceptual reality of the blot (it looks like a bear and it is green) and conceptual reality (bears are not green), subjects opt for the former. The process is similar to that encountered in incongruous combinations, and Exner (1986), in fact, scores these responses as such.

Color projection, the attribution of color to an achromatic area, is a more primitive form of response and appears to involve the same kind of pathological regression encountered with contaminations. Such responses are rooted in syncretistic modes of experience in which the "perception" of the medium merges with ideas and feelings stimulated by it. As a consequence, subjects act as if they are oblivious to the nature of the vehicle and the most basic conventions governing its use. The result is a visual representation that is analogous to a psychotic language in which individuals make up their own forms of expressions that cannot be recognized or understood by others.

Color naming is based on a different form of primitive handling of the medium. Whereas color projection, like contamination, results from severe forms of pathological regression, responses that consist of no more than identifying colors in blots are usually found in individuals with marked intellectual limitations and are often a sign of significant organic impairment in adults. As is the case with young children in Stage I, such individuals find the task of forming inkblots into representation too taxing. Adopting a concrete, truly perceptual approach to the task, they literally tell us what the card looks like.

DISTURBANCES IN LANGUAGE AND LOGIC

In addition to the task of forming a visual representation that lies at the heart of the Rorschach, the test involves secondary tasks as well. In particular, subjects must communicate responses and explain their responses to examiners. In doing so, they provide samples of their use of language, thought, and logic.

A number of special scores that bear on diagnoses of thought disorder seek to codify disturbances in these processes. They include Exner's "deviant verbalizations," "deviant responses," and "inappropriate logic"; Rapaport's "peculiar verbalizations" and "queer verbalizations" and "autistic logic"; and three Rapaport scores, Vagueness, Confusion, and Incoherence, which seek to capture degrees of thought disorganization. They also include efforts to refine and quantify these scores such as that are part of the Delta Index (Watkins and Stauffacher, 1954) and the Thought Disorder Index (Johnston and Holzman, 1976).

Because these atypical forms of language, cognition, and logic are well-recognized signs of thought disorder, they require little discussion here. It should be noted, however, that each of these processes can be approached from the same developmental perspective that has been used to understand the formation of Rorschach images.

Language is obviously a representational process and, as such, can be understood in terms of a developmental model of the symbol situation. For example, because there is a clear distinction between addressor and addressee in Stage III, words are used in conventional ways and rules of grammar are followed so that thoughts are conveyed effectively. In Stage II, subjects adopt a more egocentric frame of reference. The addressee, while still recognized as different from oneself, is treated in less objective ways and with a familiarity that may be neither appropriate nor warranted. In such circumstances, language may be used in personalized, idiosyncratic ways that are scored as "peculiar verbalizations." In states of profound regression, such as those encountered in schizophrenia, objective distinctions between self and other are dissolved; words lose their denotative reference; and bizarre, utterly idiosyncratic uses of language appear such as neologisms.

A similar form of analysis can be applied to the manner in which Rorschach percepts are justified and to the qualities of subjects' thinking in general. In Stage III Rorschachs, subjects have a clear appreciation that examiners may not see the blots as they do and that an explanation of responses is necessary. They are thus prepared to answer questions about their percepts in logical ways (e.g., "It looks like a bat because . . ."). Their thinking during both association and inquiry phases of the test is reasonably coherent and organized. In Stage II, a more egocentric approach prevails. With children explanations may be offered, but often more is left to the examiner to infer. In adults, the rationale offered for responses may become strained and hard to follow, leading to mild to moderate forms of "autistic" or "inappropriate logic" scores. At this level, too, subjects' thought processes may seem vague or confused. In the most regressed stage, again, distinctions between self and other blur, structures of logical thought collapse, and extreme forms of autistic logic are encountered, as are responses to inquiry which may not be explanations at all. At these times, thought processes that warrant scores of "incoherence" in the Rapaport system appear.

In effect, the same principles of differentiation and hierarchic integration and the same view of differing patterns of relationship between addressor and addressee used to conceptualize the task of visual representation can also be applied to these special scores.

THOUGHT DISORDER AND OBJECT RELATIONS

Conceptualizing thought-disorder signs in terms of a representational theory of the Rorschach can also make significant contributions to the assessment of object relations, an issue clinicians and researchers with psychodynamic orientations have come to believe is critical in differential diagnoses of severe forms of psychopathology (Blatt and Ritzler 1974; Kwawer et al., 1980; Blatt and Lerner 1982, 1983; Kissen, 1986; Lerner and Lerner, 1988; Blatt, Tuber, and Auerbach, 1990; Lerner, 1991).

Although clinicians make some use of impressions of the patient–examiner relationship in the course of testing when making inferences about experiences of self and other (Lerner, 1991), for the most part they rely on analyses of the content of responses. Similarly, with the exception of the Developmental Analysis of the Concept of the Object

Scale (Blatt and Lerner, 1983), research instruments created to measure object relations on the basis of the Rorschach are concerned almost exclusively with themes portrayed in the test (Urist, 1977; Kwawer, 1980; Coonerty, 1986).

Thematic analyses deserve a prominent place in interpretations about identity and relationship paradigms, but to focus on these data alone may limit and distort diagnoses. Athey (1974, p. 422) offers a striking illustration of the problems that can arise. A patient may describe in an articulate, cogent manner the experience of feeling fused with her therapist. The "thought content" points to "deeply regressive preoccupations," yet the form of the communication, the "thought process," is one in which there is a "clear recognition of the difference between 'I' and 'you.'" Similarly, subjects may produce symbiotic images on the Rorschach (e.g., Siamese twins) that are well formed and explained logically. Obviously something important is lost if assessment of object relations does not include attention to structural aspects of responses.

Several theorists have suggested ways in which consideration of thought organization can enter into such assessments. Athey (1974) contends that fabulized combinations, confabulations, and contaminations are manifestations of "modes of experience" that determine how self and other are represented. Because fabulized combinations relate realistic percepts in fantastic ways, he hypothesizes that they are likely to be prominent in records of subjects who represent self and other in arbitrary ways that approach, but stop short of, those encountered in psychosis. Blatant confabulatory protocols in which associative processes take flight are held to be indicative of psychotic modes of experience in which "overwhelming affect states and intense fantasy result in a sustained loss of the reality basis for experiencing the relationship" (p. 426). Contaminations are seen as signs of the most regressed modes of experience in which a condensation of frames of reference leads to schizophrenic forms of object relations in which there is a dissolution of distinctions between self and other and between fantasy and reality.

Blatt and Ritzler (1974) posit a similar relationship between these thought disorder signs and disturbances in conceptions of self and other. Drawing upon the theories of Piaget and Werner, they argue that fabulized combinations, confabulations, and contaminations reflect different degrees of disturbances in the differentiation or boundaries between representations and between conceptual processes. Contaminations, for example, are seen as manifestations of the most profound forms of boundary disturbance in which distinctions between fantasy and reality and between self and other are lost. Because of a concern with issues of this kind, the Yale Developmental Analysis of the Concept of the Object Scale seeks to combine measurement of the content and level of organization of Rorschach object representations (Blatt and Lerner, 1983).

When the Rorschach is treated as a task of visual representation, the range of data from which inferences about critical aspects of object relationships can be derived expands even farther. If the act at the heart of producing a response is not a private perceptual one, but rather one in which a medium is shaped to represent an idea that will be shared with an audience, qualities of the relationship to that audience influence every aspect of that process. Inferences about an implicit addressor–addressee relationship can be made on the basis of how the symbolic vehicle is used, the choice of referent, the coordination of symbol and referent, and the language and forms of explanation adopted in communicating and justifying images. As has been seen in the preceding discussion, every Rorschach thought-disorder sign provides some clue to the degree of differentiation of self and other at the time it was produced.

CONCLUSION

To analyze indications of thought disturbance on the Rorschach from a comparative-developmental perspective is not to imply that phenomena encountered in early development and in states of pathological regression are identical. Even where responses given by young children and troubled adults are similar, noteworthy differences are usually present as well. For example, DW responses and blatant confabulations are produced by both groups. Yet those of children reflect a characteristic mode of handling the Rorschach task and have amusing and even endearing qualities; those of adults occur sporadically in records containing higher level responses and are frequently provocative or disconcerting. The primitive responses of young children are determined chiefly by age-appropriate modes of cognitive, social, and emotional functioning and, as such, point to healthy development; those of adults reflect pathological processes that interfere with adaptation.

Although analyses of formal similarities in the Rorschach responses of children and adults suffering from major psychiatric conditions cannot reveal the causes or functions of particular manifestations of thought disorder, they nonetheless have important contributions to make to an understanding of how the test can be used to assess pathological thinking. First, as has been seen, both the nature of the disordered thinking inherent in particular Rorschach phenomena and the relationship of these signs to one another can be appreciated when they are considered in terms of disturbances in each of the components of the symbol situation and their interaction. Second, the principles of differentiation and hierarchic integration provide a clear rationale for assessing degrees of pathology in groups of related signs. And, finally, these principles contribute to diagnosis by providing an understanding of the co-occurrence of particular thought disorder signs at different levels of regression (e.g., the presence of contaminations, neologisms, and incoherence in schizophrenia) and the relationship of these signs to forms of disturbed object relationships.

Conclusion

What the Rorschach can teach us about preschoolers is limited. Because they are only gradually mastering the test, it is not the same diagnostic instrument for them that it is for older subjects. Yet when we look at how young children learn to negotiate the test, we discover that they have a great deal to teach us about the Rorschach.

Chief among their lessons is that the Rorschach is not a test "based on perception" as that term is commonly understood, but, rather, one of visual representation. This insight, in turn, provides the key to understanding the potency of an assessment technique that to the uninitiated looks like little more than an esoteric form of the parlor game in which it had its origin.

The test's power derives from three aspects of the Rorschach task. First, inkblots are a remarkably plastic medium; they can be formed into an almost infinite variety of images. Second, subjects are allowed extraordinary freedom in their choice of what may be depicted; the range of referents is as broad as the human imagination. Third, for all but a few subjects, the task is a novel one that lies largely outside the bounds of verbal reflective thought. Unable to rely on the conventions associated with more familiar media, subjects approach the Rorschach in fresher and less premeditated ways than they approach other projective tests.

As human beings, we are capable of making any form of artistic expression mundane, and most Rorschach responses are conventional in their own ways. Yet the richness of the medium, the open-ended nature of the task, and the novelty of the situation are such that subjects continually create vivid images that bypass the defenses and controls usually placed on thoughts.

By giving form to inchoate feelings and ideas, the Rorschach affords subjects a means of self-expression that enables them to make discoveries about themselves. For example, the "shock of recognition" experienced by the teenager described in Chapter 19 as she concretized her sense of being on the verge of decompensation in such images as a face melting and a head stretched to the point of exploding attests to the test's potential in this regard. As with other forms of artistic expression, such images and how they are explained are also powerful means of sharing such concerns with others. By examining formal qualities of this representational process, even more can be learned about how individuals structure their experience. At the same time, Rorschach images may also be a form of self-betrayal as, for example, when a profoundly disturbed adolescent blithely bares his psychosis unaware of what his responses reveal. It is, above all, the unique opportunity the Rorschach offers to witness the interplay of conventionality and originality, self-expression and self-deception, and communication and concealment that accounts for the hold the test maintains on the affection of psychologists in spite of the plethora of questions that can be raised about its reliability and validity.

Children's Rorschach responses can also help us appreciate the degree of uncertainty intrinsic to interpretation of the test. There are limits inherent in what the creators of these images are able to embody and communicate in their representations and in what we are able to read from them. In addition, we can never be entirely sure whether the meanings we ascribe to symbols and their formal determinants are ones that truly reflect what their authors have produced or ones we have read into them. In trying to understand the meaning of preschool Rorschachs and in reflecting on what others have attributed to them, we are continually reminded of how much can escape our understanding, how much we can misinterpret, and how much ambiguity, in fact, attends the Rorschach enterprise.

There is one other lesson to be learned from young children's Rorschachs. The Rorschach is often viewed as a most serious undertaking. It could hardly be otherwise given the clinical problems that bring subjects to evaluations, the anxieties attendant upon the unfamiliar nature of the Rorschach situation, and the esoteric rules that govern

Rorschach administration, scoring, and interpretation. Yet preschool Rorschachs remind us that historically the test had its origins in a children's game; that developmentally mastery of the test is rooted in the capacity for play; and that, in its adult form, like other forms of creative expression, it remains a sophisticated form of play. Children's Rorschachs teach us that for all our capacity to make the test into hard work, it may hold for those who take it, and even for those who give it, the promise of fun.

APPENDIX: COLIN'S RORSCHACHS*

Two Rorschach protocols from A. Schachtel (1944), The Rorschach test with young children. *American Journal of Orthopsychiatry,* 14:1–10.

Rorschach Record of Colin at Age 3 (1938)

Card

I   Exp: Here are some pictures that you never saw before (no explanation about how they are made). A mountain.

II   That's a red mountain. The next one. (Experimenter had explained after #I that he could look at them as long as he liked and then to tell him when he was ready for the next one.)

III   That's a pink mountain. I want the next.

IV   That's a black mountain. I want the next.

V   That's a black mountain. I want the next. (A girl nearby is putting chairs together to make a "train" and another joins her and starts singing a song.)

VI   (C pushes the picture aside) I don't want to. (He goes off to play with the girls.)

The session with the pictures above lasted only four minutes. About 1½ hours later, following several abortive efforts to complete the Rorschach, the experimenter was able to get C's attention again while he was waiting for a turn to paint. The second part of the Rorschach, which follows, was also done in the open.

VI   (Turns the card on side) A mountain.

VII   Dat's a mountain too. Why are you writing? (Exp: I want to be able to remember what you say.)

VIII   That's a pink mountain. (He plays with the card and stands it up in the crack between two tables. He and the experimenter regard this as excruciatingly funny.) The picture standing up on the table! (C laughs heartily.) The next one.

IX   That's going to stand up. (Immediately taking the card and putting it in the crack without looking at it.) Exp: Take a look at it and tell me what it might be.
A mountain. (C stands it up again after this response. It falls through the crack and he picks it up, then sits with it holding it vertically between his feet for a while commenting on this procedure.)

X   (Looks at it a little longer than some of the others). That's a
     white mountain. (He takes a look at the folder containing the
     cards.) That's all.
     Exp: Did you like them?
     Mmm! (C runs back to the painting room.)

Rorschach Record at Age 4 (1939)

Card
I   A man with pinchers
II   A bird with pinchers.
III   Peacocks. They are pulling something out of it and they are
      smack.
IV   Fountain   ⎤
V   Bird   ⎥— Peaceful phase after
VI   Another fountain.   ⎥ sharp pinchers.
VII   Goal that pinches. ⎦
VIII That's a bang, bang, bang (hitting at each color spot). They are
      walking all over it. A fountain.
IX   I hate that. That's a pound,   ⎤
      pound, pound, that pounds   ⎥— Forceful,
      people's heads. A hammer.   ⎥ play fight.
X   I hate that broken down tree. ⎥
      See where it's chopped off?   ⎥
      (He shows the gray upper color.) ⎦

References

Ainsworth, M. D. (1954), Problems of validation. In: *Developments in Rorschach Technique,* ed. B. Klopfer, M. D. Ainsworth, W. G. Klopfer & R. H. Holt. New York: Harcourt, Brace & World, pp. 405–500.

Allen, R. M. (1951), Longitudinal study of six Rorschach protocols of a three-year-old child. *Child Devel.,* 22:61–69.

—— (1954), Continued longitudinal Rorschach study of a young child for years three to five. *J. Genet. Psychol.,* 85:135–149.

—— (1955), Nine quarterly records of a young child. *Child Devel.,* 26:63–69.

Ames, L. B. (1959), Further check on the diagnostic validity of the Ames Danger Signals. *J. Proj. Tech.,* 23:291–298.

—— (1960a), Longitudinal survey of child Rorschach responses: Younger children. *Genet. Psychol. Monogr.,* 61:229–289.

—— (1960b), Constancy of content in Rorschach responses. *J. Genet. Psychol.,* 96:145–164.

—— (1965), Changes in experience–balance scores in the Rorschach at different ages in the life span. *J. Genet. Psychol.,* 106:279–286.

—— (1966), Changes in Rorschach responses throughout the human life span. *Genet. Psychol. Monogr.,* 74:89–125.

—— Learned, J., Metraux, R. W. & Walker, R. N. (1952), *Child Rorschach Responses.* New York: Paul B. Hoeber.

—— Metraux, R. W., Rodell, J. & Walker, R. N. (1974), *Child Rorschach Responses,* 2nd ed. New York: Brunner/Mazel.

Anastasi, A. (1955), *Psychological Testing.* New York: Macmillan.

Anderson, D. V. & Higham, E. (1956), The use of the Rorschach technique in child guidance clinics. In: *Developments in the Rorschach Technique, Vol. 2,* ed. B. Klopfer. New York: Harcourt, Brace & World, pp. 180–194.

297

Aranow, E. & Resnikoff, M. (1983), *A Rorschach Introduction*. New York: Grune & Stratton.

Athey, G. (1974), Schizophrenic thought organization, object relations and the Rorschach test. *Bull. Menn. Clin.*, 38:406–429.

—— (1986), Rorschach thought organization and transference enactment in the patient–examiner relationship. In: *Assessing Object Relations Phenomena*, ed. M. Kissen. New York: International Universities Press, pp. 19–50.

—— & Kleiger, J. (1993), *Revised Mayman Form Level Scoring Manual*. Unpublished draft. Topeka, KS: The Menninger Clinic.

—— Colson, D. & Kleiger, J. (1992), *Manual for Scoring Thought Disorder on the Rorschach*. Unpublished 5th draft. Topeka, KS: The Menninger Clinic.

Baughman, E. E. (1959), An experimental analysis of the relationship between stimulus structure and behavior on the Rorschach. *J. Proj. Tech.*, 23:134–183.

Beck, A. (1967), *Depression*. New York: Harper & Row.

Beck, S. J. (1930), The Rorschach test in problem children. *Amer. J. Orthopsychiat.*, 11:501–511.

—— (1944a), Discussion of the papers by Drs. Hartoch and Murphy. *Amer. J. Orthopsychiat.*, 14:17–20.

—— (1944b), *Rorschach's Test, Vol. 1*. New York: Grune & Stratton.

—— (1945), *Rorschach's Test, Vol. 2*. New York: Grune & Stratton.

—— (1951), The Rorschach test: A multi-dimensional test of personality. In: *An Introduction to Projective Techniques*, ed. H. H. Anderson & G. L. Anderson. Englewood Cliffs, NJ: Prentice-Hall, pp. 101–122.

—— Rabin, A. I., Thiesen, W. G., Molish, H. & Thetford, W. N. (1950), The normal personality as projected in the Rorschach test. *J. Psychol.*, 30:241–298.

Berg, M. (1986), Diagnostic use of the Rorschach with adolescents. In: *Projective Techniques for Adolescents and Children*, ed. A. I. Rabin. New York: Springer, pp. 111–141.

Berlyne, D. E. (1960), *Conflict, Arousal and Curiosity*. New York: McGraw-Hill.

Binder, H. (1932), *Die Helldunkeldeutungen im Psychodiagnostischen Experiment von Rorschach*. Zurich: Art. Institut Orell Fuessli.

Binet, A. & Henri, V. (1895–1896), La psychologie individuelle. *Annuel Psych.*, 2:411–465.

Blatt, S. J. (1990), The Rorschach: A test of perception or an evaluation of representation. *J. Pers. Assess.*, 55:394–416.

—— & Lerner, H. (1982), Investigations in the psychoanalytic theory of object relations and object representations. In *Empirical Studies of Psychoanalytic Theories, Vol. 1*, ed. J. Masling. Hillsdale, NJ: The Analytic Press, pp. 189–249.

—— & —— (1983), The psychological assessment of object relations. *J. Pers. Assess.*, 47:7–28.

—— & Ritzler, B. A. (1974), Thought disorder and boundary disturbances in psychosis. *J. Consult. & Clin. Psychol.*, 42:370–381.

—— Tuber, S. B. & Auerbach, J. S. (1990), Representation of interpersonal interactions on the Rorschach and level of psychopathology. *J. Pers. Assess.*, 54:711–728.

Bohm, E. (1958), *A Textbook in Rorschach Test Diagnosis for Psychologists, Physicians, and Teachers*. New York: Grune & Stratton.

Bretherton, I. (1984), Representing the social world in symbolic play: Reality and fantasy. In: *Symbolic Play*, ed. I. Bretherton. New York: Academic Press, pp. 3–41.

Brosin, H. W. & Fromm, E. (1942), Some principles of Gestalt psychology in the Rorschach experiment. *Rorschach Res. Exch.*, 6:1–15.

Bruhn, A. R. (1990), *Earliest Childhood Memories, Vol. 1*. New York: Praeger.

Bruner, J. S. (1948), IV. Perceptual theory and the Rorschach test. *J. Pers.*, 17:157–168.

—— (1951), Personality dynamics and the process of perceiving. In: *Perception*, ed. R. R. Blake & G. V. Ramsey. New York: Ronald Press, pp. 121–147.

—— (1972), The nature and uses of immaturity. *Amer. Psychol.*, 27:687–708.

Burt, C. (1921), *Mental and Scholastic Tests*. London: P. S. King & Son.

Cassirer, E. (1944), *An Essay on Man*. New Haven, CT: Yale University Press.

Cattell, R. B. (1951), Principles of design in "projective" or misperception tests of personality. In: *An Introduction to Projective Tests*, ed. H. H. Anderson & G. L. Anderson. New York: Prentice-Hall, pp. 55–98.

Coffin, T. E. (1941), Some conditions of suggestion and suggestibility: A study of certain attitudinal and situational factors influencing the process of suggestion. *Psychol. Monogr.*, 53: No. 241.

Coonerty, S. (1986), An exploration of separation-individuation themes in the borderline personality disorder. *J. Pers. Assess.*, 50:501–511.

Cronbach, L. J. (1949), *Essentials of Psychological Testing*. New York: Harper.

Dearborn. G. (1898), A study of imaginations. *Amer. J. Psychol.*, 9:183–190.

Di Leo, J. H. (1970), *Young Children and Their Drawings*. New York: Brunner/Mazel.

Dudek, S. Z. (1969), Intelligence, psychopathology, and primary thinking disorder in early schizophrenia. *J. Nerv. Ment. Dis.*, 148:515–527.

Eifermann, R. R. (1971), Social play in childhood. In: *Child's Play*, ed. R. E. Herron & B. Sutton-Smith. New York: John Wiley & Sons, pp. 270–297.

Eissler, K. R. (1965), *Medical Orthodoxy and the Future of Psychoanalysis*. New York: International Universities Press.

Elkins, E. (1958), The diagnostic validity of the Ames "Danger Signals." *J. Consult. Psychol.*, 22:281–287.

Ellenberger, H. (1954), The life and work of Hermann Rorschach. *Bull. Menn. Clin.*, 18:171–222.

Emde, R., Johnson, W. F. & Easterbrooks, M. A. (1987), The do's and don'ts of early moral development: Psychoanalytic tradition and current research. In: *The Emergence of Morality in Young Children*, ed. J. Kagan & S. Lamb. Chicago: University of Chicago Press, pp. 245–276.

Emmerich, W. (1977), Evaluating alternative models of development: An illustrative study of preschool personal-social behaviors. *Child Devel.*, 48:1401–1410.

Exner, J. E. (1969), *The Rorschach Systems*. New York: Grune & Stratton.

—— (1974), *The Rorschach, Vol. 1*. New York: John Wiley & Sons.

—— (1978), *The Rorschach, Vol. 2*. New York: John Wiley & Sons.

—— (1986), *The Rorschach, Vol. 1*, 2nd ed. New York: John Wiley & Sons.

—— (1991), *The Rorschach, Vol. 2*, 2nd ed. New York: John Wiley & Sons.

—— Armbruster, G. L. & Mittman, B. (1978), The Rorschach response process. *J. Pers. Assess.*, 42:27–38.

—— & Wiener, I. B. (1982), *The Rorschach, Vol. 3*. New York: John Wiley & Sons.

Fein, G. G. (1987), Pretend play: Creativity and consciousness. In: *Curiosity, Imagination, and Play*, ed. D. Goerlitz & J. F. Wohlwill. Hillsdale, NJ: Lawrence Erlbaum Associates, pp. 281–304.

Flavell, J. H. (1963), *The Developmental Psychology of Jean Piaget*. Princeton, NJ: Van Nostrand.

—— (1977), *Cognitive Development*. Englewood Cliffs, NJ: Prentice-Hall.

Ford, M. (1946), *The Application of the Rorschach Test to Young Children*. Minneapolis: University of Minnesota.

Fox, J. (1956), The psychological significance of age patterns in the Rorschach records of children. In: *Developments in the Rorschach Technique, Vol. 2*, ed. B. Klopfer. New York: Harcourt, Brace & World, pp. 88–103.

Francis-Williams, J. (1968), *Rorschach with Children*. Oxford: Pergamon.

Frank, L. K. (1939), Projective methods for the study of personality. *J. Psychol.*, 8:389–413.

Freeman, N. H. (1993), Drawing: Public instruments of representation. In: *Systems of Representation in Children*, ed. C. Pratt & A. Garton. New York: John Wiley & Sons, pp. 113–142.

Freud, S. (1908), Creative writers and daydreaming. *Standard Edition*, 9:141–156. London: Hogarth Press, 1959.

Friedman, H. (1953), Perceptual regression in schizophrenia. *J. Proj. Tech.*, 17:171–185.

Furrer, A. (1925), Ueber die Bedeutung der 'B' im Rorschachschen Versuch. *Imago*, 11:58–83.

Gardner, H. (1980), *Artful Scribbles.* New York: Basic Books.

——(1982). *Art, Mind, and Brain.* New York: Basic Books.

Garvey, C. (1977), *Play.* Cambridge, MA: Harvard University Press.

Gesell, A. & Ilg, F. L. (1943), *Infant and Child in the Culture of Today.* New York: Harper.

—— & —— (1946), *The Child from Five to Ten.* New York: Harper.

Gibby, R. G., Miller, D. R. & Walker, E. L. (1953), The examiner's influence on the Rorschach protocol. *J. Consult. Psychol.*, 17:425–428.

Gibson, J. J. (1956), The non–projective aspects of the Rorschach experiment: IV. The Rorschach blots considered as pictures. *J. Soc. Psychol.*, 44:203–206.

Goldfried, M. R., Stricker, G. & Weiner, I. B. (1971), *Rorschach Handbook of Clinical Research Applications.* Englewood Cliffs, NJ: Prentice-Hall.

Goodenough, F. L. (1926), *Measurement of Intelligence by Drawings.* Yonkers-on-Hudson, NY: World Book Company.

——(1949), *Mental Testing.* New York: Holt, Rinehart & Winston.

Goodman, N. (1976), *Languages of Art.* Indianapolis, IN: Hackett.

——(1978), *Ways of Worldmaking.* Indianapolis, IN: Hackett.

Goodman, N. L. (1979), Examiner influence on the Rorschach: The effect of sex, sex-pairing and warmth on the testing atmosphere. Unpublished doctoral dissertation, Long Island University.

Halpern, F. (1953), *A Clinical Approach to Children's Rorschachs.* New York: Grune & Stratton.

——(1960), The Rorschach test with children. In: *Projective Techniques with Children*, ed. A. I. Rabin & M. R. Haworth. New York: Grune & Stratton, pp. 14–28.

Harris, D. B. (1963), *Children's Drawings as Measures of Intellectual Maturity.* New York: Harcourt, Brace & World.

Hemmendinger, L. (1953), Perceptual organization and development as reflected in the structure of Rorschach test responses. *J. Proj. Tech.*, 17:162–170.

——(1960), Developmental theory and the Rorschach method. In: *Rorschach Psychology*, ed. M. A. Rickers-Ovsiankina. New York: John Wiley & Sons, pp. 58–79.

Hertz, M. R. (1936), The method of administration of the Rorschach Ink-Blot test. *Child Devel.*, 7:237–254.

——(1941a), Evaluation of the Rorschach method in its application to normal childhood and adolescence. *Character and Personality*, 10:151–162.

——(1941b), Rorschach: Twenty years after. *Rorschach Res. Exch.*, 5:90–129.

——(1951), Current problems in Rorschach theory and technique. *J. Proj. Tech.*, 15:307–338.

—— & Ebert, E. H. (1944), The mental procedure of 6 and 8 year old children as revealed by the Rorschach. *Rorschach Res. Exch.*, 8:10–30.

—— & Paolino, A. F. (1960), Rorschach indices of perceptual and conceptual disorganization. *J. Proj. Tech.*, 24:370–388.

Hirsch, E. A. (1959), The adaptive significance of commonly described behavior of the mentally retarded. *Amer. J. Ment. Def.*, 63:639–646.

Holt, R. H. (1954), Implications of some contemporary personality theories for Rorschach rationale. In: *Developments in the Rorschach Technique, Vol. 1*, ed. B. Klopfer, M. D. Ainsworth, W. G. Klopfer & R. H. Holt. New York: Harcourt, Brace & World, pp. 501–560.

—— & Havel, J. (1967), A method for assessing primary and secondary processes in the Rorschach. In: *Rorschach Psychology*, ed. M. A. Rickers–Ovsiankina. New York: John Wiley & Sons, pp. 263–315.

Holzman, P. S., Solovay, M. R. & Shenton, M. E. (1985), Thought disorder specificity in functional psychoses. In: *Controversies in Schizophrenia*, ed. M. Alpert. New York: Guilford, pp. 228–252.

Huizinga, J. (1955), *Homo Ludens*. Boston: Beacon Press.

Johannessen, F. (1965), Some aspects of Rorschach responses in a group of Norwegian children at three age levels. *Acta Psycholog.*, 24:371–386.

Johnson, J. E. & Eschler, J. (1981), Developmental trends in preschool play as a function of classroom setting and child gender. *Child Devel.*, 52:995–1004.

Johnston, M. H. & Holzman, P. S. (1979), *Assessing Schizophrenic Thinking*. San Francisco: Jossey-Bass.

Jortner, S. (1966), An investigation of certain cognitive aspects of schizophrenia. *J. Proj. Tech. & Pers. Assess.*, 30:559–568.

Kagan, J. (1984), *The Nature of the Child*. New York: Basic Books.

Kaplan, B. (1959), The study of language in psychiatry: The comparative developmental approach and its application to symbolization and language in psychopathology. In: *American Handbook of Psychiatry, Vol. 3*, ed. Silvano Arieti. New York: Basic Books, pp. 659–688.

Kay, L. W. & Vorhaus, P. G. (1943), Rorschach reactions in early childhood: Part II. *Rorschach Res. Exch.*, 7:71–77.

Kernberg, O. F. (1975), *Borderline Conditions and Pathological Narcissism*. New York: Jason Aronson.

Kerr, J. (1993), *A Most Dangerous Method*. New York: Alfred A. Knopf.

Kimball, A. J. (1950), History of form–level appraisal in the Rorschach. *J. Proj. Tech.*, 14:134–152.

Kinder, B., Brubaker, R., Ingram, R. & Reading, E. (1982), Rorschach form quality: A comparison of the Exner and Beck systems. *J. Pers. Assess.*, 46:131–138.

Kirkpatrick, E. A. (1900), Individual tests of school children. *Psychol. Rev.*, 7:274–280.

Kissen, M., ed. (1986), *Assessing Object Relations Phenomena*. Madison, CT: International Universities Press.

Kiviluoto, H. (1962), Trends of development in Rorschach responses. *Ann. Univ. Turk.*

Kleiger, J. H. & Peebles-Kleiger, M. J. (1993), Toward a conceptual understanding of the the deviant response in the comprehensive Rorschach system. *J. Pers. Assess.*, 60: 74–90.

Klein, A. & Arnheim, R. (1953), Perceptual analysis of a Rorschach card. *J. Pers.*, 22:60–70.

Klinger, E. (1971), *The Structure and Functions of Play*. New York: John Wiley & Sons.

Klopfer, B. (1945), Personality diagnosis in childhood. In: *Modern Trends in Child Psychiatry*, ed. N. D. C. Lewis & B. L. Pacella. New York: International Universities Press, pp. 89–101.

—— ed. (1956), *Developments in the Rorschach Technique, Vol. 2*. New York: Harcourt, Brace & World.

—— Ainsworth, M. D., Klopfer, W. G. & Holt, R. H. (1954), *Developments in the Rorschach Technique, Vol. 1*. Yonkers-on-Hudson, NY: World Book.

——Fox, J. & Troup, E. (1956), Problems in the use of the Rorschach technique with children. In: *Developments in the Rorschach Technique, Vol. 2*, ed. B. Klopfer. New York: Harcourt, Brace & World, pp. 3–21.

—— & Kelley, D. M. (1942), *The Rorschach Technique.* Yonkers-on-Hudson, NY: World Book.

—— & Margulies, H. (1941), Rorschach reactions in early childhood. *Rorschach Res. Exch.*, 5:1–23.

——Spiegelman, M. & Fox, J. (1956), The interpretation of children's records. In: *Developments in the Rorschach Technique, Vol. 2*, ed. B. Klopfer. New York: Harcourt, Brace & World, pp. 22–44.

Koestler, A. (1964), *The Act of Creation.* New York: Dell.

Korchin, S. J. (1960), Form perception and ego functioning. In: *Rorschach Psychology*, ed. M. Rickers-Ovsiankina. New York: John Wiley & Sons, pp. 109–129.

Kwawer, J. (1980), Primitive interpersonal modes, borderline phenomena, and Rorschach content. In: *Borderline Phenomena and the Rorschach Test*, ed. J. Kwawer, H. Lerner, P. Lerner & A. Sugarman. New York: International Universities Press, pp. 89–106.

——Learner, H., Lerner, P. & Sugarman, A., eds. (1980), *Borderline Phenomena and the Rorschach Test.* New York: International Universities Press.

Lang, A. (1966), *Rorschach Bibliography, 1921–1964.* Berne: Hans Huber.

Leichtman, M. (1988), When does the Rorschach become the Rorschach? Stages in the mastery of the test. In: *Primitive Mental States and the Rorschach*, ed. H. D. Lerner & P. M. Lerner. Madison, CT: International Universities Press, pp. 559–600.

——(1995), Behavioral observations. In: *Clinical Personality Assessment*, ed. J. N. Butcher. New York: Oxford University Press, pp. 251–266.

—— & Nathan, S. (1983), A clinical approach to the psychological testing of borderline children. In: *The Borderline Child*, ed. K. Robson. New York: McGraw-Hill, pp. 121–170.

—— & Shapiro, S. (1980a), An introduction to the psychological assessment of borderline conditions in children: Borderline children and the test process. In: *Borderline Phenomena and the Rorschach Test*, ed. J. Kwawer, H. Lerner, P. Lerner & A. Sugarman. New York: International Universities Press, pp. 343–366.

—— & —— (1980b), An introduction to the psychological assessment of borderline conditions in children: Manifestations of borderline phenomena on psychological testing. In: *Borderline Phenomena and the Rorschach Test*, ed. J. Kwawer, H. Lerner, P. Lerner & A. Sugarman. New York: International Universities Press, pp. 367–394.

Lerner, H., Sugarman, A. & Barbour, C. G. (1985), Patterns of boundary disturbances in neurotic, borderline, and schizophrenic patients. *Psychoanal. Psychol.*, 2:47–66.

Lerner, P. (1991), *Psychoanalytic Theory and the Rorschach.* Hillsdale, NJ: The Analytic Press.

—— & Lerner, H. (1986), Contributions of object relations theory towards a general psychoanalytic theory of thinking. *Psychoanal. Contemp. Thought*, 9:469–513.

Levin, M. M. (1953), The two tests in the Rorschach. *J. Proj. Tech.*, 17:471–475.

Levitt, E. E. & Truuma, A. (1972), *The Rorschach Technique with Children.* New York: Grune & Stratton.

Lichtenberg, J. D. (1989), *Psychoanalysis and Motivation.* Hillsdale, NJ: The Analytic Press.

Lindzey, G. (1961), *Projective Techniques and Cross Cultural Research.* New York: Appleton-Century-Crofts.

Lofting, H. (1967), *Doctor Doolittle: A Treasury.* Philadelphia: J. B. Lippincott.

Loosli-Usteri, M. (1952), Preface. In: *Child Rorschach Responses*, ed. L. B. Ames, J. Learned, R. W. Metraux & R. N. Walker. New York: Paul B. Hoeber, p. xi.

Lord, E. (1950), Experimentally induced variations in Rorschach performance. *Psychol. Monogr.*, 60: No. 316.

MacLeod, H. (1950), A Rorschach study with preschool children. *J. Proj. Tech.*, 14:453–463.

Mahler, M. S. (1988), *The Memoirs of Margaret S. Mahler*, ed. P. E. Stepansky. New York: The Free Press.

Masling, J. (1965), Differential indoctrination of examiners and Rorschach responses. *J. Cons. Psychol.*, 29:198–201.

Mayman, M. (1968), Early memories and character structure. *J. Proj. Tech.*, 32:303–316.

Meili-Dworetzki, G. (1956), The development of perception in the Rorschach. In: *Developments in the Rorschach Technique, Vol. 2*, ed. B. Klopfer. New York: Harcourt, Brace & World, pp. 108–176.

Meloy, J. R. & Singer, J. (1991). A psychoanalytic view of the Rorschach Comprehensive System "special scores." *J. Pers. Assess.*, 56:202–217.

Millar, S. (1974), *The Psychology of Play*. Baltimore, MD: Penguin.

Mitchell, E. D. & Mason, B. S. (1948), *The Theory of Play*. Barnes, NY: Ronald Press.

Mooney, B. (1962), Personality assessment and perception. In: *Rorschach Science*, ed. M. Hirt. New York: The Free Press of Glencoe, pp. 17–27.

Munroe, R. L. (1955), *Schools of Psychoanalytic Thought*. New York: Holt, Rinehart & Winston.

Neumann, E. A. (1971), *Elements of Play*. New York: MSS Information Corporation.

Norland, E. (1966), Children's Rorschach responses: Developmental trends from three to twenty years. *Pedagog. Forsk.*, 2–3:124–149.

Oberholzer, E. (1955), Rorschach—The man and the test. *J. Proj. Tech. & Pers. Assess.*, 32:502–508.

Olesker, W. (1980), Early life experience and the development of borderline pathology. In: *Borderline Phenomena and the Rorschach Test*, ed. J. Kwawer, H. Lerner, P. Lerner & A. Sugarman. New York: International Universities Press, pp. 411–440.

Olson, D. & Campbell, R. (1993), Constructing representations. In: *Systems of Representation in Children*, ed. C. Pratt & A. F. Garton. New York: John Wiley & Sons, pp. 11–26.

Parsons, C. J. (1917), Children's interpretations of inkblots. *Brit. J. Psychol.*, 9:74–92.

Parten, M. B. (1932), Social participation among preschool children. *J. Abn. Psychol.*, 27:243–267.

Peller, L. E. (1954), Libidinal phases, ego development and play. *The Psychoanalytic Study of the Child*, 9:178–198. New York: International Universities Press.

Perner, J. (1991), *Understanding the Representational Mind*. Cambridge, MA: MIT Press/Bradford Books.

Piaget, J. (1951), *Play, Dreams, and Imitation in Childhood*. London: Routledge & Kegan Paul.

—— (1952), *Judgment and Reasoning in the Child*. New York: The Humanities Press.

—— (1959), *The Language and Thought of the Child*. London: Routledge & Kegan Paul.

—— (1967), *Six Psychological Studies*. New York: Random House.

—— (1973), *The Child and Reality*. New York: Grossman.

—— & Inhelder, B. (1969), *The Psychology of the Child*. New York: Basic Books.

Piotrowski, Z. A. (1950), A Rorschach compendium, rev. ed. *Psychiat. Quart.*, 24:545–596.

—— (1957), *Perceptanalysis*. New York: Macmillan.

—— (1981), The Piotrowski Rorschach System. Lecture presented to the Union County Association of School Psychologists, Clark, New Jersey, May 12.

—— & Lewis, N. D. C. (1950), A case of stationary schizophrenia beginning in early childhood with remarks on certain aspects of children's Rorschach records. *Quart. J. Child Behav.*, 2:115–139.

Pope, B. & Jensen, S.R. (1957), The Rorschach as an index of pathological thinking. *J. Proj. Tech.*, 21:54–62.

Powers, W. T. & Hamilin, R. M. (1955), Relationship between diagnostic category and deviant verbalizations on the Rorschach. *J. Consult. Psychol.*, 19:120–124.

Pratt, C. & Garton, A. F. (1993), Systems of representation in children. In: *Systems of Representation in Children*, ed. C. Pratt & A. F. Garton. New York: John Wiley & Sons, pp. 1–9.

Pyle, W. H. (1915), A psychological study of bright and dull pupils. *J. Ed. Psychol.*, 6:151–156.

Quinlan, D. M., Harrow, M., Tucker, G. & Carlson, K. (1972), Varieties of "disordered" thinking on the Rorschach: Findings in schizophrenic and nonschizophrenic patients. *J. Abn. Psychol.*, 79:47–53.

Rapaport, D., Gill, M. & Schafer, R. (1946), *Diagnostic Psychological Testing, Vol. 2.* Chicago: Yearbook Publishers.

Rausch de Traubenberg, N. (1986), Issues in the use of the Rorschach with children. In: *Projective Techniques for Adolescents and Children*, ed. A. I. Rabin. New York: Springer, pp. 142–153.

Rickers-Ovsiankina, M., ed. (1960), *Rorschach Psychology.* New York: John Wiley & Sons.

Rorschach, H. (1921), *Psychodiagnostik.* Bern: Ernest Bircher (Transl. *Psychodiagnostics*, 6th ed. New York: Grune & Stratton, 1964).

Rouma, G. (1913), *Le Langage Graphique de l'Enfant.* Paris: Misch et Thron.

Rubin, K. H., Fein, G. G. & Vandenberg, B. (1983), Play. In: *Handbook of Child Psychology, Vol. 4*, ed. Paul Mussen. New York: John Wiley & Sons, pp. 693–774.

——Maioni, T. L. & Hornung, M. (1976), Free play behaviors in middle and lower class preschoolers: Parten and Piaget revisited. *Child Devel.*, 47:414–419.

——Watson, K. & Jambor, T. (1978), Free play behaviors in preschool and kindergarten children. *Child Devel.*, 49:534–536.

Sanders, K. M. & Harper, L. V. (1976), Free play fantasy behavior in preschool children: Relations among gender, age, season, and location. *Child Devel.*, 47:1182–1185.

Schachtel, A. (1944), The Rorschach test with young children. *Amer. J. Orthopsychiat.*, 14:1–10.

Schachtel, E. (1945), Subjective definitions of the Rorschach test situation and their effect on test performance. *Psychiatry*, 8:419–448.

——(1966), *Experiential Foundations of Rorschach's Test.* New York: Basic Books.

Schafer, R. (1954), *Psychoanalytic Interpretation in Rorschach Testing.* New York: Grune & Stratton.

Schlesinger, H. (1973), Interaction of dynamic and reality factors in the diagnostic testing interview. *Bull. Menn. Clin.*, 37:495–517.

Schwartzman, H. B. (1978), *Transformations.* New York: Plenum.

Shapiro, D. (1960), A perceptual understanding of color response. In: *Rorschach Psychology*, ed. M. Rickers-Ovsiankina. New York: John Wiley & Sons, pp. 154–201.

Shenton, M. E., Solovay, M. R. & Holzman, P. S. (1987), Comparative studies of thought disorder: II. Schizoaffective disorder. *Arch. Gen. Psychiat.*, 44:21–30.

Singer, J. L., ed. (1973), *The Child's World of Make Believe.* New York: Academic Press.

——(1991), Cognitive and affective implications of imaginative play in childhood. In: *Child and Adolescent Psychiatry*, ed. M. Lewis. Baltimore, MD: Williams & Wilkins, pp. 174–186.

Solovay, M. R., Shenton, M. E. & Holzman, P. S. (1987), Comparative studies of thought disorders: I. Mania and schizophrenia. *Arch. Gen. Psychiat.*, 44:13–20.

Stein, M. D. (1956), Bibliography. In: *Developments in Rorschach Technique, Vol. 2,* ed. B. Klopfer. New York: Harcourt, Brace & World, pp. 661–776.

Stern, D. N. (1985), *The Interpersonal World of the Infant.* New York: Basic Books.

Sunne, D. (1936), Rorschach test norms of young children. *Child Devel.,* 7:304–313.

Sutton-Smith, B. (1966), Piaget on play: A critique. *Psychol. Rev.,* 73:104–110.

Swift, J. W. (1944a), Reliability of Rorschach scoring categories with preschool children. *Child Devel.,* 15:207–216.

—— (1944b), Matching of teacher's descriptions and Rorschach analyses of preschool children. *Child Devel.,* 15:217–224.

—— (1944c), Rorschach responses of eighty-two preschool children. *Rorschach Res. Exch.,* 9:74–84.

—— (1945), Relation of behavioral and Rorschach measures of insecurity in preschool children. *J. Clin. Psychol.,* 1:196–205.

Terman, L. & Merrill, M. (1960), *Stanford-Binet Intelligence Scale.* Boston: Houghton Mifflin.

Tulchin, S. H. (1940), The pre-Rorschach use of ink blot tests. *Rorschach Res. Exch.,* 4:1–7.

Urist, J. (1977), The Rorschach test and the assessment of object relations. *J. Pers. Assess.,* 41:3–9.

Vandenberg, B. (1978), Play and development from an ethological perspective. *Amer. Psychol.,* 33:724–738.

Vorhaus, P. G. (1944), Rorschach reactions in early childhood: Part III. Content and details in pre-school records. *Rorschach Res. Exch.,* 8:71–91.

—— (1952), The use of the Rorschach in preventive mental hygiene. *J. Proj. Tech.,* 16:179–192.

Waelder, R. (1933), The psychoanalytic theory of play. *Psychoanal. Quart.,* 2:208–224.

Watkins, J. G. & Stauffacher, J. C. (1952), An index of pathological thinking in the Rorschach. *J. Proj. Tech.,* 16:276–286.

Wechsler, D. (1991), *Wechsler Intelligence Scale for Children,* 3rd ed. *Manual.* San Antonio, TX: The Psychological Corporation.

Weiner, I. B. (1966), *Psychodiagnosis in Schizophrenia.* New York: John Wiley & Sons.

—— (1986), Assessing children and adolescents with the Rorschach. In: *The Assessment of Child and Adolescent Personality,* ed. H. M. Knoff. New York: Guilford, pp. 141–171.

—— & Exner, J. E. (1978), Rorschach indices of disordered thinking in patient and nonpatient adolescents and adults. *J. Pers. Assess.,* 42:339–343.

Weisler, A. & McCall, R. (1976), Exploration and play. *Amer. Psychol.,* 31:492–508.

Werner, H. (1945), Perceptual behavior of brain-injured, mentally defective children: An experimental study by means of the Rorschach technique. *Genet. Psychol. Monogr.,* 31:51–110.

—— (1957), The concept of development from a comparative and organismic view. In: *The Concept of Development,* ed. D. B. Harris. Minneapolis: University of Minnesota Press, pp. 125–148.

—— (1961), *Comparative Psychology of Mental Development.* New York: Science Editions.

—— & Kaplan, B. (1963), *Symbol Formation.* New York: John Wiley & Sons.

—— & Wapner, S. (1956), The non-projective aspects of the Rorschach Experiment: II. Organismic theory and perceptual response. *J. Soc. Psychol.,* 44:193–198.

Wertheimer, M. (1957), Perception and the Rorschach. *J. Proj. Tech.,* 21:209–216.

Whipple, G. M. (1910), *Manual of Mental and Physical Tests.* Baltimore, MD: Warwick & York.

White, R. W. (1944), Interpretation of imaginative productions. In: *Personality and Behavior Disorders,* ed. J. McV. Hunt. New York: Ronald Press, pp. 214–251.

—— (1959), Motivation reconsidered: The concept of competence. *Psychol. Rev.,* 66:297–333.

Willock, B. (1992), Projection, transitional phenomena, and the Rorschach. *J. Pers. Assess.*, 59:99–116.

Witkin, H. A. (1954), *Personality Through Perception*. New York: Harper.

Zlotogorski, Z. (1986), Recent research on the Rorschach test with children. In: *Projective Techniques for Adolescents and Children*, ed. A. I. Rabin. New York: Springer, pp. 142–153.

Zubin, J. (1956), The non-projective aspects of the Rorschach experiment: I. Introduction. *J. Soc. Psychol.*, 44:179–192.

——Eron, L. D. & Schumer, F. (1965), *An Experimental Approach to Projective Techniques*. New York: John Wiley & Sons.

Zucker, L. (1958), *Ego Structure in Paranoid Schizophrenia*. Springfield, IL: Thomas.

Index